mbria at Newcastle

DOING BUSINESS IN INDIA

DOING BUSINESS IN INDIA

Street-Smart Entrepreneurs In An Imperfect Marketplace

V. PADMANAND
P.C. JAIN

Response Books
A division of Sage Publications
New Delhi/Thousand Oaks/London

Copyright © Entrepreneurship Development Institute of India, Ahmedabad, 2000

First published in 2000 by

Response Books
A division of Sage Publications India Pvt Ltd
32 M-Block Market, Greater Kailash–I
New Delhi 110 048

Sage Publications Inc
2455 Teller Road
Thousand Oaks, California 91320

Sage Publications Ltd
6 Bonhill Street
London EC2A 4PU

Published by Tejeshwar Singh for Response Books, lasertypeset by Innovative Processors, New Delhi, and printed at Chaman Enterprises, Delhi.

Library of Congress Cataloging-in-Publication Data

Padmanand, V., 1967–
    Doing business in India: street-smart entrepreneurs in an imperfect marketplace/V. Padmanand, P.C. Jain.
        p.   cm.   (c.)   (p.)
    Includes bibliographical references and index.
    1. India—Commerce. 2. Industrial policy—India. 3. New business enterprises—India. 4. Entrepreneurship—India. 5. Investments, Foreign—India. 6. Competition, Imperfect—India. I. Jain, P.C. (Prakash Chand), 1949–   II. Title.   III. Title: Street-smart entrepreneurs in an imperfect marketplace.
    HF3784. J34   380.1'0954—dc21   1999   99–44124

ISBN: 0–7619–9351–7 (US–HB)   81–7036–817–0 (India–HB)
         0–7619–9352–5 (US–PB)   81–7036–818–9 (India–PB)

Production Team: Chandana Chandra, D.C. Sharma and Santosh Rawat

Contents

PART THREE

PART FOUR

Foreword

Since the early 1970s, when some of us started working in entrepreneurship development, the social status of entrepreneurs and academic interest in the emergence, performance and characteristics of new entrepreneurs have gone through a sea change. Literature about Indian entrepreneurs, which was rather sketchy, is being enriched day by day with case histories, autobiographies and media projections. We have begun to understand the complexities of how entrepreneurs perceive opportunities, why they take risks, what skills and competencies enable them to survive enormous problems and crises, and what drives them to take up new challenges.

The Entrepreneurship Development Institute of India's contribution to understanding this process and phenomenon has also grown over time. Its first major contribution was the case study of *Self-made Impact-making Entrepreneurs, the New Emerging Giants on the Indian Scenario*, which was published in 1988. Subsequently, new Indian women entrepreneurs were presented in the book, *In Search of Identity* (1992), followed by the publication of *The Created Entrepreneurs* (1994), the products of entrepreneurship development programmes.

Not much, however, is known about the entry and performance of Non-Resident Indians (NRIs) who have set up enterprises in our country. While the capital flow through NRIs has played a significant part, how are they performing as business entrepreneurs? Do they bring in new technologies, or better management practices? Do they perform well in the Indian business environment, or do they flounder because of lack of exposure to Indian entrepreneurial styles and business practices? What are the profiles of those who return from abroad and set up businesses? What motives and compulsions bring them back to face a new business environment, with all the associated hardships and frustrations? Are these ventures really set up and managed by NRIs, or do they leave behind an uncle, cousin, brother or nephew to manage the firms, while they go back to the US or UK?

Since the country is looking for not just capital, but also knowhow, efficient operations, and well-managed companies owned by NRIs educated in or having gained experience in the USA and the UK, the mystery about the performance of NRI entrepreneurs is worth exploring.

It is a prevalent belief that business environments, business practices and styles differ so much in our country, that doing business in India would be very difficult for those coming from the USA, Europe or even East Africa. This study tests this hypothesis, on the basis of the case histories of a fairly good number of entrepreneurs, who returned to India from different parts of the world, who belong to and have located their projects in different parts of India. We hope that such a study will help us evolve workshops and seminars, also training programmes, for RNRIs and foreign entrepreneurs, so that they can be well prepared for doing business in India. This may also help to prevent a number of them leaving the country out of frustration. The publication of this book, therefore, offers value to those who wish to come to India to set up business and would like to acquaint themselves with how we do business here. The lessons learnt from those who have already gone through the drill might help many to be better informed and mentally better prepared for what is to follow.

Indeed, the Indian business environment is going through rapid changes; a lot of procedures and formalities have been simplified. But even in this 'reforming' environment, the microscenario which an entrepreneur faces within a government, in a bank, at the grassroot administrative level, is still somewhat unpleasant. This book, with its case studies, therefore, is a good guide for any aspiring entrepreneur who wishes to do business in India, and it will serve a useful purpose if it is read by a large number of would-be entrepreneurs from the West, Africa, the Middle East, or the Far East. The language and style of this book not being heavy, potential entrepreneurs should find it readable.

At the end, let me emphasize that while incentives and concessions may make the prospect of setting up a business enterprise in India attractive, ultimately it is entrepreneurial competencies which determine success. The market and the customer do not differentiate between a product made by an Indian entrepreneur, an NRI, or MNCs. NRI entrepreneurs and MNCs, like all other entrepreneurs, are welcome to play a significant role in our development, but their survival, success and growth depends on their own capabilities. No excuses can justify or wish away business failures. The book offers some surprises about the profiles and characteristics of those who succeed, and the motives and compulsions which hold some of them back. The implications for policy makers are also revealing. In some cases too much is given when less is desired and in others not much is done even when it can be offered at marginal rates. This is the story of our incentives and subsidy-based promotional policies, which we are now struggling to forego and give up.

15 October 1999

V.G. Patel
Vice President and Director
Entrepreneurship Development
Institute of India, Ahmedabad

Preface

In spite of progressive liberalization and incentive schemes, Non-Resident Indian (NRI) proposals for Foreign Direct Investment (FDI) into the Indian economy have been rather dismal, given their potential. What is worse, only a fraction of them materialize. Nevertheless, NRI remittances remain at significant levels. The first could perhaps be attributed to the relatively non-conducive or unattractive Indian business and bureaucratic environment. The second to the overly 'rosy' picture presented to investors, later quashed by an uncertain policy environment and the bureaucracy. The third could be attributed to the non-entrepreneurial background of most NRIs abroad.

There is, in fact, no dearth of evidence regarding the relatively unattractive nature of the Indian economy for the objective investor. Under the circumstances, rather than focussing just on NRI investment from investors who are doing business 'with' India, and seeking maximum incentives and repatriation-based options, the policy makers should focus on the 'nostalgic' NRIs who would like to return and do business in India. The latter provide evidence of their commitment and the 'non–flighty' nature of their investment, by going in for the non-repatriable option, which, in turn, has been given incentives in terms of wide options and relaxed ceilings. Rather than trying in vain to whip up patriotism as the reason for investing in India, citing the Chinese example, the nostalgic NRI, with his technical skill, managerial expertise and new or adapted business ideas, is a more likely preposition. And he could do wonders for the Indian economy. Returned Non-Resident Indian (RNRI) entrepreneurship, a term we adopt for the sake of convenience, is in a dismal state at the moment. Of the few hundred firms registered as NRI firms in the high- and middle-income states of the economy, with a large expatriate population of NRIs, only a fraction has a genuine RNRI in the picture. The nostalgic NRI is not coming back, and this fact, combined with relatively little evidence of NRIs even evincing interest in returning, has led the policy makers to progressively focus on the investor. Obviously, acceptance of the scenario as it is, is no way to target the anomalies that exist. One must go deeper and probe.

What is immediately evident is that, regardless of reform, an adverse scenario with regard to policy uncertainty and the bureaucracy, is not going to change overnight. The investor and the big-time entrepreneur is not going to flood the Indian economy with his massive investible surplus. Well, if we have to play on sentiments as our politicians have been trying to, why do we not focus on the first-generation emigrant, the NRI professional, or the NRI businessperson in the unstable economies of the developing world? Smaller in terms of personal net worth, he is not going to give absolute priority to country investment attractiveness ratings?

But even he would need to be presented with the economic, business and bureaucratic environment in an honest fashion. He needs to understand what it involves, acknowledge and learn from the experiences of those who have returned to do business, ask himself if he is up to it, and make a decision. Yet another sick unit, and subsequent negative impressions flowing abroad, is something we do not want!

Empirical surveys have indicated that large numbers of Indians from the USA, the UK, the Middle East, and the Far East would like to return to India. But the different NRI country typologies suffer from a 'what does one do in India?' and, 'could I do business in India?' syndrome. They do not want to give up the standard of living they are used to while living abroad. It is only business that can compensate the opportunity lost in terms of income foregone by their return. With these hypotheses in mind, we conducted a free-wheeling exercise on 'NRI'-assisting officials and RNRI entrepreneurs in the country, and identified certain 'NRI-firm' typologies. We also found ourselves in the midst of something of a controversy. NRI-assisting officials wonder about the commitment, competence and credibility of potential RNRIs, and also about the very rationale for providing anything special for the RNRI businessman. The problem of business failure occurs due to the inexperience or incompetence of the RNRI and it is not as if the environment has limitations or is non-conducive, they believe. The competent entrepreneur is not going to be attracted merely by special incentives, nor is his performance necessarily going to improve because of them. And it is the competent ones that we need! But the non-starters and failures spread exaggerated and biased, if not false, harrowing tales about the Indian economic, business and bureaucratic environment, keeping away other potential entrants. Interesting!

The NRIs have an altogether different story to tell. The controversial mud-slinging also seems to arise from the fact that there is little documented information seeking to familiarize the NRIs with the Indian environment, before their return. This hypothesis was verified when going through the literature, which seems focussed on procedures, guidelines and incentives, and not on a de-facto scenario presentation of the environment from the perspective of an RNRI. The study, hence, focussed on identifying the experiences and impressions of RNRIs in the country, and examining them by employing a case-study methodology, drawing inferences for analytical generalization via pattern matching. The study validates the hypotheses that we have put forward. The RNRIs in small and medium enterprises (SMEs), regardless of whether their performance is phenomenal or lackluster, radiate professionalism, zeal and the conviction of reaching greater heights. Handicaps have arisen from the bureaucracy and the economic and business environment, but

RNRIs have made entrepreneurial and managerial errors too. So would have any entrepreneur, especially if he was new to business, the particular business, or the environment. The fact is that they have stood on their own and prevailed in the Indian industrial environment, not as sleeping partners or as a front for Indian entrepreneurs! While the credibility of the potential RNRI, particularly in the SME sector, has always been questioned, the cases in this book, drafted in a manner so as to avoid excessive repetition in order to maintain lucidity, remove misconceptions about this breed of entrepreneurs. This study is expected to inspire confident NRIs to return, and gainfully and meaningfully do business in India. The concomitant advantages to the entrepreneur and to the economy could be phenomenal.

The awareness that this work seeks to generate is expected to encourage only those who fully realize what they may be getting into, before taking up the 'doing business in India' option. A case study, unlike a sampling methodology of analysis, can be conducted with just one case. It does not have standardized norms regarding numbers, for validity. Dozens of RNRI entrepreneurs from selected states of the country have been interviewed in order to broadbase their experiences and what they have learnt. While many of the cases presented are of RNRIs, MNCs and Indian enterprises, they have their facts and specifics modified, so as to ensure anonymity. A large number of them are presented as facts, however.

Representative cases, controlled for possible diversity in entre-preneur and enterprise background, inter-state and intra-state in terms of culture, infrastructure, and markets within India, and coun-try of domicile abroad, have been carefully selected and included in this book.

Part One introduces the reader to the Indian industrial economy, to the Multinational Corporations (MNCs), the Non-Resident Indian, and the one hundred per cent ethnic (!) potential Indian entre-preneur, or one actually doing business in the subcontinent. This part of the book highlights the attractive nature of the Indian industrial environment for an entrepreneur with a good project and business acumen, regardless of investible surplus.

Parts Two and Three introduce and then study in detail the cases of RNRIs who have been doing business in India. Their cases also highlight the possible problems that individuals and enterprises doing business in India face, in terms of familiarity with the environment, entrepreneurial experience and (often competence!), a good project, sufficient capital, the requisites necessary, and the means that are adopted for survival and growth.

Part Four summarizes the experiences of the entrepreneurs in the market, be they Indians, foreign companies or RNRIs, and draws lessons.

Limitations in field research and researcher bias are bound to taint any work of this sort. Nevertheless, the wealth of learning derived from these cases aspires to be a pioneering attempt at addressing a phenomenon, or what could become a phenomenon, if even a fraction of the millions of NRIs or the Mr Right policy maker reads this book!

Many of the cases presented are facts with specifics disguised, so as to maintain anonymity. Some have been developed from the literature, and by means of extensive interactions with and insights from experts. The impressions conveyed in many cases are the authors' alone, and are merely presented in a fashion so as to make the book interesting to read. The usual disclaimer hence applies!

V. Padmanand
P.C. Jain

Acknowledgements

We would like to thank the entrepreneurs who have made possible the detailed study of the cases encapsulated in this book. Their free and frank observations have also served as a basis for the tremendous knowledge base that was created prior to the crystallization of this book.

The academic inputs of Dr V.G. Patel, Vice-President and Director of the Entrepreneurship Development Institute of India (EDI), is respectfully acknowledged. The wealth of learning gleaned from this pioneer in the field of entrepreneurship development, across several developing countries, was a catalyst that initiated and ensured completion of this unique contribution to knowledge in this sphere.

We would also like to express our gratitude to Mr Ranjan Kaul of Response Books for his sound and timely advice that has made this book publishable.

We would also like to place on record our appreciation of the excellent editorial support provided by Ms Nalinee Contractor, EDI. The competent and sincere assistance of Mrs Bindu Haridas and Mr Deepak Upadhyay, EDI, and the contribution, in particular, of Mr S.S. Modi (Consultant), are also duly acknowledged.

V. Padmanand
P.C. Jain

PART ONE

1

A Snapshot Of A Third-World Industrial 'Superpower'

Family business dominates the Indian business scenario, accounting for about 95 per cent of Indian industry. The industry, though largely composed of the public sector, is progressively being privatized. The large industrial base and the achievements of Indian industry, even in extremely high-tech areas, has led to India being classified as an industrializing economy. Even though not 'developed' in per capita terms, the economy is often compared to the Far Eastern 'Tigers'. With over 10 airports, of over 3,047 metres in length, and relatively good infrastructural facilities in at least most of the urbanized agglomerates, the burgeoning Indian middle class has been attracting the attention of international corporates. Of course, the development is not equally dispersed, and high-income states possess far higher infrastructural facilities, literacy rates and per capita income levels than do the low-income states in the subcontinent. But then, no entrepreneur would explore the possibility of setting up a manufacturing facility in a backward area, seeking developmental finance, ignoring raw material, labour, transportation and infrastructural bottlenecks. Hence, this disparity in development has more of welfare than investment implications. Foreign Direct Investment (FDI) has started flowing into the subcontinent in relatively higher levels than the pre-reform pre-1991 years. FDI flows into India to seek new markets or to source inputs of raw material and labour, etc., at competitive levels for global markets. The advantage of direct investment over portfolio investment to the foreign investor is quite well known. Direct investments facilitate direct control of plant facilities, managerial decisions and ensure proprietary technology.

India, like many countries around the globe, has been dismantling the remains of a controlled regime. Privatization, a relatively favourable attitude towards foreign investors, deregulation of domestic capital markets and attempts at efficiency orientation of domestic economies, remains the order of the day. This may imply rather sudden increases in competition and intense rivalry in the Indian industrial economy in the short run. India, with its population of about a billion, a GDP of $294 billion (adjusted to purchasing power parity of over a trillion), and its image as a third-world superpower, almost possessing the world's largest skilled manpower base, is seemingly an attractive location. However, of the worldwide flow of hundreds of billions of dollars of FDI, a minuscule fraction flows into India.

With reduced tariff barriers, in accordance with the tenets of the World Trade Organization (WTO), and greater investor friendliness, competition in the market is on the rise. Competition may perhaps have a great impact on existing larger firms than on smaller firms, as is sometimes made out by industrial lobbies. Also, the impact of competition will be felt over a period of time, with varying levels of impact on different sectors and sub-sectors of industry and the economy. The two million small-scale industries (SSIs) of India, largely run by small entrepreneurs, also face the challenges of globalization. And, many do well. More than 90 per cent of the SSIs are, in fact, in the tiny unit category, with limited investment in plant and machinery, at most running to a few million rupees.

In fact, many small units and SSIs, particularly those operating in large industrial clusters, manufacturing products such as gems and jewellery, leather and related products, are doing relatively well. Competition, for many such potentially viable industry sectors in India, arises from China and South-East Asia. While product reservation for SSIs is claimed to be against the precepts of a free-market regime, many SSIs survive on such reservations. SSIs in industry sectors operating in market segments requiring customized products in relatively small volumes, and where scale economies have low implications, have been doing well against competition from larger units. In fact, such units operating in labour intensive sectors, with low wages and overheads, and fixed costs, operate successfully. It is the customer-market segment, rather than the geographical-market segment, that is small in many cases. That is why perhaps, component manufacturers, complementary goods manufacturers, textiles, gem and jewellery and leather goods manufacturers are doing relatively well, even in the SSI categorized sectors.

India has a population of several million people living below the poverty line. However, in the medium term, benefits of reforms, in terms of encouragement of private initiative in infra-structure, and in most sectors, excluding trade in certain essential commodities such as petroleum and wheat, is expected to trickle down to the masses. The relative rate of failure and danger of the subsidy and dole option is well known!

In the current environment in India, problems in investment evaluation and corruption are obstacles in the path of business opportunity identification, its evaluation and implementation. Accounting practices may 'in principle', and on the face of it, be in harmony with international accounting standards, but standardized auditing practices are not free from manipulations. Costs and returns can be easily boosted or depressed, depending on the requirements of a company—either to impress a banker and the public, or alternatively to evade tax. Smaller firms, in particular, can easily evade statutory rules and guidelines. The official machinery often has inadequate resources to ensure the effective monitoring and fulfillment of statutory obligations.

The power of lobbies to orient policy in their favour, against the larger 'good', is also starkly obvious. Elite cliques, often comprising big industrialists, sometimes control lobbies in small and large industrial associations. And, lobbying for increasing the ceiling of investment for the preferentially treated SSIs, for example, has often been against the interests of the really small units. Deflated prices of fixed assets often accommodate larger units into the SSI category and help reap benefits for themselves. Perhaps this is one reason why the Indian government is currently rethinking its decision on the recently enhanced SSI investment limit criteria.

India is the world's largest democracy. But democracy is not a criteria for development. South Korea did not have a democratic Government but has achieved a high level of prosperity. While China, as it moves towards prosperity, is taking steps towards setting up a democratic system. Changes in political systems, be they democratic, dictatorial or socialist, can hardly influence social values in terms of social and business ethics in a short time. Also, the enactment and enforcement of legislations has not been very effective in resolving the situation in India. The US 1997 Foreign Corrupt Practices Act is supposed to have ensured that United States exporters are considered amongst the least corrupt today. Bribes given to foreign officials to facilitate business dealings in foreign countries are deemed illegal. In India, such an enactment is often difficult to impose, implement and monitor.

Regardless of some deficiencies in the environment for absolute 'fair-play', till about 1996–97, the Indian economy has shown an impressive performance in most sectors. With progressive liberalization, growth in the mining, infrastructure and manufacturing sectors is expected. An increased base of competitiveness and export orientation has often been the focus of companies in India, even if it is only to meet statutory export obligations.

And, what about the elusive Non-Resident Indian (NRI)? In the global scenario, NRI-run businesses that are small and medium by European standards have been playing the role of transnationals in terms of presence and initiative. Mittal, of steel fame, is hardly the only operator. Many firms run by entrepreneurs of Indian origin, have been thrusting into South America, Eastern Europe and Central

Asian countries. They have been participating in the wholesale sale of factories and enterprises in Eastern Europe, and sometimes challenging even the MNCs in India. For example, Devinder Sood had initiated his enterprise in the US, with his accumulated savings of $50,000, to manufacture cable-joints by using heat-shrink technology. Plastic is treated so as to mould itself to the exact configuration of an object when heat is applied to it—basically a quick-sealing material. He has been buying small companies in different countries abroad, and is also setting up a manufacturing base in India. The localized units cater to relevant domestic markets. Sood has been targeting electricity and telecommunication departments across the globe. His group's investment in plant and machinery, spread across three continents, does not exceed $8 million. Smaller NRI-operated firms have been rearing up their heads and flexing their muscles against large firms and domestic competition all over the world. But their presence, let alone the presence of NRI 'professionals-turned-entrepreneurs', in the Indian environment, remains relatively small.

Global Players Eye The Market Of The Next Millennium

A Market Of Teeming Millions Going Materialistic

In Taiwan, the $6 billion giant, RK Inc., is considering options for implementation of its company plans to increase the contribution of its overseas manufacturing operations in the field of consumer electronics, from 24 per cent to 87 per cent of the total turnover by the year 2007. The majority of its new manufacturing facilities are expected to be based at locations in South Africa, South East Asia, Latin America and . . . India in South Asia. These locations seem favourites of 'larger' foreign companies exploring project exports, not only to avail of lower manufacturing, particularly labour costs, to target a global market, but to also effectively tap the vast domestic markets in such regions. The cumulative purchasing power of the middle class in each of these economies at least equals that of a smaller west European country. This implies the availability of a whole country on a platter, at the disposal of any potential market leader or 'niche'. In India alone, RK Inc. plans to invest about half a billion dollars in the form of project costs of production bases. 'For consumer electronics, India is going to be the largest market in a few years,' says Shelat, Managing Director of the group. China is the only other economy displaying a potential even remotely similar to India. In-house company studies in India revealed one hundred per cent growth in demand for colour televisions, refrigerators and washing machines from 1996–2000 AD. And the boom in domestic consumption is expected to increase.

Riding Piggy-Back Into The Market

Advantages for a market-leader position include a possible 20 per cent share of the growth of perhaps a million pieces in each of the relevant consumer electronics category. RK Inc. would like to have its slice of the pie in terms of the ever-increasing market requirements over the first decade of the next millennium. Many such companies from South East Asia are looking for new markets in geographic rather than segment terms across the globe. All of them face looming prospects of rising competition in domestic markets and relatively low growth in these markets, sometimes coupled with the necessity to reduce tariff barriers and increased competition in their domestic economies under the WTO regime. A 'blitzkrieg' approach and high technology, coupled with competitive pricing, is the strategy followed by many such foreign companies to penetrate new markets. Indian subsidiaries are formed if the possibility of viable joint ventures with Indian companies fail. In fact, the former may be a preferred option for many who would prefer to keep their technology proprietary. Permission from the Indian Foreign Investment Promotion Board is secured as a matter of routine, and products hit distribution channels within smaller geographic market segments India such as Delhi, Bangalore, Pune and their surrounding satellite townships in down time.

Within months of a successful launch, the product is pushed nationally. Market penetration, employing predatory pricing, is not necessarily followed. Products of similar established companies sell on the strength of product quality and distribution channels. The product is ensured to be appropriate and modified to Indian operating conditions. RK Inc. plans to follow the conventional consumer-durable-goods marketing stratagem of promotion, employing advertising and promotional campaigns. Market entry is often initiated by import of completely knocked-down kits, and later followed by greater indigenization of manufacture. This process may take a year or two in some cases. However, most entrants seem to follow the economists' precept of shifting of manufacturing bases, pursuing lower manufacturing and operating costs to cater to particular domestic or even international markets. Hence, indigenization efforts are often speeded up.

Exclusive distribution outlets, common for more expensive consumer goods' distribution, such as cars, is hardly a necessary requirement in the case of most consumer durable or non-durable goods manufacturers. The market place is not uncrowded, and building up a brand image and establishing a distribution set-up, backed by a major distributor in every large city in the subcontinent, may take about a year for implementation. As mentioned earlier, those firms who would like to initially ride piggy-back on the channels of an established Indian company, go in initially for joint ventures. Others confident of establishing their own marketing channels prefer the wholly owned subsidiary route.

The Riders To Foreign Investment . . . And The Long Haulers

Foreign players are often saddled with an export obligation of several times of the import value, with realization being required in less than a decade. Often, export obligations are met with not by the 'major' product of the foreign unit. It may be yet another subsidiary company, perhaps in the field of software development and export, or export of primary agricultural products, that may generate the required export earnings! The software professional base in India is renowned for its quality and low prices, particularly for several software consultancy and application developments that are invariably subcontracted to India by enterprises in the West. Of course, the spurt in software exports is sometimes attributed to 'hawala' rackets for converting black money to white and routing money to India. Nevertheless, the foreign exchange generation focussed policy of the government hardly ponders on these nuances. Bureaucracy has its advantages for the smart businessman earnest to penetrate Indian markets. In fact, firms who meet export obligations often meet them even at a loss to themselves! They make their margins in the domestic market.

Many global players are entering to tap the Indian market of 2020 AD for a variety of consumer products. It is often a long-term game plan of even a decade-long duration. Obviously those without the wherewithal quit or avoid the market, while the confident wait patiently for the killing of the next century! RK Inc. will wait. They know the ropes.

Sensei Electro: Market Niche Within A New Geographical Market

With the Japanese and Europeans focussing on more sophisticated products, be they personal computers or high definition televisions, the mass-market electronics industry segment is relatively untapped. Enterprising Korean firms and their like often tap such niches. Similar to the strategy adopted by some MNC-pushed traditional Indian brands, such as Lifebuoy soap, Sensei plans to launch their products at the lower end of the market, and then graduate to high margin, premium-priced upper-end products. For many, perhaps this appears to be a saner proposition in a recessionary market. While some adopt the top-down approach of initially pushing premium-priced top-end products, many others follow the Sensei approach. All firms, however, have but one objective—to carve out a market niche for themselves.

Building Brand Awareness Over Sales Volumes Even While Developing Entrepreneurs

Larger players from abroad, such as Sensei, have the ability and resources to play a waiting game. Sensei, with its parent company in Taiwan, controlled by Japanese promoters, also believes in initially building brand awareness. Their unique stratagem is in focussing on a product line within a product category or form, which is conveniently believed to be in the declining or final stage of its life cycle—for example, on black and white television sets and 'no-frills' colour television sets. Focussing on the industrially developed and high-income states of Gujarat and Maharashtra, and the half a dozen metropolitan cities spread across the subcontinent, Sensei too hopes to completely indigenize manufacture, so as to afford competitive pricing. Local vendors are planned to be developed simultaneously, and facility upgradation of these local Indian entrepreneurs undertaken from the coffers of Sensei, where necessary. 'It is in fact not just low labour costs, but more importantly an efficient manufacturing process, distribution network and logistics that are key issues,' explains Shin, a Director at Sensei. New market niches and segments may be created and developed within a smaller geographical market area. Mere geographical spread and basing facility across the globe or across the Indian subcontinent is hardly the only option in the 'globalized village'. Sensei Electronics will largely operate only in the two developed western Indian states. Perhaps this is sound business sense.

CRIL Chemicals: Losing Appetite For The Chinese Pie

Many west European global players, such as CRIL Chemicals, a 30-billion-dollar chemical giant from France, is eyeing India in a new light—as an alternative to overinvested China. CRIL Chemicals is a hived-off speciality chemicals manufacturer under an even bigger global parent. Hoechst is not the only multinational thinking of leading the Indian speciality chemicals industry. Agrochemical, pesticides and leather finishing agents and dyestuffs are booming industries in the subcontinent. And, unlike in China, foreign firms can have their own Indian subsidiary without a local partner. As mentioned earlier, this facilitates avoiding the risk of loosing proprietary technology . . . what with Indian laws, patent regimes and courts. The mineral-rich states of Orissa and Bihar could well be the base for products developed for the world market by several medium-sized firms operating the global plane.

The Fight Is Also (In) Entertainment

Few industries are left alone. Global conglomerates are also up in arms against one another for market share and leeway in the entertainment industry. Hijacking of shows by buying off producers of one channel provider by other channel providers, is usual. Hoardings and other conventional advertising media promotion of programmes and channels are a common feature. Offering a variety in fare, catering to viewers' ages and languages, is also popular.

Be it Sony Television Entertainment, with its several channels, or Zee or Star TV, it is often not just television or satellite TV entertainment that seems to be their focus. Many operators have been exploiting options in the Hindi music industry of audiotapes, and of dubbed Hollywood movies in the film industry. Globus TV is just one conglomerate that looks at synergies when penetrating the Indian market. Its activities in channels and audiotapes are closely connected to building a brand image to gain acceptance of its colour TV and audio systems.

For the consumer, the intense competition in the market has been rather beneficial. Product quality has been rising, and cost and payment terms for products, in many cases, are becoming increasingly attractive. But how are the players of Indian 'ethnicity' faring?

Non-Resident Indians
And Their Demands

Other than the foreign firms, there are our own NRIs. Indian bureaucracy is renowned the world over for what it has been . . . a bureaucracy. The NRI has been defined under the Income Tax (IT) Act, for taxation purposes, based on the number of days an individuals stay in India. Under the Foreign Exchange Regulation Act, the definition is based on the duration of stay abroad. Opening up of a Non-Resident External (NRE) bank account, the criteria with regard to duration of stay abroad, and stay in India, vary over time, as do the nature of currency holding, repatriation options and rates of interest on deposits. The bureaucracy leaves some loopholes for manipulation as usual. But in an economy groping its way towards a free market system, higher levels of implementable efficiency would take time to set up. Also, one should look upon India with an 'open mind', an oft-heard piece of rather sound advice.

Top NRI businessmen and global investors have been clamouring for greater levels of accountability and transparency in the working of the government, speedy implementation of policies and administrative revamping. The necessity for an integrated mechanism, to effectively co-ordinate activities of various relevant government departments, particularly with regard to inter-ministerial and centre–state departmental cooperation, is a regularly repeated requisite. Abolishment of visa requirements for people of Indian origin, holding Indian passports, is one of the minor requirements, while demands for a stable centre is a major requirement. Nomination of representatives of external investors and NRIs, on advisory bodies of industry, 'hassle-free' remittance of dividends on non-repatriable NRI investments, increasing privatization in the banking and insurance sectors, and many more such demands have also been 'considered' by policy makers.

The Supreme Cosmopolitans

Expatriate Indians are predominantly professionals in the US, they constitute less than one per cent of the population in Hong Kong, but account for a large percentage of exports. They own the majority of all independent outlets in the UK. Coffee-shop banter harps on the surname 'Patel', a Gujarati business class, as being amongst the largest 'foreign' surnames one finds when going through a telephone directory in the UK or the USA! Silicon Valley has its fair share of Indian multinational businessmen. While some bigtimers are exploring direct investments in India in the fields of telecommunications, transportation, power generation, infotech and steel plants, involving tens of hundreds of millions of dollars, smaller professionals and businessmen still fight relatively shy. The NRIs return to pursue or initiate large projects. There are, however, not many of them! Moreover, the big brands come often with NRI professionals at the helm of project implementation. Be it asset management companies or consultancy firms, this is often the norm. There is no dearth of NRI professionals to facilitate entry. Of course, time alone will tell if these NRI professionals are professional or 'deft' enough to handle the environment . . . smaller brands have sometimes left in quick shrift, and the scenario with regard to small and medium enterprises in particular, is hardly comforting. There are a number of 'foreign' Indians who prefer to retain their NRI identity while doing or managing business in India.

One Up On The Goliaths?

Silicon Valley players in the big league, including Bill Gates himself, are eyeing India as a base for production. Not to be left behind, several NRI professional technocrat entrepreneurs have been toeing the line of the MNCs. Hardsys is one player that recently launched its plethora of personal computers (PCs), servers, multimedia systems and notepads in India. The enterprise had its humble beginnings in California, with seed money of $10,000 about a decade and a half ago. Today it generates over a billion in revenues. Hardsys serves as a vendor to several giants in the business, and has been focussing on the development of hardware accessories and components. Today, the enterprise also sells under its own brand name. Over the years, it has sufficiently integrated to be able to manufacture a computer in toto, in-house. The enterprise founder, Deepak Vyas, has almost single-handedly built up a team of thousands of professionals, and attributes his success to offering customized products. In India, he plans to focus on a cost-based market entry stratagem. Low-cost leadership is strived to be attained, not by compromising on the quality or on the service and utility offered to the customer. It has been integrated into the product itself . . . reducing functions and utilities not really required by Indian users. The multimedia PC units cuts out the unnecessary frills, and will be distributed and marketed directly through dealers, thereby reducing the levels of channels and cutting costs. At a project cost of $20 million, the Indian base will be developed as an independent profit centre with complete vertical integration. An advertisement budget of about $2 million is slated for the first two years for brand awareness generation. The enterprise is looking for a 200-dealer network and plans to sell about 40,000 pieces a year. By dealing directly with dealers, the company plans to save on the 3–4 per cent margins to distributors, and 5 per cent to retailers. While brand building for the PC market may not be a crucial factor, with cost advantages paving the way for market acceptance, certain product categories, such as servers and notepads, may require a gestation of about two years for brand positioning and awareness generation. The low-cost launch of lower end products, could, in future, help launch top-end premium-priced products, that may face direct competition from MNCs. A viable strategy for sure! What about our own 'Indian' entrepreneurs?

Smaller Indians Ride Winners

Thirty-year old Hemant Saravat launched his 'leather goods and complements' enterprise in 1989. He generates a turnover of Rs 40 million with a current project cost of Rs 10 million. His uncle had been a bookkeeper at the Madras racecourse, and Saravat spent most of his youth as an apprentice to his uncle. Leather products and the 'feel' of leather were hardly new to him. He used to marvel at the profit margins that dealers and manufacturers of leather accessories made . . . both on the turf and outside. The high margins seemed to arise from the customized products delivered in accordance to customer specifications. Rather 'casually' Saravat decided to quote for a tender for leather accessories floated by a race club in another city. He bid in the name of a friend's firm, manufacturing leather goods, and clinched the order. There has been no looking back since then. The public school-educated Saravat built on his first deal of 1989. His presentation and negoti-ation skills were excellent and when leveraging with personal contacts, clinching corporate deals was not very difficult. The 90s saw a boom in the corporate complement industry. The complement product boom included wallets, file-folders and office accessories. Adding silk and brass fittings to leather and jute mixed products helped lend greater aesthetic and perceived value, and secure higher margins for his products. Over the last few years he has also started branding his products, which allows him to charge premium prices. Saravat has opened a retail outlet in Madras and one in Bangalore, to serve a larger clientele and to avoid excessive reliance on only institutional sales. The concept of dealing in complementary goods was relatively novel in the late 80s, but by the mid 90s, competition, particularly from innumerable small players, has become intense. However, by means of offering greater varieties in terms of product-line and possession of good contacts for manufacturing customized requirements, Beleveaux (Saravat's company) has managed to remain one up on competitors. There is no dearth of success stories that highlight sheer grit and business acumen, coupled with an 'open-mind', which have laid the foundations for successful entrepreneurship in India. Investible surplus hardly counts.

Indians Who Believe In Themselves And In Breaking Even

Caroline D'Souza completed a Bachelor in Pharmacy and felt she could never work under someone. It was hardly a leaning that was in her blood. Her family were staunch government employees, and there was nothing in her pedigree to indicate her entrepreneurial preference and pursuits after she graduated. One weekend, over a casual conversation, a friend of hers in a bank informed her of a new scheme floated by the government, and implemented by the Small Industries Development Bank of India through nationalized commercial banks. The scheme, the 'Mahila Udyam Nidhi', had been launched particularly to fund potential women entrepreneurs in the country. The equity contribution from the promoter, and collateral requirements under the scheme, were a dream for would-be entrepreneurs. Caroline's interest was awakened. Her brother worked in a senior management cadre in a leading intravenous fluid and syringe manufacturing firm. A discussion with him on her entrepreneurial inclination gave birth to a business idea. She underwent a three-month entrepreneurship development training programme in manufacturing rubber products, at the Small Industries Service Institute (SISI), Delhi. The project for manufacturing rubber stoppers for the syringes made at her brother's enterprise was implemented soon after. The investment of Rs 1 million in the project, secured under the scheme, was largely in terms of financing purchase of the plant and machinery. Caroline ensured that she could operate on low levels of fixed expenditure by cutting out unnecessary machine capacity and employees. The in-plant capacity was sufficient to service her brother's company. 'I catered to orders from two other large clients by subcontracting for them on a job work basis. I could thus operate on low break-even levels,' she explains. This foresight, in fact, helped her tide over a crisis sparked off by a temporary labour union strike in her brother's company, and subsequent fall in demand. A significant aspect of Caroline's venture is that all the machines utilized were fabricated in other equipment-manufacturing units of her associates. She could hence save on capital costs to the extent of 60 per cent. Rubber Inc. has invested considerable funds on R&D over the years, on moulds and systems. Caroline has been staunch (and perhaps lucky) in receiving and making payments on schedule. Her case reinforces the advantage of possessing one of the usual bases for successful entrepreneurship, viz., established and strong relationships either with the raw material supplier, the market and/or banker.

Resolve Of Steel

Srinath Rao, a scion of a medium-sized business family, completed his engineering education at a leading Indian institution. Subsequently, he completed a professional course on financial analysis, and worked in leading Indian engineering firms. 'I believed in acquiring valuable experience in all functional management areas,' he declares. Experience in these companies, other than helping to provide insights into the operations of competitors, helped him gain exposure to develop systems and practices in accounting, marketing and operation methods.

In 1993, he stepped into his father's shoes as head of a diversified group. The unexpected demise of his father laid a tremendous burden on his shoulders. However, the enterprise had its flagship company operating in the manufacture of steel structures for infrastructure, and had been serving as a vendor for a large MNC for years. Hence, the market had never been a problem. Soon after his takeover, misappropriation of funds by some of the top management cadre brought the enterprise pretty close to collapse. Within a few months of Rao taking over, servicing creditors and funding agencies seemed impossible. It never occurred to him to throw in the towel. He set up an automobile ancillary manufacturing unit, as an independent entity, to serve some of his existing clients, in three months flat, and to generate cash to pay off creditors. The venture was a success. The corrupt old-time employees were sacked and he brought in a cadre of professionals to handle his flagship company. Perseverance to go ahead, in spite of the looming collapse of his enterprise, gave him the opportunity to build on his experience and succeed in his business venture. It was his exposure to financial systems, during his years of working as an employee in others' firms, that helped him identify the lacunae in his books, and pilferage of funds in his own system, in time.

Holidaying Can Generate Millions

Rao's favourite holiday haunt has been the Alps. His annual vacation gave him the idea of a new diversification option . . . that of manufacturing multilayer films, with a definite product advantage of a longer shelf life. In 1996, while skiing on the Alps, a casual conversation with a professional in a Japanese firm, led to a technical collaboration with the Japanese multinational. In a year and a half, the unit located in Hyderabad generated a turnover of Rs 60 million, with a profit, after taxes, of 10 million per annum. Rao is now eyeing the automobile ancillary component industry with greater interest. The way he has been operating, there is no reason why he should not continue doing well. Most of his diversified enterprises are serving the same market segment–that is an advantage in his favour.

Creating Shelf-Space

Vineet Daruwala manufactures quilts, sleeping bags and soft toys. The enterprise touches a turnover of over Rs 20 million today. Initially, marketing the concept of branded sleeping bags was difficult to impose on the market, and distribution channels in particular. Daruwala found it tough to convince retailers to provide sufficient shelf-space to display his products. Eventually, some of the larger retail stores in Calcutta agreed to stock his brand. The margins he offered them were initially rather high. Today, he has established a brand name. A name that sells. It was easy for him to do it—he had a saleable product . . . sleeping bags with polyester, to ensure less weight and more warmth, with the advantage of zippers to tuck oneself in. The concept was adapted from the West, but the material that was used in the manufacture of the product was customized to meet Indian quality-price preferences. Daruwala's product fought for and secured shelf-space on its own strength. Creating shelf-space for itself was the fountainhead of all future successes. Product differentiation, particularly with tangible value addition and benefits over competitors, can itself be a hallmark of success.

Distinct From The Herd . . . Hertz

'Kaiser's dream' comprises a fleet of two hundred cars. The enterprise has manoeuvred its way to the top slot in the car rental industry sector in the four South Indian capitals. Anurag Dixit launched his maiden business venture in 1993, and how it has grown! The enterprise had its humble beginnings in a makeshift garage in downtown Calcutta. An acquaintance in the telephone department helped him secure a telephone. The telephone was intended to help his customers reach him in times of emergency. But it also led to a new diversification option—into a related field . . . car rentals.

Dixit had hardly any formal education in his youth. He was an orphan, adopted by an Anglo-Indian family, when he was nine. His transition from a missionary orphanage to a garage was smooth. His foster father successfully ran a small car-servicing centre, and

Dixit learnt all his professional skills for over 16 years, under his able tutelage. At 25, he launched his own garage, a short distance away from his mentor's. The small piece of land belonged to his foster parents and could not be disposed off due to legal squabbles regarding ownership between family members.

A Call Away From Success

The telephone in his makeshift garage rang one weekend, immediately after he commenced operations. Dixit's involvement in the activities of a leading political party had given him a break. The party proposed to hold a rally and was desperately looking for cars on hire. Could he help? Dixit certainly could. He promptly dispatched a dozen of the cars that he was servicing and secured an impressive rental income . . . and the blessings of political bigwigs. The returns in the rental business caught his attention and he focussed all his energies towards developing this business. He tied up with smaller hotels, wedding halls and political parties, offering low-cost car rentals. In two years, he was grossing a turnover of Rs 2 million. Immediately, he ploughed in all his profits in procuring Maruti-1000s. Fourteen of them were sufficient for him to approach a new high-price, premium market segment of corporate clients. Quality, delivery and service was the name of the game. Dixit offered all of them. He was able to squeeze out very high premium charges from his clients, who hardly had any alternatives, and felt they received good value for money. 'Kaiser's Dream' was a rather unique and catchy tag he gave his enterprise. In another three years, Dixit grossed a turnover of over Rs 10 million a year. His package tours to Darjeeling, a hill resort, became popular amongst his corporate clients.

Dixit declares, 'I insist on the frills as much as on tangible value when I offer my services. That's how I beat my American competitors at Calcutta.' He has tied up with larger motels, to ensure that his clients receive priority service in the course of long drives. Over the last two years, he has specialized in offering comfortable drives to corporate executives travelling to the North-east. His drivers sport neat and smart uniforms, refurbished Sierras have CD players, a VCR, a refrigerator and a bar, a sofa-cum-bed, and a toilet and shower to boot. Kaiser's Dream is something of a dream come true for busy corporate executives who travel a lot.

Media Satraps Up Every Alley

Ramjee Yogam worked in his father's advertising agency, even while still in his teens. Advertising was in his blood. 'Advertising was hardly a popular or established business option in the 80s,' declares Yogam. But in about a decade, he transformed the agency into a one-stop outlet for all kinds of media and related services; be it event management, print and electronic media, billboards, financial ads, or just press releases. 'This was a far cry from the almost exclusive focus on press releases in days of yore, and working for survival,' explains Yogam. 'I may not be a media moghul in size or diversity in activity, but I do well for myself as a "Satrap", all right.' He is a regional player, often working on activities sub-contracted by larger firms. But nevertheless, he runs a sustainable operation. Many entrepreneurs learn and grow with the market. It is hardly necessary to have a narrowly focussed and sustainable option at project conception. One can learn and adjust over a period of time

Quality Consciousness On The Rise

Large Indian business houses, and even MNCs, depend on Paranj-pye's laboratory for its testing facilities. Sehgal, the General Manager of CLC, a multinational from Germany, declares, 'Paranjpye's "Mettle Pvt. Ltd." has been our reliable partner for many of our analyses. Their reports are certainly professional and adequate.' Specifications and procedures for establishing a new technique of testing may be well known. However, the designing requirements to establish them are the toughest part. The engineers and chemists in Paranjpye's laboratory, test the standards of materials used in metal products, including plates and bars, and have, over a seven-year period of existence, graduated to using spectrometers worth over Rs 10 million as core equipment. An impressive growth from the seed capital initial investment of about Rs 140,000. The shift in today's market towards 'quality, standardization, exports and vendor operations is ideal' establishes Paranjpye. It is not only good for Indian industry in general, but has also been a godsend to the fledgling enterprise. There certainly is sufficient scope for manoeuvring and securing 'shelf-space' and room for the smallest of units.

The Skin Off One's Back For The Market Unsavvy

Ramachandran in Coimbatore produces different kinds of briefcases, wallets, pouches and portfolios. The enterprise was initiated in technological and marketing collaboration with an Italian firm. Unlike most of the units in the leather cluster at Chennai, the manufacturing facilities of the enterprise are almost completely automated. In terms of its in-house-upgraded splitting, sewing or embossing machines and its R&D division, incorporating its own CAD/CAM facilities, the unit is the pride of the region. 'Most of the leather garments, shoes and goods manufacturing units are based around Chennai, to avail of raw material and port facilities for export. But I focussed on the more sustainable market,' observes Ramachandran. The growing number of medium and larger enterprises in various industrial sectors in Coimbatore offers Ramachandran's 'Sergio Leathers' a large market for complementary goods in the region. The tie-up with Italy facilitates his presence in the West European markets. The units at Chennai face cut-throat competition, both in domestic markets and in the international markets. Sergio's proximity to a geographical segment of the market, facilitates negotiation, better service and delivery facilities to his target clients in India. The joint venture partnership with the foreign company, has, in fact, facilitated technology transfer. The brand of the Italian firm has been used to help launch their products in India. Ramachandran may be sharing profits and managerial control, but this is a small price to pay for the sustainable development of his organization in an industry which is currently subject to domestic and international market recession and competitive pressures.

Get Hold Of A Market To Serve

Hi-tech Arts was incorporated in 1993, with a seed capital of less than Rs 200,000. From a turnover of Rs 300,000 in 1994, it has graduated to an over Rs 25 million company in less than four years. The Managing Director, Mr Khanna, believes the market in Chandigarh is subject to severe competitive pressures, but Hi-tech has a secure clientele base. Productivity enhancement and systems implantation has been the thrust of Khanna's enterprise. 'Providing business solutions in these areas is a fast-growing industry,' claims Khanna. Initially focussing on securing maintenance and service contracts, his team today includes financial experts, transportation and logistics networking people. Like most small-scale starters, Khanna had worked for a large Indian corporate in the software development department. On his own initiative, he moved to customer service. Soon he established personal relationships with clients and understood their requirements. Over eight years of work as an employee, he mobilized a personal investible surplus of almost Rs 300,000 and went to work on his own. He had a potential client list and he knew their requirements. He could offer them what they were looking for at half the price charged by larger firms. He had it made from the beginning. The problem of building up a small team to devise system and business solutions was easily solved. He took a few of his fellow employees into his entrepreneurial venture. Six of them came in as directors. The fact that the team expanded to include mechanical and other engineers and financial experts, helped them offer a total management consultancy package to corporate clients. Their relatively low overheads helped them offer better value for money at highly competitive rates. Khanna is today planning to move away from their key target markets in Chandigarh and Ludhiana to Uttar Pradesh, Himachal Pradesh and Rajasthan . . . and this is just the beginning.

Market Sentiments Count: Let Us Make No Bones About It

Areez Godrej launched his bone china unit in Baroda, Gujarat, in 1985. Whether it is flatware or holloware, the medium-sized enterprise has been a force to reckon with in the industry. It has tied up with a government R&D laboratory for design development. The products are exported to Europe, South-East Asia and Australia. 'Our labour costs are extremely low,' vouches Godrej, 'we pay slightly more than Rs 1000 to an employee, while in the US it may cost that much in dollars.' According to him, the importance of catering to market sentiments is vital. His unit and another ancillary unit, manufacturing skin cream, have thrived on selling their products as vegetarian chinaware, cutlery and vegetarian lotions . . . the products are manufactured by means of indigenously developed technology that does not incorporate bovine and ovine bones in the manufacturing process—all perfectly suited to a highly 'vegetarian' conscious Gujarati market.

The experiences of the entrepreneurs and the enterprises encapsulated above indicates that competition and success is aplenty in the Indian business environment, and the players are large, medium and small. There are the multinationals, there are small first-generation Indian entrepreneurs, family business operators, smaller foreign firms and some NRIs. The potential of the economy and the market is obvious, as is also its limitations. Yet the NRIs who could be significant players here are few in number. The following part of the volume explores this issue in detail.

5

The Non-Starters

We have considered briefly the experiences of some successful ventures. However, businesses do fail. It is widely believed that the bulk of the smaller units who secure provisional registration from the District Industries Centre, and start operations, fail. Amongst larger units, given the scale of operations and investment levels, sickness and non-start up is to a lower degree. What this indicates is perhaps obvious. It is often a defective project or an inefficient management that leads to enterprise failures. However, circumstances, such as non-disbursement of promised subsidy, or release of working capital, with the fault lying in the support system, may also in many cases be the culprit. In the overall perspective of the environment, it is anybody's guess. But in the context of the individual enterprise, the cause for non-start up of an enterprise, or its subsequent failure, may be enterprise specific. The Indian industrial environment is hardly without its failure stories or entrepreneurial misadventures.

Hiccups That Seal Coffins

Sainath Enterprises was established with the intention of processing, grading and packaging tea. Two partners, Vivek Singh and Gautam

Rathod, launched the enterprise. The project report was prepared thoroughly by the Small Industries Service Institute located at Guwahati, Assam. However, while a thorough market survey had been completed, and financial projections were impressive, the enterprise hardly had an opportunity to take off. The State Financial Corporation disbursed its contribution of about Rs three million, as project financing, in phases. Phased reimbursement depended on the entrepreneurs' purchase of fixed assets. In two years of the installation of some of the minimum equipment required to commence operations, the enterprise failed. The partners failed to secure the required working capital of Rs 800,000 from any commercial bank. They could offer the required collateral to both the banks and the State Financial Corporation, but their projections on turnover and capacity utilisation were not acceptable to the banks, who reneged on their initial inclination and promise. Perhaps it was a case of the banks having met with their statutory quota for priority sector lending for that particular financial year, and were not really interested in financing two entrepreneurs who did not have any previous experience in business. By the time the State Finance Corporation commenced disbursing their contribution, four months had elapsed, and it was February 1994, the financial year ending for institutions. Both Singh and Rathod had about 15 years' experience each in the production department of a large Indian business house operating in the same field. Their marketing and financial competence may have been in doubt. Regardless of the banks' unwillingness to finance their operational requirements to required levels, the partners put in their own cash, and started operations with the necessary minimum equipment required. They did not want to accept lower levels of working capital that were offered by some banks, but decided to fight for ideal levels—even if it took months.

Their decision to 'fight' involved a lot of paper work between entrepreneurs and banks . . . and a lot of time. They purchased equipment utilizing their own equity and part of the contribution of the State Finance Corporation, but could operate at only 70 per cent capacity, as there was non-optimization and mismatch of line balancing between machines. Fixed assets are unfortunately lumpy.

They could neither achieve the volumes required to secure total margins to cover fixed costs, nor could they do anything to increase lowered relative margins, due to problems in line balancing of equipment. The enterprise could sustain itself for about two years without defaulting on interest obligation on term loans. That was it. The entrepreneurs ran out of cash when rotation was affected by a few doubtful and bad debts, and delay in payments from a few sundry debtors. The delay in disbursement of investment subsidy that the partners had pinned their hopes on put the final nail on the coffin of their entrepreneurial attempt.

Preconceived Notion And Misconceived Projects

The circumstances of Northern Piping are rather similar to that of Sainath Enterprise, which was initiated with the objective of manufacturing cast iron pipes, manhole covers and fittings. The promoter, Jaswant, had been in the Indian armed forces, and had acquired advanced training in metallurgy. Soft loan and priority lending schemes for ex-servicemen encouraged him to explore a manufacturing option after voluntary retirement. He also 'leveraged' a scheme in favour of his brother-in-law, Balbir. The latter initiated a unit for manufacture of poultry and cattle feed. Both units secured clearances from the State Finance Corporation in record time. Both projects were formulated at a project cost of about Rs 150,000 each. Both the enterprises received their term loans. Freight and investment subsidy was disbursed in months. Both units also secured requested working capital limits. Nevertheless, neither survived the first three months of operation. Balbir could not fulfill his commitment to meet government supply orders, as he did not have testing equipment, which had not been included in the project report prepared by the local District Industries Centre, and he had not personally followed up on the necessary requirements to satisfy an 'off-the-record' promise of regular government orders. He put in a fresh request for testing equipment to the term lending institution. The request was under consideration. Unfortunately, such things take time in India. And, material stockpiling and blocked cash turned out to be an insurmountable hurdle. Similarly, Jaswant's cast iron pipes could not be pushed either to the public sector enterprise involved in infrastructure development in Srinagar, or to the municipal corporation in Jammu. Militants went on the rampage in Srinagar, and Balbir's uncle, who held a key position in the corporation in Jammu, was transferred to Chittagong. Both units collapsed.

... And The Dropouts

Management Spitting Venom ... At One Another

Food Specialities Ltd. was established in Meerut in 1983 to manufacture biscuits. The enterprise was constituted as a partnership concern with four partners, Shantaram Naoroji, his niece, Meena Naoroji, and his brother-in-law and sister. Naoroji was a qualified food technologist, trained by the International Food and Agricultural Organisation (FAO). He had also worked as a junior scientist in the Central Food Technology Research Institute (CFTRI), Mysore, and in several multinational biscuit-manufacturing firms, for over two decades, before initiating the partnership. He and his brother-in-law were working partners, while the other two were financial partners. 'Crunchy' Biscuits soon became a household name in Uttar Pradesh. Excellent distribution channels and a diverse product line catering to different consumer price and taste segments ensured tremendous increases in profitability till 1991. That year, a personal dispute arose between the partners. Shantaram Naoroji concedes, 'Partnerships, it seems, are bound to fail. It may be ego conflicts, financial disputes, or a feeling of mutual exploitation. But something always crops up,' he continues, 'perhaps this is why financial institutions prefer to fund limited companies.' At least an account cannot be frozen by one agitated partner. This was exactly what happened. The enterprise virtually ground to a halt. Shantaram Naoroji quit, with an out of court settlement that took four months to be finalized. The unit re-commenced operations. But it was too late. Accumulated interest burden, the loss of his technical expertise and the loss of confidence amongst distributors, with regard to enterprise credibility, ensured that the unit wound up by mid-1992.

Shoddy Policies For The Entrepreneur?

Mussorie was proud of R.J. Shoddy Spinners and Processors Limited. With an installed capacity of about 600 metric tonnes per annum, and technology imported from Japan, the company provided direct and indirect employment for hundreds of locals. It converted local and imported wool to woollen yarn for the government and also for private traders. Its five years of operation, from 1985 to 1990, were a dream. But in 1991, the rupee devaluation increased the cost of imported shoddy, the major raw material for shoddy yarn. Soon after, the central government raised customs duty on imports of shoddy to 110 per cent, and the L.C. margin to 200 per cent, from the earlier 25 per cent, to discourage imports. The enterprise wound up by 1993. For about a year over 1992–1993, the promoter, Navin Mittal, made all attempts to resolve the situation. He ploughed in his personal savings, to generate cash to sustain operations. He lobbied with banks to increase his cash credit limits. But the institutions required additional collateral and proof of greater turnover. Where can an average entrepreneur provide confirmed orders a year in advance? And, how could he provide fresh collateral, when the first charge was already offered to the institutions? The Indian market place is replete with failure stories. The thrust of this volume, however, is to highlight survival and growth options and cases, and not mere pitfalls. In the next chapter, therefore, we focus on the RNRI and MNC breed, and explore their initiatives into entrepreneurship. Their circumstances and relative unfamiliarity obviously make the option of business in India the toughest for them, in relation to others.

PART TWO

6

The Patriotic NRI And Other Fables: One For The Policy Maker

We don't really want these NRIs back here. They'd be more useful to us wherever they are. It's their dollars that would be one hell of a help. We're seeking their patriotism, not them in person!

—Anonymous

Underpinnings Of A Phenomenon: Where Are All Those Dollars?

Foreign investment flows are required to fill in the country's domestic savings-investment gap. The Government of India, as mentioned earlier, had introduced several incentive schemes to attract Non-Resident Indians (NRIs). Subsequently, Foreign Direct Investment (FDI) and portfolio investment flows increased, particularly with economic reform in India. Not to potential, however. Moreover, while the initial enthusiasm following liberalisation led to investment proposals, a significant number of them remained mere proposals.

Acceptably, there is no dearth of empirical evidence regarding the rationale, either economic or sentimental, about the role played by expatriate ethnic nationals in contributing towards FDI in a relatively stable and liberalized Third World economy. Nevertheless, perception of potential market entrants, and their expectations of market returns and long-term macro-economic potential, as displayed by the relatively subdued behavioural patterns of Non-Resident Indians towards opportunity for Foreign Direct Investment, seemingly leans towards the irrational. Now, does it really? While preferential incentive mechanisms and progressive market reforms have not realized potential inflows, one should also remember that India is still not necessarily a very attractive option, or the only alternative place for the investor looking at it largely as an investment option. Even a simple deposit in an Indian bank may yield more than similar investment in many other countries would, even allowing for the possibility of the periodic depreciation of the rupee. Nevertheless, even disregarding the western economies, with symptoms of sustained recession, better alternatives exist in plenty.

Playing on the sentiments of NRIs, Indian politicians often make digs at them for not showing patriotism! Between two-thirds to three-fourths of the $40 billion FDI flowing into China every year is contributed by expatriate Chinese, they argue. But the 18–20 million NRIs, whose total worth may be estimated at $300 billion (*The Observer*, Mumbai, February 17, 1997), and who have an annual investible surplus of between $30–40 billion, have shown relatively little inclination to invest in India. Against a total approval of Rs 32.07 billion for 1995–96, only Rs 7,000 million, of FDI approvals represented NRI contributions. What's worse, less than a third of them materialized (*The Observer*, Mumbai, October 1, 1996). With respect to FDI inflows, it is not as though the NRIs are playing truant in isolation. While the Foreign Investment Promotion Board has approved $7 billion worth of total FDI in the last 6 months, it is anybody's guess as to whether investments will materialize. In fact, as against the cumulative total approvals of $ 22 billion, since 1991, only $ 4.5 billion has materialized as actual inflow.

NRI remittances, which amounted to about $ 3 billion a year over the 1980s, totalled $ 7.4 billion from 1995–96, were expected to touch $ 9 billion by 1996–97 (*The Times of India*, Ahmedabad, March 5, 1997). Why these anomalies? Investment is a business decision by NRIs and other foreign investors seeking to make a good return on capital, giving due consideration to subjective risk-return trade-offs, and the Indian business and bureaucratic environment which is non-conducive in comparison to other global options. This could perhaps explain why MNC's are getting into areas, such as consumer goods, where returns are quick and margins substantial. A typical syndrome, of investors, given an overly 'rosy' picture, quashed by an uncertain policy environment and bureaucracy, may explain the anomaly with regard to approvals and project materialization. It may also be argued that a large number of expatriate Chinese are entrepreneurs or descendants of an entrepreneurial breed, while NRI diaspora are largely professionals.

Why Invest In India? There Are Other Options Galore?

There is no dearth of evidence about the relatively unattractive nature of the Indian economy for the objective investor. *The Economic Times* (Mumbai, June 1, 1994) carried a report about the US credit rating agency, Moody's Investor Service, which, in its report entitled 'Moody's sovereign ratings: Global Outlook', had India as an Asian economy with lower than investment grade ratings, in a survey of 10 Asian nations. High fiscal deficits, high levels of public debt, and sustained recession, may keep ratings of advanced industrial nations broadly negative, and Latin America may be characterized by economic uncertainty. But why should expatriates from the rest of the world, let alone the Far East or South-East Asia, consider India as an excellent investment option? There are the Asian 'Tigers', and other options such as Eastern Europe and Latin

America. Why bet on the Indian elephant, which still has a long way to go towards export-driven economic growth, high savings and investment rates, and lower indebtedness?

The Heritage Foundation, in its 'Index of Countries', by degree of controls, ranked India 140 among 150 countries (*The Observer*, Mumbai, February 17, 1997). Under these circumstances, is it surprising that the 'patriotic' NRI, for patriotism's sake, makes a token investment in India and keeps the big money for better options? Maybe it is mere nostalgia that brings in some investment? Let alone short-term speculative investment, why should an NRI think of long-term tied-down investment in Indian enterprise? But some RNRIs do, and their rationale could be revealing. If mobilizing investors for any sustained period of time is going to be an uphill task, why should we not focus on the nostalgic NRI and get him to do business in India? He may not be a big fish, who comes in with tens of millions of dollars of investment. He may be able to afford investment only in the SME sector. But if he comes in, and is properly guided and trained, if necessary, to do business in a manner so as to ensure that he faces no monetary loss by his decision to return, and to do business, he and his money stays in India An invaluable combination that we desperately need!

Investment Augmenting Policies And
RNRI Entrepreneurship

Policies and procedures, since economic reforms in 1991, have been and are being continuously modified and simplified. Liberalization, with regard to foreign investment, includes provisions to initiate manufacturing operations of any size, with 100 per cent foreign equity participation. These new policies are open to a broad definition of NRIs, including, RNRIs, persons of Indian origin, and overseas corporate bodies. There are conditions regarding repatriable sums, such as in terms of export commitments in some cases. Repatriation-based portfolio investment had some limits on investible amounts, but by 1995, progressive liberalization ensured that NRIs were allowed to invest on a repatriable basis, in all areas except in agriculture and plantation activities. Through the automatic channel, the RBI reviews all cases for automatic approval. A Foreign Investment Promotion Board, in the Prime Minister's office, considers all proposals that are not automatically approved.

While there are repatriable options open to NRIs, an NRI may go in for the non-repatriable option, when his return to India eventually is almost certain, and he does not mind keeping some funds either re-invested in business in India, or elsewhere within the subcontinent.

Options and ceilings favour non-repatriation-based investments. Avenues for investment are innumerable with 100 per cent equity permissible on investments on a non-repatriation basis in a proprietary/partnership firm in any industrial, commercial or trading activity. This non-repatriation-based option is more attractive to the nostalgic NRI, who is returning, or would like to return to India someday. NRIs can operate ventures, perhaps with a working Indian partner (initially), or return and do business on their own. It is for the nostalgic NRI, who intends to return to India 'sometime', that policies should be progressively tailored, not for the 'patriotic' NRI, who is looking for better and more favourable repatriable options. We need to tap the person with more commitment to his 'home'. His investments are likely to be less 'flighty', and returns more likely to be ploughed back into productive investment in the country. While desperately seeking the multi-billion dollar institutional investor, and the 'big-time' NRI, the policies seem to be progressively ignoring what the 'smaller' RNRI can contribute. NRI technical professionals, management professionals, technocrats and entrepreneurs have a lot more to contribute to the national economy than mere fund investment in hard currency. Their technical skill, managerial expertise and new or adapted business ideas, if properly harnessed and channelized, could do wonders for Indian industry, even while contributing to their own material success. It is the NRI who returns and personally involves himself in some entrepreneurial activity, the RNRI entrepreneur, who is doing business in India, who contributes positively to the growth of the Indian economy. Portfolio investors and investors of direct investment, emphasizing on the repatriable option, are merely doing business 'with' India. We desperately need the RNRI!

RNRI Entrepreneurship: A Dismal Scenario

By focussing on FDI, the policy maker reveals his disdain for speculative portfolio investment in the stock market, which may remain mere 'hot' money. He is talking hard currency, long-term direct investment in Indian enterprise. What he needs to focus on is RNRI entrepreneurship. Only between five to ten SME manufacturing firms, registered as NRI projects (manufacturing firms), go on steam every year, even in a developed state like Gujarat. High and middle income states throughout the country, largely seem to have a similar inflow and start-up rate. The situation is pitiable. Amongst the various states, with regard to NRI project approvals, Maharashtra tops the list, followed by Gujarat, UP, Karnataka, Andhra Pradesh, Haryana and Delhi. And, influx of NRIs from most countries abroad, is often closely related to the volume of Indians based there. With this background, focussed promotional programmes, organized by state level and all India level nodal agencies in these countries, seem to have largely failed in their slated objective. Delegations from state governments, and chambers of commerce and industry, conduct promotional tours and programmes in the US, Canada, the UK, the Middle East and South-East Asia, but little comes out of it. An NRI exploring the possibility of resettlement in India, and the business options there, sums up his impression rather succinctly, the Government of India is talking of efforts made to promote FDI of hard currency into the Indian economy, even while we wonder whether we are 'Non-Required Indians.' As mentioned earlier, of the number of 'NRI firms', only a few hundred registered as such in the state of Gujarat, and just a small fraction had a RNRI in the picture. The plot thickens! We contacted banks, both Indian and foreign, and term-lending institutions, seeking RNRI entrepreneurs, who may have by-passed the NRI categorization, or have got into service or trading activities. There was a reasonable sample procured in this manner. And without much ado, we proceeded to examine the situation.

Doing Business In India? Haven't Given It A Thought!

While the policy makers seem to have relatively ignored this nostalgic breed of potential RNRI entrepreneurs, it could perhaps also be due to the fact that there were insufficient numbers of them so as to make the effort hardly worthwhile. V. Krishna Murthy conducted a study on the 'investment preferences of expatriates from India' for the National Council for Applied Economics and Research, in 1994. The study explored the vexation factors weighing against Indian expatriate investment in the subcontinent. The study in terms of expatriates' broad country of domicile abroad (*The Observer*, Mumbai, February 17 and 24, 1997), indicated that most NRIs seem apprehensive about the risks of repatriation, fall in exchange value of the rupee, and about the taxation rules and procedures, leading to red tape and corruption. It also indicated that inadequate banking standards and information facilities served as impediments to industrial investment. Further, the study also highlighted the fact that dual citizenship and tax incentives could also perhaps attract investment. While radical reforms in these areas may encourage investment in general, curiously, the attitude of most NRIs implies that the bulk of them are merely looking at India as an investment option, at best as 'sleeping' partners.

Few evinced concern about infrastructural facilities, labour laws, industrial subsidies, or urged reduction in term-lending rates. Rather than taking it for granted, by attributing this attitude to their non-entrepreneurial background, should we not go deeper and probe?

7

Free-Wheeling On The Dilemma Of The Nostalgic NRI, And An End To Contradictions

They come in with one foot in India and one abroad, expect things on a platter, and display scarce commitment or credibility, quite unlike the typical entrepreneurial breed. They fail, fly back and crib to all the world about anything and everything but themselves!

—Anonymous

The Small And Medium Is Beautiful! Why?

As indicated in the previous section, the large NRI businessman-investor, the 'overseas business house', may well look into country credit and risk ratings, and about securing the best bargain in terms of incentives before investing, with large options for repatriation in medium- or long-term proposals for investment in Indian industry. Also, we may as well accept the fact that the uncertain policy environment in a democracy such as our's, is often not even in the hands of our policy makers, and that the bureaucracy will remain a bureaucracy, in the foreseeable future at least! Forget the investor and the big-time entrepreneur! Why do we not encourage the smaller NRI (smaller in terms of personal net worth), to return and do business in India? If politicians are to play on sentiments, they should play on those of NRIs who have an inherent inclination to return home—perhaps the first generation emigrant, the NRI professional, the NRI businessman, in unstable economies of the Developing World, who can return and initiate a SME in India, an enterprise he cannot set up in the developed West, given his investible resources, potential scale of investment, or if he would rather do in his motherland. Policies targeted at this breed need focus not only on providing priority regarding clearances and facilities, but on presenting the environment—economic, business, bureaucratic and social—honestly, from those who are or were their peers. And let them understand what it involves, so that they can learn from the experiences of the Returned Non-Resident Indian (RNRI) entrepreneurs in the subcontinent. Let the NRI understand the environment, ask himself if he is up to doing business in India, and take heart. If he does lose heart, no regrets! India has enough sick SMEs, without additions from abroad! It is in the light of this argument that this book proceeds in its mission.

What Does One Do In India? Business, Of Course!

A large number of Indians living abroad may like to return and settle down in India. In a recent survey conducted by the National Council of Applied Economics and Research, on a cross section of NRI families in the United States of America, the United Kingdom, the Middle East and the Far East, nearly four-fifths of the persons surveyed declared their intention of 'eventually' returning to India.

However, the ratio was found to vary depending on their country of domicile abroad. While 80 per cent of Indians settled in England wanted to return, only 60 per cent in the USA wanted to. Now, traders and industrialists may have clear options, they can always return to do business in India. But the NRI professional may not really want to return in a hurry, unless there is a negative push from his country of domicile abroad, or there are worthwhile opportunities in India. The 'working class' NRI, at the lower echelons of the professional ladder may suffer from homesickness, as he is often alone, with his immediate family left behind in India. He may want to return as soon as he has made a small 'fortune' abroad. He builds a small house for himself in India, and return home to do some odd job or 'tiny' business to keep himself busy. But the professional wonders, what does one do back in India? The NRI entrepreneur wonders, can I do it in India, too?

To put the dilemma in the right perspective, we shall formulate a hypothesis about NRI typologies in terms of NRIs' emigration specifics and background abroad, in the following box.

The 'What Does One Do In India?' And, 'Could I Do Business In India' Syndrome

A first-generation emigrant, a professional or a trader-business-man, has made his money abroad. He is in his 30s and 40s. This is a stage where an individual is often beset with a mid-life crisis, if we are to believe our psychologists. He is plagued by feelings of restlessness and nostalgia for his home and his family back in India. For those NRIs in their 50s, the feeling may be even stronger. The first may like to return, and bring up his pre-teenaged children with Indian values, and the latter may like to return to retire. But both would prefer not to loose the standard of living they are used to while living abroad. The younger would like to remain at least as successful, professionally and materially, as he was while abroad, while the older one would like to build a home and do something to be 'meaningfully occupied'—perhaps business.

The rationale for returning to India is often subjective. The 'backwardness' of working life, and the dearth of professionally satisfactory and remunerative opportunities, may keep the professional away from returning to India for 'a few years', perhaps in perpetuity. But with success, material comforts and sizeable savings from his work abroad, his feeling of uneasiness increases. He wants to return. But to what? Business? He wonders.

A third type of NRI, the smaller trader or businessman, with strong family linkages in India, would not 'mind' returning, he can always do business. But he may not want to risk an unfamiliar business environment. He too has heard 'horrendous tales' from those trying to do business in India. Both the professional and the NRI businessman are in a dilemma, exploring opportunities and ideas . . . and postponing their return.

A preliminary survey conducted amongst select officials assisting NRIs at the state level and RNRI entrepreneurs in the country, helped us go further and develop typologies of NRI firms in existence.

A 'Firm' Typology

Our free-wheeling exercise indicated, that while there are NRI segments who do not have the knowledge or skills required to do business anywhere in the world or in India, there exist typologies of NRI firms in existence. First, there are NRIs with a business family background in India. They have an 'inside' view. Though not directly involved with business in India before migration, they have kept in touch with the business environment here, with support institutions, utilizing their family knowledge/skill/network resources to overcome minor disadvantages caused by their absence from India. They have returned to set up business. Second, there are NRI business houses, which operate a string of businesses, mostly in African and South-East Asian countries. Such a business house, at the owner level, may or may not have an adequate understanding of the ways of doing business in India. It, however, normally operates through an Indian chief executive. The owner is distanced from the day-to-day operations. The chief executive is invariably an Indian, and is very likely to be at home in Indian business conditions. Third, an NRI/RNRI joint or partnership venture is often set up. Both are actively involved in the business. The Indian partner is expected to cover gaps, if any, in terms of understanding ways of doing business in India, while the NRI/ RNRI performs a similar role, either in taking care of certain functional aspects of management, or those in relation to the non-Indian environment. Fourth, an all-pervasive model appears to be an NRI who has invested into an enterprise because of family, friendship or business connections. He is not at all involved in operational management; he does not live in India. There are numerous kinds of arrangements. One extreme probability is that even the investment money does not belong to the NRI, though it is made out to be so. The NRI involvement varies from participation in strategic decision making, to no involvement at all. The NRI may plan, in some cases, to return to India, and take over or directly involve himself in the management of the enterprise at a future point of time. Fifth, an Indian business group, by virtue of the nature of its business, and with one or more family member living abroad for a reasonable spell of time, also qualifies to become an NRI enterprise.

Some NRIs are thoroughly integrated into the socio-cultural system of the country of his or her residence, but have decided to return and launch an enterprise in India. Some have lived abroad, but have changed little in terms of orientation. For example, a technical worker in the Middle East may have very often visited India over the period of his stay abroad, but may not have been very much in touch with the local socio-cultural environment.

It is in the light of the hypothesis given above, with regard to the 'nostalgic NRI', and 'syndromes', and based on the indicative typologies, that this study proceeded. We found ourselves in the midst of a cross-fire!

Apathy Towards The RNRI? A Controversy Unearthed

As a part of our free-wheeling exercise, we probed the 'assisting' officials even deeper. What do they have to say about RNRIs initiating and doing business in India? NRI-assisting institutions largely perceive that RNRI entrepreneurs look down upon the Indian assistance and support system. They subject support officials, by recommendations from powerful quarters, or by name dropping, to pressures that are disproportionate to the developmental import-ance of ventures proposed by them. RNRI entrepreneurs convey the message that they are doing a favour to the country by launching an Indian venture, while assisting officials believe that the venture decision is based on the RNRI's own self-interest. Some RNRIs have a shady background and perpetrate frauds on financial institutions. It is difficult, in comparison to the case of Indian entrepreneurs, to ascertain the truth in respect of an RNRIs financial standing or credibility. Some RNRIs are too vague and impatient in terms of their project or expectations, while many are disinterested in learning about inter-institution allocation of responsibility, or assistance procedures, and expect things on a platter.

We also observed that it is only in some states that nodal agencies for assisting NRI entrepreneurs exist. For all practical purposes, they are non-existent in most states. Even in states where there is an official in a state industrial promotion organization 'assigned' the portfolio of assisting NRI investors, NRIs largely by-pass their office. 'It is not mandatory that everybody, including NRIs, come to us. They can go directly to various offices and departments. Anyway we largely serve as guides,' says an official who would like to remain anonymous, for obvious reasons, 'most RNRIs have their private consultants in the market, to route them to SFCs, SIDCs or all India financial institutions.' In fact, there is very little rationale for distinction between RNRI and NRI projects, officials believe. For example, there is by no means anything significantly different in terms of causality between a sick firm of an RNRI, or that of an Indian entrepreneur. Largely, it is not the economic, business, environmental or cultural differences between the environment that an RNRI is used to abroad, and that in India, that lead to sick enterprises. Often the inexperience of a first-generation entrep-reneur, or deficient project planning and management, are the culprits.

The example given in the following box illustrates this.

Many NRI Units Are Classic Recipes For Sickness

As an example, an official cites a typical case. Three RNRIs were lured by incentives offered by the government to set up units in a backward district towards the latter half of the 80s. An investment subsidy of 25 per cent was offered, when normal subsidy levels were only 10–15 per cent. The promoters' equity component was highly reduced due to the extent of the subsidy component. They had to put in only two-and-a-half million as equity. The subsidy was two-and-a-half million, and the balance of ten million rupees was in the form of term finance. It seemed a good bargain and a wonderful idea to the inexperienced entrepreneurs.

The backgrounds of the three entrepreneurs were diverse and complementary. Two were from the state of Tamil Nadu. The third was a local of the state where the unit was located. One was a plastic technologist, the other a mechanical engineer, and the third was a chartered accountant–all very perfectly matched to set up a manufacturing unit for plastic disposable syringes. But though the project was technically feasible, the market collapsed. Transportation costs were high, due to the location of the unit. Availability of skilled labour locally, and willingness of skilled labour from other regions to move to the backward region, was a problem. Labour in the region lacked professionalism, work ethos, and shirked work. And, to top it all, the market collapsed. The project report prepared by the chartered accountant showed considerable demand for the product. It indicated India's population, health conditions, the advantages of disposable syringes, the production capacity to replace conventional types of syringes, and the tremendous demand the product would generate under such circumstances. However, while government hospitals bought the new product in plenty, the private ones did not. Exports to other states were attempted, but Sales Tax in the state of location was already high, at 13 per cent, and the Central Sales Tax for intra-state sale made the effective sales tax 17 per cent. The product was low-margin-oriented, there was not adequate demand, to help the unit reap economies of scale, and once the breakeven point was not attained, the unit wound up. In four years' time, since commencement of operations, it collapsed. Today, there is another unit manufacturing the same product in a nearby location. It is doing very well, though people still continue to speak of the earlier one's quality. Those syringes were perhaps the best quality ones ever manufactured in the country. But it was slightly ahead of its time, and people were just not aware of its utility, let alone quality. Failure was the result of a number of factors. It was not because the project was run by NRIs that it failed. Anybody else could have failed too, if he had inadequate experience in handling business.

The bureaucracy are of the opinion that the business environment in India and countries abroad is not very different. NRI projects fail, or do not even take off, due to the defective entrepreneurial capabilities of the RNRI entrepreneur. And, to explain away their failures, or their inability to do business, the environment, the bureaucracy, all are blamed. Negative impressions flow back abroad, and NRIs keep away from doing business in India.

Perhaps, this is why less than a dozen SME NRI manufacturing firms are set up every year, even in our 'developed' states, or that only a small fraction of them are really run by an RNRI? Perhaps, this is also why our policy makers, rather than looking for the crux of the problem, merely highlight them, and run after investment, rather than encourage direct entrepreneurship. This is no way to address and solve the problem. We continued with our exploration and randomly met a few RNRI entrepreneurs in the country, to make a preliminary comparison with the official viewpoint. They seemed to contradict the official version. Broadly, NRIs and RNRIs feel that there is inadequate, imperfect information concerning production, market, trade, and supply sources; that the day-to-day environment in India for doing business bristles with uncertainties. Abroad, at least in the developed economies, there are powerful trends and upheavals, but no day-to-day uncertainty. Power shortages, labour unrest, 'over-zealous' factory or excise inspectors, bad debts, or an 'offended' banker, are all part of possible exigencies. So, a certain proportion of time in India is devoted to suddenly surfacing problems that may prove to be fatal. Most RNRIs also believe that the interpretation and implementation of laws and administrative guidelines in the larger sense are archaic; that legal, technical and business consultants in India often do not have knowledge about what they supposedly specialize in; that the mental and psychological stress associated with doing business in India is far greater than that in advanced countries, for the inexperienced entrepreneur; and that the supply of raw materials, utilities, manpower, services, and credit in the Indian business environment is far more problem-ridden than in the West. An Indian entrepreneur is normally able to devote less attention to marketing his product than his counterpart in the West can. He is too busy trying to handle labour, the bureaucracy, inadequate infrastructure and utilities, to focus on his product and his customer.

What the NRIs viewpoint indicates is that there is much in the bureaucratic and business environment that an RNRI, unfamiliar with the Indian business environment, would know about. If he is more aware, he would be prepared, and would have a better chance of making his entrepreneurial venture in India a success. Training and information could perhaps help. Information is but the starting point that this book strives to provide. Let's begin with what's lacking about the information that exists or is disbursed?

Where's The Literature?

The existing sources of information provide knowledge about the macro-economic rationale for FDI in the Indian economy: in terms of benefits to the economy, and to the investor or entrepreneur. It provides information regarding the rationale for entrepreneurship, and about the managerial aspects of business in general. But the fact remains that the decision of an NRI to do business in India, and his success, are also dependent on the information data available with and provided by the government, industry, promotional and support agencies, private agencies and consultants. These docume-nted material, unfortunately, are largely concerned with procedures and guidelines, facilities and assistance, or are merely theoretical or conceptual rationalizations. They provide little information about the facilitating and hindering factors for RNRI entrepreneurship in a de-facto perspective. The existing sources of information may be useful to NRIs who get into partnership arrangements with 'reliable,' local businessmen, who, have a direct feel of the Indian business environment. But there is a lot that remains to be told to RNRIs, who attempt to initiate and manage an enterprise in India, largely on their own.

The relevant body of literature includes books and papers regarding the development and personality of the entrepreneur, entrepreneurial psychology, the stages of business growth, and the problems and rewards of small and medium business entrepreneurs. But these are about doing business in general in the Indian environment. A 'Nabhi's' series, or Indian Investment Centre Newsletter, largely focussing on policy and guidelines, or newspaper articles, may not completely meet the requirements of the NRI trying to evaluate his capabilities for harnessing the potential for business opportunities in India. Home pages, hosted on the 'Net', merely makes available access to information regarding contacts and statutory provisions more accessible. Do RNRI entrepreneurs see a positive business environment in India? This is but one question. Little work has been undertaken in the perspective of the RNRI, few studies that he could relate to.

So What Are Our Questions?

The RNRI businessman in the small- and medium-scale industry— who is he? Why did he choose to come to India? Why did he choose to go in for independent enterprise? How did he go about the whole process? What were the mistakes he made and the hurdles he overcame at the stage of entry, at the teething stage of business, and at the growing stages of his enterprise? What are the lessons he has learnt, the advice he has to give to his peers, to the novice RNRI entrepreneur and the authorities! These are just a few of the questions this book seeks to answer, by documenting and evaluating his experiences and impressions.

There is also the question of fitting in culturally, which may be indispensable for achieving success in business in India. Do culture, social and business ethics serve as an invisible barrier that comes in the path of potential RNRI businessmen and entrepreneurs in India? RNRI entrepreneurs, who have lived abroad 'too long', may not know how the Indian mind works. Do those who have stayed abroad for decades know how to handle support institutions, business associates, customers or labour in the Indian business environment? If not, how does one learn all this?

While institutional, structural anomalies and deficiencies could help rationalize the dismal RNRI entrepreneurship phenomenon, one also wonders about the role played by NRI entrepreneur specific deficiencies in contributing towards the relatively lacklustre performance of many NRI enterprises. The impact of negative feedback of failed RNRI entrepreneurs, or potential entrepreneurs, cannot be disregarded. Though there are a large number of enquiries regarding business prospects and support facilities by NRIs, is it negative perceptions and lack of serious motivation, or the lack of information that stalls RNRI entrepreneurship? Is it the environment, or the entrepreneur, who is to blame?

RNRI Entrepreneurship: Examination Of The Phenomenon

The information regarding business in India is based on a two-year long study undertaken by the Entrepreneurship Development Institute of India, encompassing primary and secondary data analysis of select upper- middle- and lower-income states in the country. This categorization is expected to intrinsically control infrastructure, raw material, market and cultural, and entrepreneurial personality variation, and inter-state and state-level industrial policy diversity. The NRI/RNRI cases analyzed encompass a wide diversity with respect to personal background and specifics regarding domicile abroad, so as to account for cultural competence and environmental variation. On the basis of addresses procured from nodal agencies, the Prime Directory and other sources, NRI firms and information sources were identified. Discussions were held with officials in the Indian Investment Centre, state-level industry promotion bodies, nodal agencies and financial institutions. A large number of the cases are based on factual information, with specifics diagnosed, so as to maintain anonymity, while others are developed. Select NRI projects located across about half of all districts in Gujarat' were studied, to control possible intra-state variation. Units in Maharashtra, Karnataka, Andhra Pradesh and the Punjab were also scrutinized, given the relative plethora of RNRI SME entrepreneurs in these states. In low-income states, officials threw up their hands when it came to even identifying a handful of genuine SME RNRI projects in their state. Mailed questionnaires to about 200 NRI firms, NRI bodies and financial institutions in India and abroad, provided some insights, which culminated in the collection of unique experiences and impressions by means of personal interviews with above 30 RNRI/NRI business people. Dozens of other cases and snippets of experiences have been developed, considering other larger foreign investors and Indian entrepreneurs. This is to facilitate comparison, and generate more information on doing business in India, while also ensuring that this book is of use to a larger audience.

The study adopts the case study approach, viz., a multiple case study analytical methodology. Research strategy in the social sciences are classified into experiments, surveys, archival analysis and case studies. We adopt the case study methodology, as we ask a 'how' or a 'why' question about a contemporary set of events over which the researcher has no control. The why and how of NRI entrepreneurship is considered, so as to derive lessons regarding success formulae and techniques to avoid potential pitfalls. Case studies and experiments are generalized, regarding theoretical propositions, and not about the population or universe. The multiple case study approach does not represent samples, and our goal is to expand and generalize theory, or the propositions propounded, by means of analytical generalization, and not to enumerate frequency, that is, statistical generalization. We merely match patterns or observations. We do not cover the question of how many and how much with regard to entry and success, investment levels or sector specifics. This information 'may' be available from select promotional institutions, or NRI nodal agencies at the state level, or can be procured by means of a survey methodology, by those interested in it. Such data, however, is likely to suffer from the common limitations of reliability and accessibility! Given the fact that potential entrepreneurs in the SME sector are those who face the brunt of information and resource crunches, this book is primarily meant to serve as a complement to their entrepreneurial efforts in the Indian subcontinent.

The information presented until this stage also highlights the foundations of the research design adopted in the study. A research design attempts to draw a set of conclusions from an initial set of questions, and serves as a guide in the process of collecting, analyzing and interpreting observations. It seeks to investigate the influences concerning causal relations among the variables under investigation, and also defines the domain of generalizability. We have already elaborated on the former. With regard to the latter, we take the study as indicative of a larger population, viz., RNRI entrepreneurship in India in general.

The questionnaire schedule, that doubles as a discussion format, focussed on, (a) the entry dynamics, viz., indicatively, the who and why questions with respect to enterprise initiation and crises during start-up; (b) the personality profile, family profile, socio-economic background, motivational factors that encouraged the NRI to continue, in spite of his own personality-related or environment-related deficiencies; (c) the project profile, viz., the project idea selection, environment scan, extent of information search, matching of RNRI competency and resources with the project, business style and success strategies of RNRIs; (d) the doing business in 'India' rationale, viz., as to whether it was positive pull factors or negative push factors from the country of domicile abroad that encouraged his return. The former factors include the need for independence, the advantage of starting off with a relatively low level of investment, in an economy with relatively less competition, urge for creative expression, or a risk-taking attitude, to fulfill either psychological or material aspirations, all combined with emotional linkages with 'home'. The latter factor also includes political instability, or job-related dissatisfaction abroad. The role of support institutions in facilitating and hindering RNRI entrepreneurship is also explored. Do financial, developmental and support institutions act in a sympathetic, considerate manner? Does one approach term-lending institutions directly, or through a 'liaison' agent? Do contacts with bankers aid loan sanction, speed up paper work and ensure quicker processing of applications for industry registration? Are RNRI entrepreneurs more honest and reliable? These are some of the aspects that were covered, the focus of enquiry being in a historical perspective.

PART THREE

Never Say Die . . .
In The Bad Old Days

In the era of the License Raj, profits were assured through the mechanism of licensing. If you could manage to get one without much 'trouble', that is.

—Anonymous

Karmic Influences On Business And The Entrepreneurial Personality

Are you an NRI wanting to do business on a small or medium scale in India? Maybe you have already resettled in India and are exploring business options, or perhaps you are still abroad, and are pondering over the idea of doing business in India. Maybe you are an independent professional, have perhaps worked for somebody abroad in some functional management, technical or research area, or you may be a trader or manufacturer in your country of domicile. You may be nurturing an idea for a new and unique product perhaps, or a service that you are certain will help you earn adequate money, to at least help you maintain the standard of living that you were used to while abroad. You wonder what managing a business in India will involve? What are the factors that could make or mar a successful enterprise? Will it be a piece of cake? You ask yourself, first, whether your abilities, training and confidence ensure success, or, second, is there something in the business environment that could mar your performance? This chapter presents two cases, which introduce the prevailing business environment, which could bring to naught your sincere efforts, and nullify your skills and abilities. This includes business-related adversities, policy changes, institutional deficiencies or corruption. These elements were perceived to be particularly strong in the controlled regime, the 'License Raj' that prevailed before reform in and since 1991. The cases also present lacunae of the entrepreneurial or managerial sort that affect business performance. The cases highlight the fact that regardless of whether it is the environment, bureaucracy, or business environment, that is to blame, it is the personality of the entrepreneur that makes him persevere, confident of eventual success. The typical Indian philosophical attitude of being resigned to one's fate attributing success and failure in business to an exogenous 'Karma', is a fatalistic attitude which has no place in the make-up of a successful entrepreneur. Entrepreneurs are made of stronger mettle: a mix of perseverance, commitment and confidence, regardless of adversities. It is these kind of people who invariably survive and thrive. The following cases highlight these issues.

Shivam Computers

The Moment of Decision

Born and raised in Ahmedabad, Kiran Kantilal Shah, the son of a textile trader, graduated from college in 1966, and proceeded to the United States for higher education. He completed a Master of Science degree in Electrical Engineering at the Steven Institute of

Technology, New Jersey, and worked with leading American firms during his sixteen-year stint in the US. From 1967 to 1983, he could visit India only about five times on short holidays. However, Indian culture and values, and close parental affinity remained firmly etched in his psyche. Also, as the years passed, Shah's in-laws in India were ageing and physically ailing. He and his wife were needed back home. There was no indecision. He merely waited for the right opportunity to return.

A 'Sure Thing' With A Captive Market

The opportunity to do business in India crystallized in April 1983. He returned, because of the insistence of a close acquaintance who had returned to India, and was associated with a large public sector unit (PSU) in Gujarat. He promised Shah, on behalf of his company, a large market order for computer equipment. Shah started his business of manufacturing computer-related products, and Shivam Computers was put on rails, with an initial project-investment of Rs 1 million. Kiran Shah invested about Rs 400,000 and the rest came from his kith and kin in India. Most pre-initiation formalities were initially taken care of by him abroad, and also when he returned to India. The project report was prepared by a consultant, but the licensing formalities and necessary liasing with the Department of Electronics (DOE), he did on his own. Thinking back, he muses, 'The major problem with licensing that I encountered during the erstwhile License Raj was my liability in starting small.' Statutory requirements regarding equipment, such as soldering irons, micro processors and testers would have excessively burdened his project costwise, and were rather unnecessary, given his investment potential, scale of business and promised market. Shah felt it would be a waste of time and money to initiate business involving larger amounts of equipment and investment, but it would have given him access to a diversified clientele. His investible funds were rather low, the concept of computers was relatively new to the Indian environment, and bureaucratic procedures for securing statutory clearances would have been even more longwinded. He avoided this option, and instead focussed on equipment and investment, so as to serve his promised market. The application and procedural aspects of business initiation took about two and a half years. In anticipation of this time lag, he put in about one and a half years of project-related preliminary efforts, on meeting bureaucratic formalities from abroad, prior to following it up on his return to India. Over this period, his brother, in India, had helped, by following up on necessary formalities, such as procuring a license. He had also personally initiated considerable correspondence, seeking to identify products and their applications. Nothing can really go wrong, he thought initially, 'I have a promised buyer, and I am starting very small, with my own money.' Hence, the perceived psychological risk of doing business for the very first time in his life, was very small. But it was not to be. One major problem after the other cropped up. His case is one of perseverance, when many others would have adopted a fatalistic approach, and thrown in the towel.

An Elegy While Teething?

A virtual deluge of adversities almost upset the applecart. His application to the Department of Electronics, for manufacturing electronic products, also covered the requirement for the approval of necessary imports, given the 'statutorily restricted' nature of the items. This, and the requirement of an industry license for manufacture, became a stumbling block . . . the first. The procedural lag in sanctioning the project heavily strained working capital during the period preceding actual manufacture. This hurdle having been crossed, he was faced with a problem that almost drove in the final nail in the coffin of his maiden entrepreneurial adventure. His colleague had 'verbally' promised him a contract and a captive market for his products. The deal fell flat.

The 'verbally' promised requirement on behalf of the public sector unit was for 'automatic ledger posting systems', an eight bit computer, referred to as such because of the organization's union's stand against computerization. The requirement was for about one hundred pieces. This was a large order. However, an order for only 25 machines came through. The central government had meanwhile issued a notification to PSUs to go in for a 16-bit and not 8-bit computers. Unfortunately, the latter was what Shivam had designed and was equipped to deliver. The public sector unit cancelled the promised order, and only 25 machines were taken. Of course, there were other smaller customers, but this initial blow left a permanent gash on long-run unit profitability.

'The shock was bad enough to have killed the venture,' says Shah, 'as the firm had been initiated and designed tailor-made to serve one larger major buyer.' The fundamental error on his part was identifying and initiating a business activity with high asset specificity, without ensuring a mutual dependence with respect to his buyer and based purely on a word of mouth promise. The mistake blocked up about Rs 500,000 to Rs 700,000 of working capital and there was an immediate cash crunch. Twenty machines were taken first, and five more were taken piecemeal by the public sector unit over the period of a year. So money was a problem. This was a difficult time, a phase of severe adversity, even at the teething stage of a business, when most would be RNRI maiden-entrepreneurs pack up their bags and baggage and return to work abroad. But Shah stayed. 'Those days IBM was not in India, and I got into selling Apple machines,' he muses. 'Selling Apple machines generated revenue that helped the firm survive.' He realized that he had lost about Rs 2 million during the first year of operations, due to the failure of the public sector unit to honour its commitment. Most of the machines he had manufactured, even today, lie unsold in his godown. They have remained there for more than a decade since they were manufactured. 'Nobody wants the mechanical stuff and integrated circuits,' he says sadly.

Always A Survivor, With Family And High-Margin, Product-Mix Decision Lending A Helping Hand

Shivam Computers sold about 15 Apple machines on a retail basis over 1987–88. In 1988, IBM came in, and the market for Apple machines dried up. By then Shah had decided to start assembling and selling machines under Shivam's own name. It was clear, that in spite of waiting and hoping for the best, no more orders would come from his promised client. He decided to plough in more family money in order to survive. 'We also decided not to depend on somebody else, but market our product on our own' he observes. 'Personally, I did not want to invest additional money out of my family's pocket.' But he had no choice. 'A business could never have survived under the circumstances of the strong money crunch that affected us then,' he rationalizes. The investment did not go down the drain.

In 1994 and 1995, Shivam's return on investment averaged about a gross of ten per cent. This was a precursor to strong recovery and growth, Shah believes. The unit currently manufactures computer system and video terminals, but a crucial generator of net earnings is his focus on providing computer after-sales servicing to a wide clientele. The total gross volume of revenue generated from service operations may be low, but in terms of net margins, it is much more lucrative than realization from products sold by his firm. 'This is how we survived from being wiped out,' he says. 'This kept us alive.'

Economic Reform And A Manufacturing Strategy: The Man And His Vision

Kiran Kantilal Shah even today manages all the financial aspects of his firm himself. His is a top and middle-level management, one-man show, and his travails over the years have not affected either his pleasing personality, or his long-term vision. When he first entered the Indian market, Shah was manufacturing 'IC by IC', with about 15 employees involved in the process. Today, he has only two technically specialized personnel. There is sound rationale behind this. He feels that a crisis confronts the domestic computer industry. Technological changes are extremely rapid. If a firm is involved in manufacturing work-in-progress, or in building up inventory or stocks, which may be a necessary outcome of a manufacturing strategy, turnover of inventory and rotation of cash will be affected. Survival from a situation of being short of cash would depend on the ability of a firm to work on practically zero inventory. 'What we did and are still doing is controlling inventory,' he notes. 'In order to ensure that we do not have large cash outflows, we take credit from suppliers for 15–20 days. We ensure that debtors turn over faster.'

The potential for crisis, he believes, arises not only from technological change, but also from the entry of Multinational Corporations (MNCs). Survival depends on diversification in the style of business activity. Manufacturing of computer systems, given the entry of MNCs, will prove to be dangerous, he perceives. Their prices, networking and promotional muscle cannot be matched by domestic competitors, large or small. It is better to join them rather than fight them. Various relevant options must be explored. Right now, domestic producers are competitive, as they are focussing on assembling and not on manufacture. Removal of tariffs and entry barriers for foreign competition could change the scenario completely. Selling, distribution and service would be the feasible options for the medium-scale operator in the SME sector.

'Today, marketing is not much of a problem,' he declares. 'In 1988–89, a lot of marketing was necessary to sell the idea of computers. Now there is no need for this. However, price competition is a crucial aspect in business in India.' Shivam intends to meet, and has been tackling competition from other SME firms, by giving due consideration to this factor, providing better services and value for money to their clients.

Little Goodwill Towards Doing Business In 'Grey' India!

Shah has never entered and has no intention of entering the 'grey' market, which he believes accounted for about 80 per cent of the total computer industry in the country in the closed 80s. While he concedes that this market may be shrinking today, he knows of many businessmen in the computer industry operating in this market for profit. Regardless, he has never believed in avoiding taxes and import bills. He claims, 'I do not want to put a blanket on the legal way of doing business and go illegal. It does not fit my style.' He has, hence, focussed on providing 'better service' to his clients, as his survival strategy.

Even before returning to India with his wife and children, he knew that he could lose, perhaps in terms of standard of living and potential savings. His wife had also been earning handsomely abroad as a doctor. He may have lost heavily in terms of potential earnings, but has survived, and is bullish about his business prospects and entrepreneurial skills. 'There was little goodwill with regard to doing business in India those days,' he observes, 'but I tried doing it.' On the basis of good faith and word of mouth agreements, he returned and invested his hard-earned savings in business. His experiences have left his faith in Indian business ethics rather shaken, but he has survived, and his faith in his own business style, with regard to honesty and ethical standards, has not changed.

A Gentleman And An Indian At Heart—A Potentially Winning Combination

He believes that economic liberalization now bodes well for India, himself and other small entrepreneurs. Earlier, it was only multi-million dollar companies that could afford to focus on aspects such as quality in products and services. Now, all firms have to be quality conscious to survive. This implies that intrinsically and morally quality conscious people, like himself and other RNRIs, especially those returning after a long stay of close to a decade or two in the West would have a definite edge in building customer loyalty, while doing business in the tiny and SMF sector.

He feels that while he may be an expert at survival, he has still to learn the ropes regarding expansion and growth. In his small organization, after all these years of survival, he believes that a successful business style lays emphasis on delegation of authority . . . and on the market. Today, he does not depend on contracts or job orders, but sells directly to the market. He has always believed in providing quality service, and that, he feels, is the secret of his survival, despite adversities. 'It was the higher margins from the service contracts that provided a breather,' he concedes.

Soft, Straight And Steadfast . . . Not Go 'Bad' For Success

Jovial and friendly by nature, he believes that machine and equipment theft does occur in his office sometimes. Perhaps his own employees may be at fault. He has, however, never punished even suspected culprits. Instead, he has striven to instill moral and ethical values amongst his staff, by giving them sound and reasoned advice. He believes his soft mentality, not exactly 'the corporate raiding', 'kill competition' or feudalistic boss type, whips up and sustains employee motivation and triumph in the long run.

He tries to avoid mixing business with personal relationships, as he does not want to be exploited, or taken advantage of by his employees or business associates. Shah believes that violation of norms and regulations, minor or major, should not be seen as a sort of imperative to doing business successfully in India. He also believes that identifying and exploiting loopholes, and evading various statutory norms, so as to amass black—unaccounted— wealth is by no means the only route to success in business. He has not done it, and believes that a conservative image, promises that can be fulfilled, good service, and sincere and diligent effort is the secret of successfully doing business in India.

Bear With Bureaucracy And The Environment . . . To Feed One's Soul

Shah is still not attuned to spending more time in bureaucrat's offices than in business. He had problems in identifying sources of information regarding business opportunities, finance, aspects of management and procedures, guidelines and norms for doing business in India. He fortunately did not get lost in the maze of licensing and other procedural problems, and with the 24 agencies, that he, as an entrepreneur, has to deal with even today, including with excise, sales tax and labour authorities. He feels that thumb rules in the functional aspects of management are employed by the business and bureaucratic community—not exactly financial ratio-based decision making! All these make the environment very difficult for the uninitiated entrepreneur.

He realises that earlier his immediate family had great difficulty in adjusting themselves to the quality of food, prices and the general social and business environment in India. However, Shah now has no regrets about his return. He may have lost financially, mostly due to exogenous factors (policy change) that affected his business, and in terms of his income if he had continued working abroad.

Yet, he believes that an individual should 'not always feed his stomach alone, he should also feed his soul sometime.' His heart and soul were in India. Of course, his young children were not happy when he returned to India after seven years abroad, but he tried to help them adapt themselves to the Indian environment, with the support of his wife and extended family. And he succeeded!

As a survival expert in doing business in India, Shah believes that the skill imperative for successfully doing business here is the marketing ability of an entrepreneur. Also important is the ability to deal effectively with taxes, financial institutions, the labour-related statutory and policy environment. Problem solving and networking skills are equally important. He does not believe that pure creativity is of much use in the Indian environment. It is the implementation of creative ideas that counts. It is the functional marketing ability that is the crucial success determinant.

The Confidence Of 'Never Resided In India' Indians

The Confidence Of A 'Never Resided In India' Indian: Given A Business Background And Perceived Economy Advantages

Of Indian blood, but born and brought up in Uganda, where his grandparents had migrated from Jaipur, in Rajasthan, Sunil Mukherjee returned to do business in India. In 1977, at thirty-four, he initiated the process of setting up a wireless equipment manufacturing unit near Udaipur. In all his years abroad, prior to his decision of doing business in India, he had only once visited India in 1966. During his visit he explored business options in India, and somewhat familiarized himself with the environment. But it was several years later that he returned with a business idea, linked to his training, expertise and perceived core competencies.

Armed with a Bachelor of Science degree in Electronics Engineering from the UK, he had worked as a project engineer for an electronics giant at Birmingham, UK, from 1964–76. For four years after that, he carried on trade in the electronics business in the UK and in Africa. Mukherjee was, therefore, no novice in doing business, nor was he a stranger to business environmental dynamics in a developing economy. Relative institutional deficiencies, imperfect markets with respect to competition and access to support facilities and credit, were certainly not new for him. He believed then, as he still does today, that while in the developed West, the time involved in setting up an assembly line operation may involve relatively smaller gestational lags, advantages for entrepreneurship with new or adapted business ideas and opportunities from the West, exist in India.

Pooh-Pooh To Corruption

He scoffed then, as he does now, about the widely acknowledged problem of corruption. 'Leave corruption ratings and indices regularly presented by international agencies be!' he declares. The widely acknowledged problem of corruption in Third World economies, like India, and the low business ethics in such environments in general, he feels, is understandable, given the various institutional limitations and resource constraints. More lightheartedly, he ponders, 'the difference in ethical standards amongst developing and developed economies is not with respect to the pay off or cash up-front requirement to finalize business-related deals. Thumb rules of global investors, in evaluating between investing in alternative high-growth Third World economies, rest on analyzing the quality of the job done, and the performance and implementation of the job, for which formally unaccountable payments have been made. This, in fact, may indicate a realistic scenario and approach, though it may be rather subjective.' He explains, 'One cannot change ethics, business, bureaucratic or social values in a day.' Mukherjee believes that the first generation entrepreneur, or a first time entrepreneur may be shocked, but the difference between the West and developing economies, like India, is not as great as is often made out to be. He says, 'Problems and hurdles in the business environment should be taken as a challenge in a truly entrepreneurial spirit, and not as a lame and exaggerated excuse to avoid doing business altogether.'

Tanzania And Britain Was Out . . . India Offered Financial Support And A Nephew To Hold Fort

Political turmoil in Uganda, and the widely perceived second class citizenship in the West, particularly in Europe, served as a negative push, encouraging the decision to do business in India. A positive push was provided by the 1977 government delegation team from Gujarat to the UK, with promises of returning and resettling NRIs, of priority and special facilities for their children's education, in the allotment of telephones, assistance in project funding, and in the speedy procurement of industrial licenses. His decision to come back to India was almost a return to India at any cost decision, strengthened by the offer of a local partnership option and financial support from his nephew and family in India. With family funds and a reliable partnership option in India, he was confident that the initial gestation lag in project approval and initiation could be handled without his presence. Like most other returned NRIs, who explore the manufacturing option, family financial support, and, crucially, the presence of a committed confidante in India, working on the sometimes 'emotionally tiring' and time-consuming project initiation formalities and securing relevant clearances and financial support from financial institutions, strengthened his resolve to do business in India.

The Economic Benefits Regarding Location

He initially adopted an objective viewpoint while deciding on the selection of location for his proposed venture. Indians like Mukherjee, born and brought up abroad, seem to be more rational about the selection of the ideal location to do business in India. He had, in fact, first considered Bangalore, in the South, but he realised the importance of a partnership, family business, and his bureaucratic contacts in Baroda. His decision regarding location was, hence, not on the basis of psychological affinity to a particular state, city, or town of origin or former stay. Mukherjee observes, 'Indians born or reared in India may favour a particular region to do business, even if specific language barriers don't exist. However, people like myself are more interested in the economic benefits of location.' Those who return due to a negative push from abroad, and are looking at the business option as a very serious make or break factor, or have a sound business background, are rational in their approach to business. The SME RNRI entrepreneur, particularly a first generation one, would like to live and work close to the place he perceives as home, within the multi-lingual, multi-ethnic subcontinent that is India. This has often more to do with seeking emotional rather than any tangible support in the business. Of course, if he has the fortune of having someone trustworthy and competent, in a particular region, to work on the business idea, before he takes the ultimate decision to return, his choice is obvious. This is understandable. Today, with the removal of the License Raj, informal linkages, business, or bureaucratic, and emotional support-related contacts might be useful at an early stage of project initiation, if they are really strong. So does formal networking. But sound economic rationale, in terms of infrastructure availability, market and input supply, should not be forsaken for mere sentimental reasons. A competent entrepreneur can personally develop his own network. Business should not be a mere half-hearted corollary to the decision to return home. Sentiment wears away in a couple of years, and loosers wonder why they left their choice of location to their hearts rather than to their minds!

Commencement Of Operations—An Eternity In Itself

Mukherjee believed, as do most RNRIs returning to do business with a reliable Indian counterpart, that the stage would be set, and business operations would commence by the time of his return. He was confident. However, confidence and sound business acumen are not sufficient for successful entrepreneurship in the Indian subcontinent. His confidence and bullish stance till date, about doing business in India, scarcely conceals the problems he has faced in the Indian environment during the erstwhile License Raj. The project report was submitted in 1977, with his nephew designated as his official partner. For four years, from 1977 to 1981, it went back and forth between the partners and the authorities. Being a restricted item, the registration and licensing with the Department of Electronics (DOE), and negotiation with funding institutions, entailed several visits on his part to India. He made about ten trips, at the rate of about two visits per year, between 1977 to 1981. However, Mukherjee utilized this period productively, to the extent possible. It was over this period, during his frequent visits to India, that his business idea, technology, location and financing plan streamlined, and licensing formalities accomplished. During the same period, Mukherjee conducted further discussions with the state nodal institution for industrial promotion, and intensively analyzed the Department of Electronics' reports regarding the market for his proposed products. Towards 1981, his investment had to be upgraded, along with the project cost. This was in order to ensure that the project came under the purview of the State Industrial Development Corporation. This, in turn, was due to the 'sensitive' nature of a wireless communication project, and to attain scale economies, as per the advice of financial institutions. Still later, it was believed that the project could be a 100 per cent government venture. He fought and won against this option, going to the Prime Ministerial level, utilizing contacts, and organizing open NRI audiences in Delhi, chaired by the Prime Minister. After 1981, the problem of government takeover of the project died down, but the gestation lag and uncertainties had taken a heavy toll on the cost of the project. Unpaid interest burgeoned. All the above adversely affected the enterprise. The time lag also witnessed the entry of new competitors. Earlier, there were just one or two competitors in India, but this increased to about five in number, over the several years that it took him to cross all the barriers along the way to project initiation and stabilization of production. Thus, the possibility of near monopoly and first entrant advantages were lost.

A Better 'Today', If One Utilizes Tips Regarding The Bureaucracy, Labour, Business Ethos, And Networking, From Those Who 'Bucked' The System

Mukherjee is confident, that the shift from the early License Raj to a more liberalized economy, makes things easier for the potential RNRI businessman of today. Nevertheless, he continues to believe that the success determinant of doing business in a Third World economy, is not mere professionalism, but also management of

'Indian' labour, and efficient handling of the myriad bureaucratic support systems, that are equally crucial. It is the method of understanding and dealing with the support and external environment, financial and regulatory institutions and business environment, in terms of practices and norms, that is a critical success determinant. For example, Mukherjee has learnt, that in India, an entrepreneur should make provisions and allowances for delays as far as even simple meetings, appointments, or outstanding bills are concerned. 'We have lost about Rs 3 to 4 million in bad debts and bounced cheques,' he smiles drily. However, Mukherjee sticks to his guns regarding his own business ethics. He believes that labour work ethos is not very strong in the Indian subcontinent, and a feudal approach, employing a carrot and stick technique, may ensure positive productivity levels. Labour management, particularly with regard to less qualified and uneducated employees, should be liberally peppered with the use of 'rough and ready' language.

Though he has persevered despite tremendous adversities and without connections with the bureaucracy, he believes such connections and networking could perhaps have helped him voice his grievances so that they were heard quickly in the erstwhile License Raj. They could have helped him anticipate and tackle crises at an early stage. Mukherjee is of the view that the importance of networking and connections, specifically unethical influence mechanisms, are not unique to India. 'Business is business, and ethical perception and norms vary from country to country, and may be relatively woeful in most developing economies. Things may be shocking for the inexperienced new entrepreneur, but not for a businessman.'

Market Reorientation With Quality Orientation, With Market Price-Quality Configurations As Underpinnings

Mukherjee is confident of turning around his loss-making unit in the near future. Project cost overruns, lag periods for licensing, and competition from the government market resulted in the firm remaining a loss-making one. The firm, in 1991, had a turnover of Rs 7.5 million, while in 1995, the turnover was about Rs 25 million.

He believes success in his venture lies in long-range planning, now that the survival stage has been crossed—a stage which has taken more than a decade. Ninety-five per cent of his market included government agencies and the public sector. This, he feels, warrants change, as a safe hedge against market saturation, lower margins and demand due to competition. He intends reorienting his market focus accordingly. He plans to tap the household and business market in a big way, first testing the local district market for wireless telephones. His current strategy of shifting away from a convenient government and public sector buyer's market, to providing innovations in service so as to facilitate flexibility, and to cater to the needs of private businessmen, could give him an edge in the market. With his wide exposure to European and African markets, quality in production and services, he is resolute, should be tailored to market requirements of price-quality configurations. It should not be a unilateral decision, ignoring this relationship.

Marketing And Networking Without A 'Closed Mind'

Having been in business, specifically trading abroad, he was confident of succeeding in manufacture. His strong resolution and confidence, in spite of being strapped with a currently loss-making company, is reflective of the potential of returning NRI professionals for doing business in India. Success ingredients, for potential RNRI entrepreneurs, he believes, lies in their marketing and creative ability, in their capability for fund procurement and management, and in their personal and formal networking arrangements.

He is also of the opinion that most RNRIs who return to do business in India in the SME sector are often first generation entrepreneurs. They should remember, he repeats (that) business is business. It is not for weaklings, losers, the faint-hearted, the wailers, or for those with a 'closed-mind' with regard to social norms or business and institutional related ethos in a rapidly advancing Third World economy like India's.

The cases of Mukherjee and Kiran Shah indicate the nature and source of hindering factors in the initiation and processes of doing business in India. Where do problems arise? The RNRI or the environment?

Whodunit? The Entrepreneur Or The Environment?

Kiran Shah's case provides ample evidence of his possessing (or having developed) several entrepreneurial competencies, including persistence, initiative, information seeking and opportunity identification, concern for high quality, self-confidence, and care for employee welfare. However, his project, while initiated in 'good faith', was not without certain managerial lacunae. Business without product or market flexibility is a dangerous game. Kiran Shah was perhaps forced by circumstances to make an error in the conceptualization of his project. His manufacturing base suffered from excessive asset specificity. He should have decided on equipment and investment levels, so as to either facilitate manufacture of alternative products with the same equipment, or ensured the presence of alternate markets for the same product. His business idea suffered from the absence of market risk diversification. Kiran Shah's association with an employee of a potential large customer, led him to believe that he could avoid marketing-related problems for his computers—especially since the product was relatively new to India. He did not, and perhaps could not, ensure that the dependence between him and the potential buyer was natural, or that there was a firm agreement. Even if his potential buyer had not reneged right at the start, he could have been exploited, by say, payment delays, which would have stretched his working capital requirements. Large firms in India have often used their vendors or suppliers as sources of working capital, the Delayed Payments Act notwithstanding.

And, as a technically qualified professional, it seems that it was not just the marketing aspect he was initially not very comfortable with. Financial structuring of the project was also not exactly his forte. Kiran Shah had invested his own and his family's money in the project. The 'perceived risk' was low, he believed. But management philosophy tells us that a firm should have a right mix of debt and equity in its capital structure.

Seeking subsidy and tax holidays should not cloud the decision-making of an entrepreneur, to the exclusion of considerations regarding accessibility and availability of raw materials, utilities, labour and markets. Similarly, seeking maximum debt financing from financial institutions could also be risky. While increasing financial leverage, and the shareholders' earnings per share (EPS), or return on equity, it also increases the firm's risk of bankruptcy, as it increases the extent of variability of earnings. Nevertheless, interest on debt has a net tax advantage. An extremely conservative financing policy, without debt, may give independence from financial institutions, provide financial flexibility and minimise the financial risk. But the promoter's wealth is not maximized.

Ideally, in the case of a sound business idea, with (almost) assured sales and volumes, debt financing would have been preferable. The earning capacity and ability to generate cash flows, and stipulations regarding debt-equity mix, play a crucial role in deciding about a project's capital structure and means of finance. Of course, Kiran Shah had no firm contracts, but if he had faith in a 'word of mouth' promise, he could have taken the debt route. But the entrepreneurial logic is unfathomable. He wished to manufacture and sell high quality products. That was it. Period!

Anyway, he was perhaps lucky that he did not!

Mukherjee suffered due to the bureaucracy and the policy environment. His attempts at initiating his project had been delayed by several bureaucratic constraints, that resulted in a long pre-initiation lag. But it may not have been entirely due to unilateral and arbitrary bureaucratic requirements, as it may seem, but sound banker rationale. The stipulated enhancement of the investment, required for his proposed unit, prior to the sanction of a term loan, also contributed to the lag period.

Consideration regarding the capacity to be installed is often judged on the minimum viable size, potential for scale economies, projected cost of expansion, number of shifts and working days, on pre-empting competition, which may affect market structure and long-term profitability. The support institutions that recommended increase in investment, may have considered those options before recommending the same to Mukherjee. Project viability is critically affected by these parameters.

To Mukherjee, it did not make any difference, industry categorizationwise. But the fact remains that some entrepreneurs myopically and artificially 'tailor' these parameters, so as to ensure that they fit the SSI category. The advantages include exemption from excise, up to a certain annual turnover, low interests, lower promoter's margin, and preferential prices if sold to the government. Mukherjee and Kiran Shah had the option of these advantages. Wireless equipment and computers, being restricted and relatively new entrants to the economy, offered them the advantage of ruling a market with a relatively new product, perhaps with preferential prices. If backed by solid, medium-term contracts, it could have given their projects immense potential. Fate willed otherwise. But the future brings hope, as it should, for the confident and diehard entrepreneur! The cases of Mukherjee and Shah seem to indicate managerial lacunae in some aspects of their projects, be it project size, product-market decisions or capital structuring. They also seem to have not been very familiar with the Indian business and bureaucratic environment before they launched their enterprises. If Mukherjee had been more exposed to the environment, he would have anticipated the lags and the problems that could arise in getting a 'sensitive' project cleared in a 'controlled' economy. But bureaucracy and the License Raj hurt him. Both these, as well as policy changes, also harmed Kiran Shah. The contribution of bad business ethics in adversely affecting their projects at the teething stage is also evident. Therefore, it is often difficult to exclusively blame either the environment or the RNRI for his project running into trouble while doing business in India. It is invariably a complex, cumulative effect. What explicitly emerges from these cases, is that regardless of the source of calamity, it is only the 'never say die' attitude of an RNRI entrepreneur, and his resolve regarding success, that can sustain a business. Those were the bad old days of the License Raj! There has today been a lot of fanfare regarding the so-called liberalized environment. Has the bureaucracy, the potential for policy change, or business environment changed? Not much, it seems, and, simultaneously, there is now, intense competition from globally competitive, large business houses, or their products, from within and outside the country. Haren Shah faced something of a crisis with the reforms.

Trouble With Reform!

Though not given much consideration in India's development strategy until the early eighties, the government, since the crisis in 1991, is pursuing a proactive policy to attract Foreign Direct Investment in general, and NRI investment in particular. The new industrial policy of 1991, and subsequent amendments, offer a relatively liberalized policy framework to attract NRI investment into the country. Many of the regulations prevalent earlier, by way of restrictions on equity participation, areas of operation, etc., have been favourably revamped.

NRI investment is today being progressively encouraged in all sectors. But, the dismantling of the License Raj, and the new industrial policy, brings with it its own advantages and disadvantages in doing business in India. For example, protection in the domestic industry is being removed, in turn increasing competition. The advantages of a protected domestic market are going away or gone. Market-determined interest and exchange rates could lead to uncertainty for the purpose of business planning in the short run.

Training And Saving Precedes Entrepreneurship

Haren Manharlal Shah initiated himself in his maiden role as an entrepreneur at the age of thirty, in 1989. Before he returned to India, he worked as a first line manager, viz., a staff engineer for a leading American information systems' firm.

His return to India in 1987, and his initiation into entrepreneurial activity, were all pre-planned. He wanted to train himself abroad, earn some cash, and return to India to do business. No other option had ever been considered. His technical knowledge and financial savings from abroad provided invaluable support in his attempt to do business in the subcontinent. In his decade's stay in the United States, he completed his studies, before working for a few years, and gaining valuable experience.

His business idea of 'modem' manufacture developed from his own educational background and from his perceived market potential. During his visits to India, he formulated the business idea, decided on his technology and location. Even while Haren was based abroad, all details were finalized unofficially with his partners in India. His Indian partners contributed financially to the project, but contributed little towards managerial aspects, once the firm started operations. He had also built up a network in the region, and sought information from state-level industrial promotion agencies and from the state-level Technical Consultancy Organisation (TCO). This was, as mentioned broadly with regard to location and promoters' contribution, all of which were finalized during his visits to India, and through correspondence before his final return. He returned, finalized his means of finance, and commenced initiation formalities. He was in business.

Partnerships Make Life Easier

Belonging to the Kaira district of Gujarat, the electronics estate at the state capital, geared specifically to meet the needs of the electronics industry, encouraged him to locate his firm there. Initially, at the business conceptualization stage, he was worried about selecting a good business opportunity. Networking and correspondence solved that problem. Later, at the teething stage, he wondered if he had selected a good business idea, and also about the marketability of his products, computer modems. Fortunately, towards the fag end of his stay abroad, his Indian partners did some useful legwork, securing information on procedures and guidelines for business initiation and also regarding the viability of the idea. His two Indian partners and collaborators were close friends of his parents in India, and Haren had tied up with them from the stage of the conception of the project. While he was abroad, partnership ties, including financial commitment and moral support, gave him the mental peace to plan.

Haren had little hands on experience in entrepreneurial activity. However, support from reliable partners, helped boost and maintain morale at the pre-initiation stage. The encouragement and advice from his Indian partners, on his return, also helped in the quick progress of the commissioning of the project, and his enterprise was initiated at a project cost of Rs 2 million, and with a 50 per cent term loan from the state financial institution. The combined, committed efforts of Haren and his partners ensured that he returned with some confidence to India, and started on his business venture in earnest.

Reform Reads Doom . . . Almost

From 1989 onwards, the unit performed wonderfully, with a focus on producing high quality products. However, being in the Small-Scale Industry (SSI) category, and with his limited investment potential, Haren could neither invest large sums of money on in-house R&D, or in backward integration. His final product, hence, relied heavily on imported components. A major strategic error he made was that he did not expect the potential for policy change. The near bankruptcy of the Indian economy, and policy reforms in the latter half of 1991, led to reductions in tariff, progressively reforms, and made his products less price competitive. He should have gone in for products, which do not require a great deal of imported components. He should have also considered the price and market requirements. Hence, profit in absolute terms and margins, remain unimpressive, since the initiation of the new economic policy regime in 1991. Regardless, he continues doing business successfully. How? With a focus on quality, in the tradition of the truly ethical entrepreneur, and in meeting his obligations, not only to customers, but also to other entrepreneurs, creditors and suppliers on time. His focus has been on developing goodwill and customer loyalty. Potential lower margins were offset by these measures which helped realize relatively higher margins. 'Reputation, brand image and customer loyalty return success', he says. 'Policies in the reforming Indian economy are changing so rapidly, and liberalization, licensing, policies, etc., metamorphosise so fast, that long-term planning is next to impossible'. . . or so, he declares! But there are avenues, certain fundamentals. His sustainable focus and strategy in firmly entrenching himself in his customer's psyche, to thwart progressive increase in competition, has helped him live and thrive with reform.

Know Your Environment And Prepare Yourself

Haren has observed, that given the stringent and often redundant/ unrealistic rules and regulations, various bureaucratic loopholes are exploited. Malpractices are believed to be rampant in the SSI sector in India. 'Double-book entry' book-keeping, the maintenance of an absolutely unrepresentative statement of accounts for the authorities, and a true statement of accounts for oneself and one's trustworthy chartered accountant, are often observed to be the norm. It seems to be the usual practice amongst some entrepreneurs to make their employees sign for higher wage amounts than they are paid. The labour seem to be happy to get a job of their choice and salary, and the employer is happy to have filled up his labour requirement without straining his working capital. Minimum wage legislations and other rules and guidelines do not seem to be adhered to always. This is the environment in which the RNRI entrepreneur may have to compete in, he warns. This kind of environment is not necessarily always the norm, but is not an exception either.

The ex-professional entrepreneur has learnt to avoid mixing business with personal relationships in the Indian environment (it never gets anywhere), and to handle labour with strictness, to ensure productivity, and to occasionally adopt a feudal style of employee management. Some entrepreneurs may flow with the tide, with respect to business ethics, but others, like Haren, employ more ethical and sustainable strategies to do well in business. It serves no purpose to be shocked or disillusioned with the environment, but one must not ignore it either, he believes. It is only if you can understand it that you can beat it.

Recognize The Trade-Off And Tap The Benefits

Haren believes that the key to successfully doing business in India is to have a 'flexible approach' towards the authorities. Returned NRIs should not stick to their own views regarding delays and about crossing institutional hurdles to secure various facilities. They must understand that authorities too are hard-pressed, and the institutional incentive mechanism does not encourage dynamics of extraordinary effort on the part of support authorities to promote industry. Hence, the method of dealing with the external support environment and state boards should be tempered with flexibility and an open mind. Returned NRIs should not expect 'things' to move as smoothly as they do in the developed West. 'You get facilities, such as subsidies and various incentives and waivers for SSI, that you don't get in the developed West, the level of investment and manufacturing costs in absolute terms is low, market competition for products/processes, new to India, but old to the West, is low. Likewise, the time and infrastructural resources with the authorities may also be relatively lacking in some cases. A trade off exists,' he rationalizes.

One May Be Careful, But Need Not Be Crooked. Ensure Competence And Be Aware

Haren has learnt one important lesson in all these years of doing business in India—'Don't take anybody or anything at face value, be they project reports, contracts, promises; be they authorities, bureaucrats, partners or business contacts'. One needs to be careful, but need not be crooked to handle business in India. He does not believe that a successful businessman in India should ignore the black or white colouring of company returns, to ensure or sustain success. He believes it is excellent marketing, planning and quality focus that lead to success. Will the changing environment make things easier at least at the point of entry? At the point of entry into the subcontinent, Haren had wanted to explore the feasibility of various business opportunities. Sources of information, however, were lacking. He believes that most returned NRIs, seeking business options, lack reliable information regarding the financial aspects of business, the financial structuring of the project, about the financial incentives available, about market potential and means of assessment of the same, and about the various 'field-level' aspects of doing business in India. However, he corrects himself, 'the largely technical education and experience that I secured abroad made it all the more difficult for me, those with well-rounded managerial and technical exposure could perhaps find things a lot easier.' The major skills, imperative for successfully doing business in India, Haren believes, are individual marketing ability, creative foresight, problem-solving skills to manage unexpected business-related disruptions, and the ability to manage Indian labour and all business-related support institutions. 'Make sure you have all or most of them before you try!' Haren's enterprise has tied up with a marketing agency based in Mumbai, in order to tap the market potential in India, and is going places.

NRIs See Red

The bureaucratic environment has witnessed considerable change with economic reforms since 1991. But there has not been, by any means, a 'sea change'. Reforms have hardly eliminated red-tapism. Maintaining records, paying up levies, and claiming incentives and exemptions, is by no means a cakewalk. Valuable time and energy have to be spent on bureaucratic formalities. For example, excise duty levied on goods manufactured in the country covers over 1300 items. The number and complexity of excise procedures remain seemingly immense. The procedure of payment is longwinded and offers ample scope for harassment and arbitrary behaviour. The procedure includes the application and procurement of a registration certificate for the factory, an electronic control code, filing declarations, maintaining a daily register of goods and raw materials, in a prescribed form, to be pre-authenticated by the excise authorities, obtaining permission to operate a personal ledger account from which excise payments are to be made, and invoicing and endorsement of movement and transshipment of goods. And more, copies of all invoices and returns are to be submitted every 10 days, or monthly, depending on the scale of operations. Similarly, the process of obtaining approval for export of goods is equally longwinded. Between filing an application and becoming an exporter, there is many a slip. It begins with registering the company with the RBI, obtaining an RBI code, an export–import code, registering with the local export promotion council, submitting documents for proof of an export order, procuring inspection and insurance, ensuring clearance from a clearing and forwarding agent, and securing clearance from the port officials and superintendents. These are to be followed by obtaining a bill of lading, a certificate of origin, procuring payments through a bank, and applying for a duty drawback.

Price-competitiveness and efficiency, in spite of exemption from excise and customs duties, sometimes remain adverse, due to the fact that extensive procedures to claim exemptions from excise duty, for example, may delay dispatch of consignments; many exporters just go ahead, as they cannot afford to wait.

Requests for exemption from duties requires goods to be invoiced, several forms of varying colours have to be filled up, signed by the excise authorities and submitted to customs officers and commissioners. A certificate requesting central excise exemption has to be submitted. And, if duty exemption on components is required, yet another form has to be filled in and submitted. Smaller units are exempt from some of these longwinded essentials of doing business in India. But they have more than enough to chew themselves.

Now, while the institutional set-up may continue having vestiges of the License Raj, even while going the 'market' way, the entrepreneur has his travails heightened by increasing competition from within and outside the country. For example, business efficiency is indicated by the cost and profit structure of a business. Efficiency of production, selling, financing, pricing, administration and tax management, in a holistic sense, is indicated by the profit margin ratios of a firm. The ratio of contribution to sales, viz., excess of sales over variable costs of manufacture to total sales, indicating surplus generated after break-even level of output is generated, was low for Kiran Shah's manufacturing line. The same problem developed for Haren Shah. Both of them being in the computer electronics field, had a high proportion of imported components, due to their emphasis on producing high quality products. Value-addition was not very high. Margins had to be reduced, as India reduced import tariffs on products in the field of computer electronics, as part of its liberalization programme. Both enhanced their quality and the service provided for their product line, as a remedial measure. Kiran Shah realized high margins by providing computer servicing to customers. A monopoly producer, like 20 MICRONS, whom we consider later, even if not integrating backwards, so as to ensure high-input value addition, need not worry, as he can secure good margins anyway as fixed overheads are low and foreign competition is not envisaged. The managerial imperatives may be product and market specific, and the changing environment may not make things easier for the RNRI entrepreneur. From the bureaucracy in earlier times, it is increasingly the market that is master now! Those like Kiran and Haren Shah, and Mukherjee, who realise this in time, and act accordingly, avoid disaster.

Use of debt finance could have helped Kiran Shah offer products at lower prices by forsaking some of his declared profits secured by leveraging debt. If he was worried about the price-based competition but confident of the ROI and rate of interest on loan differential, he would have considered the debt-financing option more seriously. Kiran Shah was perhaps lucky that he did not, as his 'promised' market collapsed initially, and even investment in a flexible manufacturing option, at a higher project cost, may not have helped him get through the teething stage. Computers then were a new concept, and pushing them in the market would not have been easy. The interest burden of debt could have killed his enterprise initiative in months.

For the Shahs, reforms in 1991, with lowered tariffs, and subsequent competition from abroad, offered a tremendous challenge for survival. Both also found that the bureaucracy takes its own time, something like a year or two, for putting their units through the statutory requirements and legislations. But bureaucracy and policy had also kept away competition for a few years of their firms' operations. They perhaps appreciate that! A reforming economy is not necessarily going to make it immediately any easier to do business in India. The bureaucratic environment retains its vestiges, and ethics in business, and labour and bureaucratic ethos remain relatively dismal, in comparison to the developed West. But the cases, impressions, and the confidence of the RNRIs indicate the advantages and potential of the economy for a viable business opportunity.

10

Institutional Incentives Vs. Business Sense

Established institutions in India are a comfort—for example, the legal remedy in India, as against 'good faith'-based business in China. But, of course, a dispute may take decades to be resolved through Indian courts! Incentives are also there aplenty. At least on paper! But no business can survive on these alone. Values, the product, and the market, deliver sustainable competitive advantage.

—Anonymous

The current policy regime with regard to NRI investment is quite comparable to that of several Asian countries, which have been quite successful in augmenting investment inflows from expatriates. The regime offers a wide variety of incentives to attract direct investment. These include industrial estates, special economic zones, export-processing zones, and technology parks, which have attracted considerable attention. In addition, a broad spectrum of financial incentives, particularly in the form of tax holidays, subsidized sites, and business services, are offered by central and state authorities, to encourage economic development. The incentives, especially for small-scale units, are substantial, but should not cloud sound business rationale. Hemrajani seems to have selected a rather convenient project, as would perhaps most finance professionals with relatively meagre technical knowledge. He also sought to secure ample institutional incentives and support for his project. And, the project seems to be doing fine. But, as we shall see, it is business sense, with regard to the specific industrial environment, infrastructure and the market, that counts.

Injecto Plast Industries Pvt. Ltd.

Jivan Hariram Hemrajani, a qualified chartered accountant, returned to India after 16 years in Nigeria. With funds mobilized from friends, and some of his junior staff abroad, he started manufacturing plastic automobile products and household items.

He initiated his project at a cost of Rs 3.6 million, 1.6 million of which was in the form of a term loan Injecto Plast secured from the state financial corporation. With little family contacts or past involvement in business, the returned professional involved his younger brother, a commerce graduate, in his maiden business venture. The organization now employs about a dozen personnel, and has recently diversified into 'injecto acryl'.

A Negative Push, Macro-Market Estimation, And Business Opportunity Identification

Hemrajani's return was the outcome of a negative push factor, with risk to life and limb, in a strife-torn and relatively destabilized African country. It was not just worry about racist or burglary-related attacks on Asians and foreigners, but also the poor economic condition of the country, and the currency risk, that encouraged his return to India in 1988. His decision to do business in India was a corollary to a 'return to India at any cost' decision, and his commercial exposure. How did he go about his market search regarding business opportunity identification? He carefully analyzed newspapers, journals such as *India Abroad*, published from the US, chemical newsletters and journals, and chemical and oil-related literature in general. There was a plethora of these in Nigeria, an oil-exporting country. From amongst the literature, he discovered that in India, per capita plastic ratio, with respect to availability and consumption, was low. A macro observation served the purpose of estimating market demand. Or so he believed. However, as he discovered later, this was no substitute for a specific market analysis. Given his small-scale scope of operations and target market segment, such a broad market analysis should have been treated with caution. But it was not. Nevertheless, his broad observation helped him focus on an idea, and he was worried only about the technology to be incorporated, and about the financial aspects of the project. Hemrajani corresponded with government promotional agencies of the state, and with financial and industrial development corporations, before locating his unit. His brothers in India had followed up with these institutions, prior to his return. One brother handled the wholesale division, prior to leaving India for the USA. But his business idea, that blossomed due to his browsing through relevant literature in magazines in Nigeria, met with disaster. 'The market was the problem,' he declares. What went wrong?

Subsidy Seeking . . . A Potential Killer! Flexible Manufacturing . . . A Saviour!

The firm did not take off. Seeking subsidy, he had located his firm at an industrial estate developed by the industrial developmental agency of the state, without adequately testing the targeted local market, and without considering the 'sometimes' dismal record of authorities regarding the provision of promised infrastructure, utilities and capital subsidy. Further, there was relatively little value addition to imported raw-material inputs in his line of business, which in turn, affected margins. Fortunately, however, even at the start, he had carefully considered various manufacturing alternatives, such as injection and blow-moulding options, and related technology and manufacturing process alternatives. His broad intention was to enter the field of plastics, with equipment to manufacture diverse product lines, if necessary. He had narrowed down on the injection-moulding alternative. From manufacturing plastic buckets, he moved over to the manufacture of other products, including radiator fan blades for automobiles. The planned flexibility of his manufacturing equipment saved his firm from collapse.

Hemrajani believes his early error of seeking subsidies, available at specific sites, to the neglect of giving due consideration to local market potential and related costs including transport diseconomies, resulted in the lasting 'relative' ill-health of his business venture. 'It is infrastructure availability and the market that one needs to focus on, and not on looking for ways and means to reduce initial financial commitments,' he emphasizes, 'it is business opportunity identification, with reference to specific scale and area of operations, that is crucial.'

Is The Indian Environment Different? Not From Other Developing Economies!

Hemrajani perceives, that in terms of macro-economic instability, in terms of interest rate, exchange rate and currency fluctuations, the difference between India and a developing economy like Nigeria, is not very significant. This is true even on the social plane. 'Twice every three years there is a major outbreak of violence in some corner of the country, and politics and the bureaucracy are riddled with characteristically similar problems,' he says. The common belief about the scope of employing influence mechanisms to avoid delays, speeding up the activity of support institutions, or to move files, is by no means a unique phenomenon peculiar to India, as is perceived by some. While the business and economic environment is not very different in India and most other developing economies like Nigeria, the only difference for an NRI is the widely acknowledged and real possibility of racist, targeted burglary attacks, and often, higher political and economic instability, in some African countries. 'Dismal business ethics is something one has to live with, 'says Hemrajani. In some cases, where his buyers' power is strong, and market competition intense, some distribution outlets have to be 'encouraged' by special incentives, and their unethical exploitation, say, in the form of delayed payments, ignored. Bounced cheques have to be taken in the 'right spirit', to avoid antagonizing the debtor, as a sort of distorted public relations imperative, so as to not scare away customers. All developing economies face problems regarding business ethics and value systems. The problem is cultural and psychological, as well as an outcome of resource constraints for monitoring. Enforcement of contractual agreements is a problem, time and money have to be spent and wasted, often beyond the abilities of small entrepreneurs. Hemrajani believes that a method of avoiding delays and facilitating the movement of a relatively slow administrative machinery, is to deal directly with the heads of industry-related administrative departments, and to convince them of one's firm resolution to do business, and highlight the problems faced. He hears from others that the threat of going to the media, or dropping 'names', often works. The mental strain, relating to the market, and in business administration, can be tremendous, in the case of entrepreneurs who are shaky in their resolve to do business.

Values And Business? Competitive Advantage Stems From The Former

Reviewing his experience in his maiden role as a businessman, Hemrajani is of the view that his business style has been oriented towards maintaining a high level of professionalism, particularly regarding quality, keeping up business commitments, and his approach to people. The latter is crucial, he stresses. Hemrajani emphasizes on the diligent handling of labour, by means of incentive-based motivation, with strict accountability, and in establishing and maintaining goodwill with suppliers, buyers of his product, with support institutions, and the administrative machinery. He is resolved to progressively emphasize on product quality, in order to be one up on his competitors. Regardless of bitter experiences, he will continue to maintain his own personal values in discharging contractual obligations. He says he may not be able to control his debtors from delaying payment for credit purchases, which they do to avail of the interest advantages of the outstanding sum, or to use it for their own working capital requirements, to the maximum extent possible. But he prefers to maintain his principles.

Hemrajani's transition to a businessman has led him to trust associates, employees and other entrepreneurs less. He feels he now 'starts off with mistrust, till the other person proves himself worthy of trust and an ethical relationship'. It pays to be careful.

He believes that a positive approach towards aspects, such as keeping up a time schedule, whether an appointment, or the delivery of goods, is crucial. The record of others towards these aspects is often woeful. 'But there is no excuse for me to follow suit.' He realizes that in India today, and progressively in future, it is competition that will determine success or failure, and the source of competitive advantage stems from sticking to one's values. Entrepreneurs often ignore some of these seemingly rather pedestrian requirements. This, in turn, ensures the collapse of a business enterprise.

Forget The Support System, Focus On The Product And Its Market

Hemrajani believes that the slow process of the initiation of a business venture in India, and the negative experiences of inexperienced (in terms of business) returned NRIs, often dissuades entry of potential RNRI entrepreneurs. But the complaints, often with regard to the bureaucracy, by no means present insurmountable hurdles. A small scale of operations rarely causes serious difficulties or interaction with administrative machinery in any phase of business management. That is, so long as interests on borrowings from funding institutions are paid on time and more than a score of different types of returns have been filed regularly.

This excuse is not necessarily tenable even if in some cases valid. The slow pace of initiation is only a preliminary phenomenon, and is by no means necessarily, or always slow. Another complaint is regarding dismal business ethics. But one can take preventive measures. Hemrajani has been careful in the selection of customers, with a focus on creditworthiness and ethics, as he has heard of even court summons being disregarded by unscrupulous business, offenders, by availing of system loopholes that exist in plenty.

Efficient management of working capital, to tide over teething problems and market demand fluctuations, are crucial for small-scale manufacturers. He realized this from his initial errors in product identification, and in market estimation, for his scale of operations. However, the last few years have seen him progressively and innovatively select manufacturing processes, so as to cater to a diverse range of customers with the same machinery.

Hemrajani has always believed in being strongly conservative, and in presenting a positive image to his clients and maintaining good public relations, given the crucial role of marketing in his line of business.

The environment is not necessarily an excuse for avoiding the business option, he believes. It is entrepreneurial skill for doing business in India, which includes strong problem-solving skills, the ability to project a solid image, and strong skills in financial management, that counts. These skill imperatives are valid for any professional getting into business. Marketing ability, innovativeness, and networking, are crucial competencies to market products depending on broad consumer segmentation and channels of distribution. Not everybody is lucky with a captive market!

Being One's Own Consultant

Hemrajani's case also highlights the necessity for an entrepreneur to be involved in the preparation of an 'honest' project report or business plan, before initiating a project. Entrepreneurs often select an option linked to their background, and one in which the return is high and is dependent on the ability and effort they put in. Evaluating the option from the financial, technical and market perspective requires some competence and training. Giving the job to a consultant to work at it almost independently, as a sort of package deal, is no solution. But then, most finance professionals, such as Hemrajani, do it themselves . . . and sometimes land themselves in trouble!

Generally speaking, the genus of trouble may be isolated in most cases. Once the RNRI has selected the business idea, he has to make a business plan, highlighting the steps to be taken to operationalize the concept, including initiatives necessary in the project pre-initiation stage, before actual commencement of operations, and the projected performance of the project. The business plan considers the product, its features, the plant capacity, product lines, the market prospects, selling price, arrangements and cost of selling, the production process, technical arrangements, plant and machinery, suppliers, the cost of equipment, the location, infrastructural facilities, raw material-related aspects, manpower, working capital requirements, project cost, capacity utilization, estimates of business income and expenditure, profit levels, tax liability, risk element in the specific business, and policies, statutory legislations, clearance requirements, and the gestation lag for establishing the enterprise. The business plan is essential to procure assistance from lending institutions. Unfortunately, often that is all that it is prepared for, regardless of whether it is a consultant, or the entrepreneur himself who works at it!

In the course of preparing a business plan, if one is really interested, he gets to know the intricacies of the market, and possible lacunae in his idea. Hence, it is ideal if an entrepreneur is personally involved in the whole process, rather than merely use it as a tool to procure finances from funding institutions. Unfortunately, while the latter is achieved, the former imperative is rarely given the attention it deserves. The entrepreneur does not seem very interested in knowing the 'real' viability of a project estimated, by means of scientific methodology, with respect to the market, for example.

If the promoter has prepared a project report himself, or has at least been involved in its preparation, to a reasonable extent, its authenticity invariably improves. Assuming, of course, that he analyzes all aspects of feasibility in an honest fashion. But, as we shall observe throughout this book, not many bother to do so, hardly appreciating the necessity for going beyond filling in standardized information, so as to secure a term loan! There is often a lot more to the environment than even an approved project report reveals. For example, an Indian entrepreneur developed a spark plug for the two-wheeler industry. The quality was better than that of others in the market, in the price segment at which he positioned it. The quality of the product was his main focus. His proposal, prepared by a chartered accountant, for institutional support, was sanctioned. The business should have done well. But the market relied on wholesalers, who were not interested in product quality. A product with a shorter lifespan would have sufficed. What was crucial was a long credit period. The market was also characterized by practices of dishonoured commitments and bad debts. Financial planning and market demand projections can go haywire for the uninitiated. This is especially so if reliable wholesalers are not easy to identify, and are not 'bought' away from competitors, perhaps via influencing the employees of the wholesalers. This entrepreneur did not attempt to implement the measures discussed, or even hedge against it. The project collapsed. Business practices played a crucial role in that industry, but was not even considered at the stage of project feasibility and evaluation! Preparing a report, even by oneself, is worth nothing, unless ground-level market information regarding practices, nature of competition and customer requirements are understood. These are but some aspects. Of course, at the stage of implementation problems may surface anywhere, perhaps with the technical adaptability of equipment.

Other than involving himself in the preparation of an honest project report, an RNRI can work as an employee in a related industry in the Indian environment, and familiarize himself with the specific business and its environment, before he starts out on his own. But few have the inclination or the patience to do so. Another alternative to reduce business risk is to rope in an experienced partner, familiar with the business environment in the subcontinent. But such partners are barely available for the asking!

Hence, the least an RNRI can do is to give serious weightage to a business plan. In conclusion, one should understand that it is factors like business acumen, and awareness of practices and competition, within specific markets, that count. Institutional incentives and financial support may be procured by plans which are excellent on paper. But excessive reliance just on these plans, will, by no means sustain a business proposition.

Buying Oneself Into Business

Many RNRI entrepreneurs, who have been doing business in other Third World economies observe that the practice of employing unethical and even illegal payoffs in some cases, while clinching business contracts and in seeking institutional support, is not unique to India. Such practices prevail all over the world. To varying degree, though, RNRIs with exposure to doing business abroad, find that the extent and incidence of corruption may be higher in developing economies, due to the ethical and cultural psyche of the populace, monitoring, control, and resource-related problems of the regulatory system. People believe that if an Indian entrepreneur is forced to pay Rs 500 as a bribe for a job to an underling of the utilities department, to ensure 'speedy' connections, an RNRI is forced to pay Rs 5000. Being unfamiliar with the environment, many complain of having being taken for a ride. A few RNRIs confess, though not on record, of having successfully employed unethical and illegal influence mechanisms at the stage of project report submission, when seeking institutional funding. The standard methodology is to get it done through an agent or a consultant—perhaps a recognized project consultant, with 'contacts' within the bureaucracy. Establishing contacts with well-referred and credible, experienced consultants, through referees, could help the 'broad-minded' RNRI entrepreneur explore avenues to take advantage of such practices, in areas where they are prevalent.

Some RNRIs do not bother to hide their disgust with the environment. Project proposals and documents move at an excessively slow pace, unless 'speed' money is disbursed among the right authorities, some believe. But one need not take things lying down. When junior officials harassed some RNRIs, who were installing a utility connection to their unit, did not cave in. They took the matter up, with righteous indignation, with the superior officers in the concerned department, and rid themselves of harassment-seeking bribes in a jiffy. Nobody wants a scene or bad press! If one is getting into business at a medium scale of investment, it is sufficient to interact with senior officials of support institutions, and avoid the corruption at the grassroot level. This is an option that merits serious consideration.

A tough RNRI, using all his entrepreneurial competence, projecting a credible image and project, can avoid giving in to corruption, so as to exploit it to his advantage. Hemrajani did not. Name dropping and employing influence strategies, perhaps through networking, have helped some, while others have fought it out, by, for example, organizing open RNRI conferences at Delhi to voice their complaints, coupled with arduous follow-up. Merely keeping in touch with the Indian Investment Centre at Delhi, and state-level nodal agencies, has helped keep many RNRIs appraised of such events.

A few RNRIs see dismal ethics and corruption as an adverse element of the environment, as often 'speed money' and 'file-pushing' incentives to authorities go down the drain, and there is nothing one can do about it! Some RNRIs, who would like to use illegal and unethical influence mechanisms, are frustrated, as they do not know how and on whom they should 'work on', and hence, feel that their competitors have an advantage over them.

For many RNRIs, however, the whole issue is an exaggerated excuse by unprepared, incompetent and novice first-generation entrepreneurs, to justify their failure to start and sustain a viable business venture. They themselves have not paid graft, and do not feel they have suffered because of it. Nobody says corruption does not exist. It certainly does. But one need not give in to it. Hence, for most RNRIs, it is a question of ethics. Under no circumstances will they knuckle down to the 'ignominy' of doing something illegal or unethical.

Corrupt practices are widely prevalent in several industrial sectors or institutions. It is by no means the rule, but it is not the exception either. Confidence, commitment, and attacking the problem head on, is the only way of tackling the system! Hemrajani was a fighter, but then, so many RNRIs, it seems. They have had no intention of getting a defective project through, by exploiting corruption, where it exists.

The discussions and cases we have considered till this stage largely concentrate on aspects relating to the preliminary stage of preinitiation. What about business growth?

11

The Indian Business Environment: Phenomenal Potential For Exponential Growth . . . With The Right Strategy!

*It is not that support institutions are always corrupt.
They may be well-meaning, but they have their own
resource constraints. And where institutions and
regulatory bodies are unethically or illegally
influenced, it is often the businessman who is the
culprit! It is business ethics and practices that one
should be wary of. One need not adapt to the
environment, but one cannot afford to be blissfully
ignorant and live in a fool's paradise either.*

—Anonymous

Invariably, it is the starting phase of initiating a business, and
surviving the teething stage, that is often difficult. But, while market

entry may have been relatively easy for some 'lucky' RNRIs, the fact remains, that a smooth entry does not necessarily or automatically ensure a sustained performance. There is a need for vision for constantly seeking out innovative ideas and for being on the look out for developing sustainable competitive advantage in business. Keeping in view the emerging environment, characterized by the continuous liberalization process, the potential RNRI entrepreneur should be aware of strategic options and be prepared to adopt them. He should regularly ask himself several questions, keeping his resources, the market, and the general environment in mind. 'What is my existing business?' 'What should be my business?' and 'What will be my business?' If the answers to all these questions are the same, the entrepreneur should continue in the same business. If different, he should either give up a part of his business, or start a new business altogether. In a dynamic business environment, various generic strategies may be successfully and periodically modified and followed. The following three cases amply highlight the available options. (a) An expansion strategy involves the addition of new products or markets to the existing ones. Companies may diversify into unrelated or related areas of business, seeking returns opportunity and diversification of risk. The case of D.R. Industries provides an example of the successful implementation of this option. (b) A stability strategy is followed by a company, which is doing very well in its line of business. The company should focus its resources where it can develop or maintain a meaningful competitive advantage in the narrowest possible product-market function scope, consistent with its resources and market requirements. By building effective entry barriers, efficiency, and constant innovation, it should try to maintain and build a competitive advantage. 20 Microns has been following this strategy effectively for a decade. (c) A retrenchment strategy may be adopted when a part or the whole of the business unit is unprofitable, or when the opportunity cost of being in that business is very high. A retrenchment strategy is a decision to get out of such a business, by divestment or liquidation. However, the entrepreneurial breed devise unique methods to avoid failure, or write off their investment and try to successfully develop their enterprise. Chandresh Parikh's United Foam, and Dr Anang

Shah's, Oceanic Chemicals, serve as excellent examples. Let us consider these three cases in isolation.

D.R. Industries: Always Seeking, With Vision

The Man And The Lady Behind His Throne

Nattily dressed, in a manner exuding success in business, Dhirubhai Desai is constantly pursued by media personnel who dog his footsteps. He matter of factly declares his ultimate goal of establishing a global network of manufacturing operations and offices. Under his able stewardship, and guided by his strategic vision, the Chicago Group of Companies are forging ahead in leaps and bounds. Currently employing over 300 employees, the flurry of activity in his office is indicative of a firm on the threshold of stupendous growth. Over the years, various awards have been conferred upon this RNRI entrepreneur, honouring his excellent performance in business. These include the Udyog Ratna Award in 1990, the Vikas Shree Award in 1992, and the Rajiv Gandhi Excellence Award in 1993. His wife, Manjulaben Desai, is herself a highly qualified professional. An MBA in marketing, she works as the Managing Director of D.R. Industries. Manjulaben also handles the financial services company, Chicago Future Markets and Financials Ltd. She had gone to the USA in 1972 to join her husband, and has played an active role in his entrepreneurial career since.

The financial performance of the group is excellent, and massive expansion and diversification plans are always in process. From its initial investment in the texturing of synthetic filament yarn, the company has already grown into a multifaceted organization, with interests in textiles, food processing and real estate. Desai is firmly entrenched in his role as head of the management team.

Entry And Growth . . . As Smooth As Silk

An official delegation from Gujarat that visited the USA attracted the husband and wife team. They returned shortly to set up business in India, with no problems. Desai's exposure to business, his specialization in finance, and his financial resources, facilitated entry.

No middlemen, consultants or chartered accountants were employed by the couple to smoothen their path in initialing business in India. It was all smooth sailing. The fact that they had returned to India at the special invitation of the delegation headed by Mr H.K. Khan, and Mr Shelat, later Chief Secretary to the state government, to invest in industry in the state, and their scale of proposed investment, helped.

D.R. Synthetic Limited was set up in record time. The procedures and formalities of initiation were completed in three months, and the unit texturized and processed synthetic yarn by the year 1980. From an initial investment of about Rs 25 million, and a turnover of about, Rs 150 million, the unit matured into D.R. Industries Limited, and then into the Chicago group of compaines. Mr Desai is confident of developing his company into a Rs 10,000 million company by the year 2000.

Impressions From A Success Story: Don't Look For Excuses For Failure Even Before You Start

The entry of businessmen like Desai into Indian manufacturing is facilitated by the subsidies and other industrial development incentives offered in the country. 'Where in the developed West do you get all these incentives and subsidies?' he demands. 'Some NRIs in the SME sector, particularly those who are not doing too well or are failures in business, complain of corruption in the system. I have not seen anything of it!' he declares. Often, it is the lack of civic sense and the perceived unethical code of conduct of some local Indian businessmen, and their attitude and activities, that shocks some NRIs returning to India after working as professionals in a middle-level management cadre in a developed economy. Talk of corruption and preliminary hurdles to doing business, Desai believes, is 'losers' talk', by people who do not possess entrepreneurial qualities, or are inexperienced first generation entrepreneurs. 'People who do not have a commitment to stay in India, but keep one foot abroad and one in India, and try to do business, will get nowhere. They only look for mundane excuses to convince themselves to go back.' He elaborates, 'planned risk-takers, who burn their bridges behind them, and return to India to undertake entrepreneurial activity, do well'. People with business experience abroad can do very well in India, with the expertise gained in the West, with new business ideas adapted to Indian needs, and their years of training and skill abroad in a relatively much more competitive environment. Desai is of the opinion that eventual success in business is determined by committed hard work and positive thinking and an appreciation of the advantages of doing business in India. Not by harping on limitations in bureaucratic, market or infrastructural aspects, to justify one's own incompetence!

A Recipe For Success In Business

This veteran, of a decade and a half of experience in entrepreneurship in India, is expecting a growth in terms of hundreds of times, within two decades of doing business in the subcontinent. What is his secret? His style! Desai believes that right 'presentation' is a crucial business style that must be adopted for successful growth in business. It is the approach and image that one projects to the external environment and to business-related players that counts. However, presentation does not imply a blown-up image, or media hype, but a solid, conservative profile. This helps in one's efforts to mobilize funds from institutions and the public in a growing firm. Focus on presentation and a solid image implies the necessity of maintaining the functional management area of marketing as a priority area.

What has he got to say to the potential market entrant? Desai thinks back to his own experience. For a potential RNRI entrepreneur, the information required most crucially is regarding financial incentives and statutory guidelines that apply to business. Business ideas need to be probed into and shortlisted. The institutional machinery can only give options. The entrepreneur has to link available options to his core competencies. Desai believes that a person skilled in finance and marketing can do well in most fields, if he is a good organizer of resources, and builds up a management team which includes experts related to a specific business sector. 'Marketing and management capabilities remain paramount factors for success in business,' he adds.

The Confidence Of A Success Story

The company has gone in for backward integration and expansion beyond the state of Gujarat. This is in terms of location of manufacturing bases seeking incentives and sourcing raw material. Dhirubhai Desai, who returned to India in 1979–80, after more than 10 years of working in prized jobs in Fortune 500 companies, including General Motors, Dupont and Price Waterhouse, is bullish regarding the growth of his enterprise, about the Indian economy, and about his doing business in India in general. Desai believes that India will be a leading economic superpower by the year 2010. His training as a Chartered Public Accountant (CPA), MBA from the USA, and his work experience with leading Fortune 500 companies, have given him the confidence and the competence to successfully do business in India. The liberalization of the economy and the dismantling of the License Raj have served to reduce the possible incidence of institutional barriers and constraints to doing business. 'It will serve to reduce the "blown-up" versions of the possible incidence of institutional corruption, spread by some incompetent would-be or had-been entrepreneurs,' he declares. Desai does not believe that business ethics in the corporate world of the developed West is vastly different from that of a developing economy like India's. Business is business. In a nutshell, Desai is of the view that his success stems from his focus on providing quality goods and services to customers, backed by his personal drive, motivation and presentation, supported by sound financial management. There is little difference in the skills required in a businessman in India and in a developed economy like that of the USA, he says.

The implicit similarities in the views of an expansion strategist and a stability strategist are evident from the following case.

Strike Pay Dirt And Hold It!

A Sustained Monopoly . . . With Happy Employees And Customers

At 51 years of age, Chandresh S. Parikh has been running 20 Microns for nearly eight years. 'We have no competitors,' he says with a wry smile, 'we retain our employees, we ensure loyalty to the organization and keep our manufacturing process close to our chest.' A suspicious look flickers across his face, but he quickly dispels it with an apologetic glance. The firm manufactures micronized minerals used by paint manufacturers and the plastic industry, for example, as fillings of PVC pipe manufacture. Even today, after all these years of operation, the firm has no competition throughout India. Quality goods 'everybody' is ready to buy is manufactured, and Parikh believes that the firm can continue to manage its marketing and promotion completely on its own. 'We don't need anybody else to build up our image, our product does it for us,' he emphasizes. Customers are generally not happy with traders and with intermediaries between customers and manufacturers in the plastics and paints industry. Some unethical traders adulterate the product with cheap substitutes so as to secure greater margins for themselves, and get away with it. It is perceived, that in many cases, if the material supplied to the final consumer gets rejected at the quality control stage, traders often pay some money to quality control officials, and the material is passed. However, ultimately the customer suffers, and consequently, the company is the loser in the long run. This rationalizes Parikh's decision to undertake direct marketing and selling.

Bad India Is Not So Bad If You Want To Remain Indian, With Committed 'Business' Partners, Not Family

Parikh was informed about the negative aspects of doing business in India, from NRIs who had tried to and failed, and from friendly Indian businessmen. But his resolution to do business in India was strong. He had obtained a Green Card in America, but the decision to surrender his Indian citizenship, and acquire a British or an American one was strongly opposed by his family. 'When you can make money in India, why live as a second class citizen in the West?' His wife argued. Several years of stay in the UK, and the West in general, had only strengthened his resolve to return to India at some point of time. His major motivation to do business in India was not merely the availability of an opportunity to tap, but a decision to return to India at any cost! He had been abroad, frankly speaking, 'only to generate savings,' as he was of humble family origins in economic terms. Resettling in India had always been a pre-determined conviction.

The first generation entrepreneur believes that his strategy of avoiding relatives, and collaborating with other NRIs who have returned to India, and with friends and acquaintances in India, who have ploughed in their own funds, is a smart move. The motivation of his partners is ensured by their financial commitment, and a 'professional relationship', thus contributed significantly to the progress of the business and its exemplary performance.

An Idea Strikes Pay Dirt And Is Pushed By Local Partners

How did his 'opportunity to tap' develop? Bhanu Patel, currently a partner in the enterprise, was earlier a manufacturer of paints in India. He brought to Parikh's notice problems regarding the quality of raw materials used in the manufacture of paints. The business, therefore, developed from the point of view of fulfilling a perceived consumer demand. The promoters explored the idea of producing micronized minerals, and initially contacted all mine owners in India to gauge their impressions and ideas. They received one equivocal response, 'Mitti me kya paisa milega'! Nevertheless, the partners got together and went ahead with the project, finalized the business idea, technology and location, and the company was started at an original project cost of Rs 7 million. Four Indian partners and an NRI contributed towards the capital of the firm. The term loan amounted to almost Rs 4 million. Parikh's partners in India managed the show initially, while he was still based abroad. They also helped him on his return, as he felt he was totally out of touch with the style of working in India.

Adapting An Idea, And Partnership Synergies

'Initially, when 20 Microns got off the drawing board, every two or three months I was in India for a month, exploring and re-exploring the market, and handling bureaucracy-related problems. I wanted to know about and be sure of the potential of the product in India,' says Parikh. The original project was prepared by a consultant in Germany, and the project cost was estimated at Rs 50 million. If a full-fledged mineral project even with Indian machinery, had been initiated, the cost would have been too high. The right way of manufacturing mineral powder is a complex and expensive affair, of owning mines, mineral operators, crushing, grinding and surface treatment equipment. But Parikh decided to avoid excessive backward integration, and focussed the project to meet the requirements of the relevant manufacturing process involved. This reduced overall project cost to a tenth of the estimate. The raw material, however, was available in abundance, and the stage was set.

Currently, 20 Microns is the flag-ship company of the group, and other firms, such as Hi-tech Minerals and United Foam, all produce similar products, micronized minerals. The differentiation was to help avail of term loan facilities and other government incentives allotted to SSIs. A colleague of his, Sudhir Parikh, worked as the group's financial controller. He is a qualified finance professional. The partners were persons experienced in the different aspects of manufacture, and in the management of the product and the firm, the Indian partners were involved in manufacturing and trading in paints, and the two NRIs in finance, administration and marketing. The management thus combined their synergies in the major functional areas of managing an enterprise.

Growing Teeth Late In The Market

The firm, initiated in 1987, did not do well in the absence of Parikh. He returned in 1989, to bring about a turnaround of the firm. While abroad, he had been in complete charge of Africa-based operations, including the marketing assignment of a leading Indian business house. It was not very difficult for him to develop systems and streamline marketing operations. The initial prolonged teething problems, faced by 20 Microns in 1987–89, could have been avoided if he had come immediately after registering the company, and provided personal supervision. His wide personal exposure could have saved the firm from an adverse turnover of Rs 700,000 in the first year of operations. But the past is past, and he has no regrets, as everything has finally turned out well. The group is poised for major expansion.

How Have They Been Able To Make It?

Parikh believes, as do all professionals, that quality regarding products, marketing and service, is crucial for success in business. He, like Dhirubhai Desai, believes that it is crucial to project and maintain a solid image of the company. If a customer is not satisfied due to a defect in the product, the firm accepts, returns and rejects at its own cost. Employee loyalty to the organization is also important. This is particularly so, as the firm is a monopoly operator and potential competitors would like to know their trade secrets, including their manufacturing process. Parikh has developed several simple techniques for gauging employee loyalty. For example, he periodically advertises in leading local newspapers, posing as a multinational company, seeking employees with experience in related fields. Only one employee in all these years has tried to change jobs! He analyzes discontentment and gives a fair deal. Employee promotions are rapid, in keeping with fast corporate growth. Monthly meetings of the key personnel are organized to sort out problems and explore suggestions together. All this has ensured that his management of people has been a resounding success, in terms of morale and loyalty.

Blessings, Qualms Of The Fresher . . . And Determination

Parikh was lucky not only because of his success in business, but also because of his being 'blessed' with a wife and teenaged children, who also despised their second class citizenship in the West. The only cause of worry, when he started his business, was not his unfamiliarity with overall business operations, but the possibility of failure in his maiden entrepreneurial venture. He believes that many NRIs would love to come back to India and stay with their friends and relatives, once they have mobilized sufficient funds and experience, but they face similar worries. Several of them attempt to do business, but experience problems akin to that of any first generation entrepreneur. Some fight it out, while some say their goodbyes, blaming project-related gestation lags and the bureaucracy. But everything has a way out, Parikh argues. Some successful RNRIs avoid administrative delays and bureaucratic problems, by taking the matter up confidently with top state and national level officials and politicians, even if they do not possess formal contacts. The necessity for such action is not common, but an entrepreneur is one who has to use all means at his disposal to emerge successful. Those who do not possess a truly undying entrepreneurial spirit, fail!

A Jack Of All Trades Or A Jack For Each Trade

The starting crisis that ruins many an enterprise just after the initiation stage, often occurs due to underestimation of project cost, working capital requirement, relative neglect of the market or of taxation. The cash crisis occurs due to the entrepreneur's concentration on profits rather than on cash, which is necessary to maintain activity levels and to meet marketing obligations. Tying up funds in fixed investment and unplanned expansion may also culminate in a crisis. Any of these and many more such crises may occur due to lack of all-round managerial exposure. D.R. Desai, of the Chicago group of companies, was aware of these pitfalls because of his experience abroad. And 20 Microns was well-equipped with partners experienced in diverse areas of the particular industry. Two were locals with experience in trading and manufacturing and the two RNRIs together possessed expertise in financial management and in overall marketing and administration. This smoothened the entry and growth of these enterprises.

Several RNRIs initially tie-up with a local partner in India, (unfortunately) not necessarily a person who can fill in the gaps in managerial exposure, but someone who can do a bit of follow-up and 'running around' during the pre-initiation stage. Invariably, it is a trustworthy relative, viz., a 'trustworthy and available Jack', and not necessarily a competent or qualified one. The NRI delegates the responsibility of project initiation, preliminary and pre-operative activities to this person, and returns when the project is close to taking off, or at some later stage, when he is ready to return. If he can find a reliable and experienced partner, who can fill in the gaps in his background, as far as the Indian environment is concerned, and in specific functional aspects of management, it is ideal. But such people are hard to find.

Being a Jack of all trades, viz., possessing skills in various or all functional aspects of management, does not necessarily make a successful entrepreneur. Managerial skills are essential in the early stages of enterprise initiation, as the RNRI may not be in a position to locate and employ competent professional managers. And, depending on the scale of investment and on the extent of personal stake in the enterprise, it may be necessary for the owner manager to develop a management team with expertise in all functional aspects of management. Several first generation RNRI entrepreneurs have adequate experience in overall project management, which has been very useful for entrepreneurial activity. But it is also necessary, that apart from managerial skills, the promoter/s should possess entrepreneurial competencies. These may include initiative, opportunity evaluation, information seeking, concern for work quality, commitment to work contracts, efficiency orientation, systematic planning, problem-solving skills, self-confidence and the ability to employ various influence strategies. An entrepreneur, unlike a manager, seeks opportunities, regardless of his resource base. His competencies develop not from training or exposure to hard skills alone, but from soft skills and competencies imbibed in his psyche. The crucial element is commitment to enterprise!

Fragmentation Favours Stagnation

Initially, starting off 'smaller' has its own advantages and problems. Perceived financial risk is smaller for those new to business or to the environment. The RNRI can make lower investments and could hold back more of his savings for unforseen expenditure and working capital requirements. It is cash shortage that is the killer in most cases. SSI also provides flexibility and speed in decision making, and the special needs of market segments can be targeted. But unit costs of production may be high, though overheads are lower, due to presence of scale economies in the industry and difficulties of investing in R&D. Often, it is not these considerations that determine scale of investment, but exemptions from several statutory requirements and protection which attract entrepreneurs into the segment.

Parikh had invested in the sector because of his capability of contributing to promoter's equity. He realized the foolishness of spawning too many small firms, and seeking advantages associated with an SSI status, specially in the face of the rapid growth of his project. Excise duty, sales tax and labour advantages existed, and he could have set up any number of small units, even within the same compound, different only on paper! But he ensured that he built a flagship company, 20 Microns, which did well, with its performance reflected in its financial statements. The group of firms under his able stewardship included United Foam and Hi-tech Minerals. He is not adding on any more firms, but is building up 20 Microns. 20 Microns is a solid firm with great potential. Funding from the banker or going public would be no problem. This explains and ensures its sustained growth. Entrepreneurs in India often forget that spawning too many small firms, different entities only on paper, but in reality parts of the same manufacturing process, underspecifying profits, carrying on non-recorded transactions, etc., only serve to evade or avoid statutory levies in the short term, or if one can get away with it, even in perpetuity. But such strategies affect future growth prospects, as the image of the firm with respect to the market and potential financiers is not as impressive as it should be! Smart operators realize this before it is too late.

Dhirubhai Desai and Chandresh Parikh have been doing well. But what about firms that have not been doing too well? A retrenchment strategy for an SME entrepreneur may simply imply that he winds up his entrepreneurial adventure! The tenacious RNRI entrepreneur is not going to stand for it! He looks for options to help sustain his enterprise and builds on it. The entrepreneurial spirit comes out strongly in Sudhir Parikh's and Dr G.R. Patel's case.

United Foam: RNRIs Together In Business

Entrepreneurship For Posterity

Sudhir Parikh had worked for Banco Products (I) Ltd., directly associated with overseas operations in an overall supervisory capacity. From 1981 to 1987, he was largely based in Tanzania. He supervised the operations of localized manufacturing plants of polyurethane foam, detergents, paints, glues, etc. Chandresh Parikh was his superior, in overall charge of Africa and UK operations. Over this period, Sudhir Parikh visited India two to three times. The immediate rationale for his return to India was provided by the health problems of his eight-year old son, who had developed bronchitis and faced a severe asthma problem due to the coastal location and climate of his base in Africa. He also wanted to set up a business and leave a legacy for future generations, in keeping with his India-based elder brother's advice. 'I decided that even if I lose all my savings, I would do business in India,' he recollects. Sudhir returned to India and set up 'United Foam', at a project cost of Rs 3 million. The state finance corporation provided 70 per cent of the project cost. About 50 per cent of the equity capital was provided by Sudhir Parikh, and the balance by Chandresh Parikh.

Being One's Own Boss On One's Own Steam . . . Though It May Involve Mistakes Aplenty

Sudhir Parikh loved the idea of being his own boss. He had complete independence in decision making, while organizing and finalizing contracts in Tanzania for Banco. He thus had a good experience base for entrepreneurship. On his return to India in 1987, he conducted a personal search, made enquiries in furniture and furnishing materials and automotive industry, and being a person of qualified financial background, in terms of education, prepared his own project report. It took about two years for the project files to be processed and sanctions from various support institutions to be received. He concedes that not engaging the services of reputed consultants with contacts could be the reason for this. But he did not want to jump the queue, or resort to unethical means like some other entrepreneurs.

He had initially been worried whether he was selecting a good business idea, whether he would be able to market his product, and where he should set up his unit. But by means of his own painstaking efforts, his business idea, technology, means of finance and location of his unit were all finalized after his return to India. The stage seemed set. But there were other problems that he had not bargained for. He encountered difficulties at the initiation stage. He was surprised to have his application for a term loan rejected on the grounds that the project was on the banned list for SSI. It was a wrong conclusion drawn by the institution and it took them four to five months to rectify their mistake. This delayed project initiation. But he went ahead without much ado.

Being One's Own Boss . . . Ahem! Apart From The Market And Business Environment That Is

Sudhir Parikh is of the view that the business environment in Tanzania, where he was engaged in overall supervision and coordination for Banco's unit, was not very different from that in India. He believes that the widely perceived corruption in a developing economy is by no means restricted to the Indian environment alone. And, the greatest bane of a business enterprise is the market, anywhere in the world. It is problems in the marketing function that serve to undo most business ventures, as was almost his case regarding United Foam, and not institutional problems and limitations, he believes. By the 'market' he does not imply satisfying the final consumer alone. Sudhir Parikh elaborates that, practically speaking, it depends on the market you have to work in. Sometimes it is possible to broadly categorize customers' requirements. In the north of the country, it is cost consciousness that prevails, in the south it is quality consciousness, and in the west it is a mix of both. Hence, it is first necessary to understand your market. But this alone is not sufficient. Business practices within specific sectors play a crucial role. He could not match the unethical business practices followed in his industry. The distribution outlets were cornered by entrepreneurs operating on unethical and unaccountable cash transaction-based arrangements and settlements. Entry was difficult, and United Foam's performance was adversely affected.

Other Aspects Of The Environment Are Also Almost The Same—But RNRIs Can Always Turn Messiah

He has experienced corruption both in the bureaucracy and in business in Africa and believes the problem to be more severe in some developing countries than it is in India. But this does not imply that bureaucratic and business ethics in India are not wanting, as it is the latter that almost sealed United Foam's fate.

Sudhir also feels that in the changing Indian environment, long-term policy and planning by an SSI is ruled out. Every budget change necessitates changes in strategy. Taxation, excise duty, interest rate and other policies change periodically. The scenario is akin to the economic instability in several African economies. Government rules pertaining to taxation and other statutory norms are not liberalized enough in developing countries, as to serve as an encouragement to entrepreneurs to earn an honest income. He does not believe that payoffs and underhand dealings are necessary for success in business, though the industry in which United Foam operated in, was based on a distribution network influenced by these practices.

As a matter of fact, he is also disillusioned about employee ethics, as he is about business ethics in India. Several times, even upper management grade employees, sent to collect cash from debtors, returned, claiming to have lost the sums collected en route. Often the sums exceeded Rs 100,000. But what could he do? He sacked them, but that was all he could do. All these factors cumulatively affected his unit's performance. Nevertheless, he was both smart and fortunate. His partnership with fellow RNRI, Mr Chandresh Parikh, and consequent modification in the manufacturing base and process of manufacturing micronized minerals, as was the practice in other firms of the group called 20 Microns, came to his rescue. Sudhir Parikh doubles as financial controller for 20 Microns, and his relationship with it has its foundations based on a long-standing mutual trust between the two of them.

Information And Training For The RNRI

Parikh believes that the most needed information required by the RNRI is regarding rules and regulations and government procedures and guidelines. But more importantly, he also believes that first generation entrepreneurs need information concerning all applied aspects of functional management, project ideas, technology, bureaucratic procedures and guidelines, and specifically about product-wise business practices. They need training. RNRIs must realize that thus need to anticipate and make provisions to overcome the significant problems that thus are likely to face even at the pre-initiation stage. This is necessary, to avoid losing their savings and investible surpluses before the entrepreneurial adventure is set on a firm footing.

Innovative Strategies To Beat Sickness

Several of the firms discussed in this book are performing in a rather poor fashion. In most cases, the RNRIs operating the show are confident of a turnaround. However, some cases are not very viable from an independent financial point of view. In such cases, unique options have been successfully explored by entrepreneurs Sudhir Parikh got an opportunity and utilized it. Dr G.R. Patel, with his chemicals unit, developed the available opportunity. Defective implementation has invariably been a result of the market environment.

A Chemist With An Entrepreneurial Bent Of Mind

Dr G.R. Patel started his business initiative in India at an 'official' project cost of about Rs 5.5 million. His factory was set up in the Panchmahal District of Gujarat in 1986. About Rs 4 million of the project cost was provided by the state financial corporation. The firm today manufactures pharmaceutical products and bulk drugs, and undertakes R&D activity. It focusses on formulating catalysts and processes. Today, this unit has Rs 200 million worth of processes to sell. The unit, however, has not been doing very well financially. The problem stemmed from defective market assessment and competition. However, Patel rationalizes the firm's long-run utility, by declaring his enterprise 'Shirag' to be an R&D base, even if not a profit-seeking venture. This is evident from his subsequent initiation of Hindustan Nitro Products Gujarat Ltd., with a capital investment of Rs 550 million in 1994, and another proposed 'close to the chest' project of Rs 1 million on the anvil. The process developed by Shirag can be used by both the (other two) projects.

The Stage Was Set: Competence, Resource And Exposure-wise

This PhD in Thermodynamics, viz., Engineering Physics, from the US, had completed his Bachelor of Science in Chemistry, in Gujarat, before proceeding to complete his MS and doctoral degree at New Jersey. Since 1967, he had worked with leading international firms, both in the research area and in the selling division. He had frequently visited Indian government and public sector units, such as Indian Petro-Chemicals Corporation Ltd. (IPCL), Gujarat Petrochemicals and Madras Fertilizers, to sell processes. Thus, he had the opportunity of acquiring a unique training, both in the technical aspect of product R&D and also in the marketing of the same. Moreover, over the period of his stay abroad, and particularly from 1974-85, he must have visited India about four to five times a year. Hence, the Indian social, cultural or business environment was not new to him. This served as a definite advantage when he ventured into entrepreneurship in India.

His major motivation to return to India was his long-standing decision to return to his homeland, and the 1977 Gujarat ministerial delegation, led by Mr Shelat, later Chief Secretary. He was also confident of his technical knowledge, supported by ample financial resources of his own, given his proposed scale of operations and his commercial exposure. Even before he initiated his maiden entrepreneurial venture in the subcontinent, he had some exposure to small-time entrepreneurial activity in the USA. In fact, even while working abroad, he ran a private laboratory with his brother. He had developed his own process for peroxide, and he manufactured catalysts and sold them. His market included pharmaceutical and chemical firms in the USA.

An Idea And Its Location

Long before returning to do business in India, Patel was a voracious reader of the *Gujarat Samachar, India News,* the *European Capital News,* and CNN publications regarding market potential in countries like India. He also browsed through chemical news bulletins regularly. And prior to his return to India, his business idea and technology had crystallized. A native of Gujarat, his home was Gujarat; its culture, language and people, his. However, his decision regarding settling close to Baroda, was based on the availability of investment subsidy and on the promised provision of natural gas and water.

Since his decision to initiate business in India, he moved back and forth, over a period of two years, prior to his resettlement in 1986. His project financing plan, capital structuring and location were decided upon during his visits. Shirag was initiated.

Patel has a sincere bit of advice. He believes that new entrepreneurs, particularly NRIs, should not decide on the location of their units, based on the availability of subsidy, but they should be absolutely positive regarding infrastructure and utility availability, before project initiation. Shirag suffered because of this mistake. Learning the hard way, Hindustan Nitro Products, another firm initiated by Patel, is more rationally located.

A Deep Dive—Watch Out For Boulders!

Even before returning to India, like most NRIs planning entrepreneurship, Patel was worried about the success of his technology, about the soundness of the business idea, its viability, and as to whether he would be able to attune himself to the change in ethos, be it business-related, bureaucratic or social. He had no 'contacts', either in Indian bureaucracy or business, which he had 'heard' could favourably affect entrepreneurial activity in India. But he does not believe that it is at all necessary. Patel was confident that he could set up and successfully manage a business enterprise in the subcontinent, through hard work and his competence. 'If I burn money, it's my own. So it is okay to take the plunge,' he reasoned. He feels that the widespread notion that corruption is all-pervasive in the Indian environment is an exaggerated misconception. His persistence and steadfastness have ensured his success, with potential for immense returns in future. If he could do it, so can anybody else, he argues. Shirag may be a relative financial failure due to locational misassessment and the market scale-economy relationship was also not given the consideration it deserved, but it could still be used as a base for his current and future plans.

Entrepreneurial Woes Regarding The Business And Industrial Support Environment . . . And A Conviction

Hindustan Nitro Products manufacturing aniline has dye manufacturers in Gujarat and Delhi as its market. The firm blossomed as a result of the base developed by Shirag. As in the case of Shirag, which had taken something like two years for project implementation, Hindustan Nitro Products also took a long time— four years. Patel faced problems regarding the supply of gas. Almost none was available, and what little was, was consumed by other units. He then attended an NRI conference in New Delhi in 1991, and voiced his problems to the Prime Minister. In 1993, though natural gas was still not provided, naphtha was preferred as an alternative.

Regarding the market and competition-related adversities in the case of Shirag, Patel feels that he should have perhaps returned to India not in 1986, but ten years earlier, when he could have been a monopolist with no competition in the country. Unfortunately, today competitors have increased in the field of process technology. Nevertheless, Patel is of the opinion that with focus on technology and quality, with the processes developed at Shirag as his base, his entrepreneurial activity is bound to gain a sure boost. He has, however, suffered at the hands of the Indian business environment. For example, at the stage of construction, construction contracts resulted in only 80 per cent of the work being completed. The balance was not undertaken at all. He has learnt to be more careful the hard way. He now hires only quality and well-established contractors, and does the construction phase-wise, even if all these entail enhanced budgets. Similarly, bills outstanding from debtors take time to be realized, but he does not harass creditors, as a matter of principle. His convictions have borne fruit and his reputation as a businessman remains strong, providing credibility at the time of public mobilization of funds, and in harnessing funds from other NRIs abroad.

A Word Of Advice For The Uninitiated

Patel is of the opinion that earlier long-term business planning in India was based on a budget to budget strategy. For example, some believe that one pays and gets a license—the payment being made in terms of one's financial resources and in accordance with one's time schedule. And then abruptly, delicensing was enforced. Rapid policy changes do not encourage planning, he feels. He also observes that it is perceived by RNRI entrepreneurs that locals shirk work. Hence, outsiders, viz., natives of southern Indian states, from Kerala, for example, are often preferred as employees. He is not too sure whether it is the local, casual lifestyle, or work ethos in general that is a problem. Regarding employees' skills, he feels like most other RNRI entrepreneurs in the North, that 'the more towards the south of India the better'. He also realizes that one should not explicitly trust one's employees regarding commitment, but should check on them regularly—watch out for policy change and watch the people who work for you!

Patel believes that as the scale of initial investment by an RNRI tends towards medium and larger size categories, the better would be firm performance and more important would as many believe political support and bureaucratic contacts. But increased credibility, by means of increased investment levels, could help in securing the latter.

Patel is confident that NRIs abroad would be benefited by understanding the ground realities regarding the business environment in India, and gaining access to easily comprehensible guidelines for doing business in the sub-continent. Not everyone has the good fortune of visiting India something like 50 times over a period of 11 years, prior to final resettlement!

Conservatively Financing New And Untested Ideas and Markets . . . And Oneself

Most entrepreneurs, regardless of their being high or poor performers, emphasize on the importance of projecting a conservative image in the Indian market place. This has implications regarding capital structuring, cash-flow projections, and determining the cost-volume-profit (break-even point) level. G.R. Patel believed, 'If I burn my money, its my own'. But he was also smart. He had about 3/4th of his project cost funded by a term loan from the state financial institution. He was careful, and his consultant gave him sound advice. The problem with the market did not bring down Shirag, in spite of the high debt component in its capital structure.

As seen, first-generation entrepreneurs, particularly professionals who do not have a finance background, do not realize the importance or the intricacies of capital structure planning in enterprise creation and its viability. However, Patel also realized that a planned and optimal capital structure ensures efficient use of funds and maximizes return on the promoter's equity. The optimal capital structure varies between sectors, industries and individual firms. The average debt to total capital ratio in an industry should be taken only as the reference point, and maximum use of favourable leverage (employing debt) should be sought, after giving due consideration to other requirements, such as flexibility, solvency and norms set by financial institutions. With increasing levels of earning, before paying interest and taxes, return on equity will increase at a greater pace, with a high degree of leverage. However, if the probability of earning a rate of return on the firm's assets, viz., revenues, is less than the cost of debt, perhaps due to low sales realization, or increased raw material costs, the equity route should be preferred. Sales in some industries, such as in consumer goods industries, may show wide fluctuations. 'Excessive' debt may not be preferred in such cases. But Patel's project was tailored to the needs of industrial consumers, though it was not very conservatively financed with a very low debt to equity ratio, it seems to have been conservative enough to service its fixed charges, under any reasonably predictable adverse conditions. The expected ratio of net cash inflows to fixed charges was not fixed at levels high enough to take the firm into bankruptcy.

Any smart project planner, at the stage of project formulation, and as a continuing exercise, carries out a simple cash-flow analysis, indicating whether a decline in sales results in prompt decline or losses, so as to cause cash inadequacy. Even when sales and profits are increasing, a growing firm may face cash inadequacy to fund its inventories and receivables. When the market is not bright, or due to financial mismanagement, it may collapse. All the high-growth manufacturing firms, be they 20 Microns, or the Chicago group of companies, had taken advantage of options for financial leverage, but their capital structure was conservative, given the industry levels, and so were their cash-flow projections. Image is crucial, as Desai says . . . but it should be a conservative, stolid one, especially when one is going public!

High-growth companies rarely borrow to the limits of their capacity, some unused levels are maintained for raising funds in future, in order to meet unexpected exigencies. An accounting system of direct costing would, also, be convenient. This would indicate the splitting up of assets into fixed and variable components. The margin of safety between break-even sales and anticipated or existing sales could be periodically reviewed. If the ratio of revenue to sales increases beyond the break-even point, a substantial change in sales volume is necessary for it to have a significant effect on profits. This implies that additional working capital requirements, to meet the increase in production capacity, may not be met with from an increase in profits or retained earnings. Firms in such a condition face a problem during their growth or expansion stages.

The break-even point is reached faster at a lower sales volume, in a firm with a lower fixed cost. But, once the break-even point is reached, the rate of profit earning is greater in the company with a higher fixed cost base. The low fixed cost base company has a larger safety margin, but its rate of earning profit is lower. A conservative project plan, specifically regarding a new concept or product in a relatively untested market, needs to give due consideration to these aspects, at the time of finalizing the scale and type of investment and sources of funding. A Chartered and Cost Accountant, with some exposure to financial management or project finance, is a great help to an entrepreneur at this stage.

Anything For A Good Consultant

It took Sudhir Parikh of United Foam, a financially qualified professional, more than a year to get pre-initiation formalities cleared and term loans procured. This was perhaps because he did not utilize the contacts of a consultant, but did everything on his own. A consultant is by no means a mere liaison agent. Mr Pujari, who is mentioned later, says, 'Where there is a will there is a way,' in the process of achieving the dream of being one's own boss. But one can use all the help that one can get! He was advised by an official of a support institution to return with a larger and more viable project. Sound advice like this could be a 'make' or 'break' factor for an entrepreneur. If he had not been given this advice, Pujari could have faced the typical problems faced by manufacturers of plastics in the SSI sector. Though readymade project reports are plentifully available, machinery and equipment are highly automated and easily available, and high levels of technical knowledge is not necessary at the manufacturing stage, the market is one of low margins. Volumes, contacts and middlemen are critical factors in the highly competitive business environment. Unethical practices and influence mechanisms characterize the market, and failures in the sector are a dime a dozen.

Most RNRIs, whose cases we have studied until now, have often found it difficult to get information in new projects, to procure reliable information regarding product markets, and about project viability. Most project profiles, if available, were redundant. And regarding new products, there was very little information available in terms of even sketchy viability. Readymade market survey reports do not really mean much. They are often contributors to 'recipes for sickness', as proven by officials. A consultant could help, and support institutions have a whole list of accredited consultants whom one can meet, scrutinize and employ for the pre-initiation phase. It is relative unfamiliarity with the environment in general, and within specific sectors, that affects projects adversely. New concept selling can work only if the project is technically viable and the market can be tapped by hard work. Many RNRI entrepreneurs invest in chartered accountants, or consultants with 'contacts', to push their projects through, and some are lucky enough to locate a good product or process consultant. But few look for a good market researcher. It is not as if they do not exist. The time taken for a reliable market survey, its cost and reliability, seems to be a negative factor. Nevertheless, it is the market which makes or breaks an enterprise, and relevant research is well worth the time and money spent. Most realize it too late, however.

Most of the cases studied until now are of first-generation entrepreneurs. Vast numbers of RNRIs seem to belong to this category. Their lack of family networking in business, and inadequate exposure to a business environment, have made it difficult for this breed to do business in India, at least during the initial stage of their entrepreneurial venture.

12

Entrepreneurial Roots

The toughest part of doing business in India is understanding the culture. People promise to meet you at 10.00 a.m. sharp the following day and they may turn up a week later, often not even displaying sheepishness! People confidently assure you that the job will be done when they probably do not even know what it is all about . . . and you realize it too late!

—Anonymous

The fact remains that while an entrepreneurial orientation is often shaped by family attitudes and background, it is not necessarily or always so. Several of the cases presented in this book testify to this. First-generation entrepreneurs take to entrepreneurship by several pull factors, perhaps in conjunction with several push factors. Nothing is more revealing of this fact than Pujari's and Shama Bhat's experience.

The Temple Of Entrepreneurship: Priesthood To Mercantilism

Opportunities At Home And A Disapproving Society

When he initially returned to India in 1984, exploring business options, his family in India and acquaintances wondered, 'What is this guy doing? Is he a failure at work abroad? Why is he giving up good job prospects abroad and coming back?,' Pujari says wryly. But Pujari was resolved to do business, and he knew that a venture like the one he had in mind, would come off with great difficulty in the United States, where development banks, institutional support, incentives and required investments levels are either not available, or do not match the requirements and capabilities of a person of his means. A professional abroad, and a technically qualified entrepreneur like himself, can get neither seed capital nor capital subsidy. These would have increased the personal finance risk in business options abroad. He ignored the warnings of acquaintances in India, believing that 'where there is a will, there is a way', and returned to do business. It was not easy. His wife had joined him in the USA in 1979, when one of his children was three years old, and the other just born. His decision to return to India was supported by his wife, but his elder child still wonders, 'Hey, what are we doing here? This is not a picnic!' But he realized that time could attune a young mind to a new culture, and hence, did not let it lessen his motivation regarding entrepreneurship.

Small Is Not Really Beautiful . . . Think Medium

Pujari had initially returned to India in 1983 to explore business options, and considered setting up a project at a cost of Rs 6 million, manufacturing plastic buckets. However, he was informed by experts in financial institutions, TCOs, as well as by private consultancies, that there were scores of others in the same line in the region. He was, therefore, advised to focus on a product tailored to a niche market, an ideal strategy for a SME. He says, officials at term-lending institutions warned him, 'You are an NRI, well-qualified, if you need supportive funds, come to us. But pool-up with other NRIs and invest funds, a little over Rs 150 million of promoter's contribution, and you will be like a sturdy small boat on your own in the business arena.' He went back abroad and mobilized several NRI stockholders, three of whom were large contributors for the new project. Partners for his venture were garnered through personal contacts among NRIs abroad. Two or three of his colleagues in the US linked up with others in the UK, Middle East and Africa to fund the project.

A Consultant Identifies The Project, For A Change

Initially, for preparation of a project report, identification of Indian collaborators and for organizing a term loan, he visited accredited consultants in the region. During his visit, exploring the plastic bucket option, he came in touch with a private consultant, to whom he paid Rs 7,000 a month as retainership, over a period of a few months, for project, process and product identification and finalization. On satisfactory completion of the report, Pujari paid him Rs 20,000 as fee. Normally, consultants employed by potential SMEs, are either Chartered Accountants with contacts in the bureaucracy, or consultants associated with state-level TCOs. So, how did he get in touch with the private consultant, who identified his business opportunity? Simple. He talked to the IDBI and to state-level industrial promotion agencies, asking for lists of approved consultants and contacts in this field of electronics. Identifying the right person was not difficult after that.

Entrepreneurship . . . An Entrepreneurial Environment And A Self-Made Individual's Cup Of Tea

Belonging to the state of Karnataka, Pujari had completed his Masters in Mechanical Engineering in the USA, and worked as a site engineer for a reputed firm in Houston. His job was related to construction of nuclear power plants. He returned to India to his firm, with a personal contribution of Rs 6.5 million, in a total project cost of Rs 100 million. Pujari's upbringing in an environment of 'bania', mercantile-class culture, in the state of Gujarat, where his parents had settled to practice medicine, he feels, helped him develop an attraction towards entrepreneurship. The difficulties he faced in the United States during his education, gave him confidence. Going back in time, he explains how, when unexpectedly, he realized that he was short of funds, he decided to work, both to survive and to fund his education. On his third day in the US, he worked in a restaurant. 'When I didn't know how to make a cup of tea,' he laughs, 'why should I not be successful as an entrepreneur?'

Mental Blocks And Being One's Own Boss

Hunting for temporary jobs in the US . . . 'a Pujari looking out for anything that would help him make a few dollars' . . . he walked into a meat shop. Even the mention of meat was taboo back home, but he worked in the shop. Thus, mental and psychological blocks that often hold back potential entrepreneurs, particularly first-generation first-timers, were removed. He experienced all this when he was just 26 years old. Therefore, he declares 'If you have your own original thinking and freedom to do what you want there is no way you can go down in business, or in life, in general.' In Baroda, he had social interaction with the Patels, a class of successful businessmen of Gujarati origin in India. In the US, he had close interaction with people from different Indian communities, cultures and states. All this honed his entrepreneurial spirit, he acquired a versatility in languages and a broadminded attitude to life and people.

He feels that success in business, whether it is in India or abroad, is determined by the desire to be 'your own boss'. He knew it would not be easy, but he did not consider any other option, not even working with MNCs operating in India. It is not self-perceived impressions about his own entrepreneurial competencies alone that encouraged his return in 1990. A major motivation for his 'doing business' rationale, was his large personal savings and access to financial resources abroad. His father-in-law, a civil servant in India, was also of some use in establishing contacts and networking with various support institutions.

Pujari believes that an RNRI, with a flexible personality, easily adjustable to different social environments, can do well in the

Indian business environment. But he also believes that perseverance, hard work, and an undying spirit, as opposed to the typical Indian's convenient resignation to his fate, *karma*, needs to be nurtured.

Impressions From A 'Globalized' Entrepreneur, About Wetting His Feet

At the moment, Pujari's electronics firm is facing teething problems. However, while his current turnover is just about Rs 10 million, he confidently talks in terms of achieving a Rs 1.5 billion turnover in ten to fifteen years' time. He expects his turnover to touch Rs 100 million by A.D. 2000. The major rationale in doing business in India, he confides, was, first, 'the decision to wet my feet in India, and then expand abroad, because there are well-protected Indian banks and institutions, which provide infrastructure and all necessary facilities. A promoter's risks are considerably reduced, and India is not far behind the West,' and secondly, regarding his wife and children, he says, 'We are a globalized family.' His wife had no problem about returning to India, as she felt that opportunities for women in developing countries were better. In fact, it was she who said, 'Let's go.' His wife and children are American citizens, but, as he was in and out of the country, with considerable property in India, he never really cared to acquire a green card, specially given its tax liability.

An honest, 'no-nonsense' type of person, Pujari believes that technical capability, entrepreneurial skill, professionalism, and one's positive approach to the external environment, are the ingredients for doing business successfully in India. However, these alone will not ensure success.

Beware Of The Employee And His Laws

While he has always believed in having a democratic set-up in his organization, he has, in the process of doing business in India, learnt from fellow RNRIs to trust people less. Their trust in their employees is shaky, and he sadly observes that work ethos in the country, in comparison to that in the developed West, is perceived by RNRIs to be rather poor. It is widely believed in the entrepreneurial community that employees often shirk work, and always come up with stereotyped and occasionally lame excuses, to cover up their incompetence.

The Indian environment could do with some positive change, he feels. Many believe that labour laws in India are all wrong. This is specially regarding an employer's impotence to ensure employee accountability, and retain the discretionary authority to sack employees. It is difficult to implement either, and factors like these seriously hinder industrial development in the economy. RNRI entrepreneurs should remain wary of these problems.

Understanding And Exposure To Cultures Is The Key To Entrepreneurship

Pujari believes that at the stage of opportunity identification, it is vital to secure information regarding new business opportunities, along with information about the cultural and sociological profile of entrepreneurs in the market, and also regarding human resources and interpersonal relationship management in the subcontinent. NRIs exploring business options in India, need to make sure that they have access to information about all these factors, before taking the plunge into entrepreneurship. Being something of an idealist, he waves aside the need for thorough familiarity with (support) institutional aspects, such as tax management, and to favourably exploit these. 'You got to pay, you got to,' he argues. According to him, playing around with books is rather myopic. Marketing, quality and process control are the heart of any manufacturing firm. NRIs have a definite edge in operating a globalized company from a cheap manufacturing base like India. This is particularly applicable to those handling an export-oriented unit in the small-scale sector. Handling of foreign clients, planning utilitarian travel abroad, is the forte of an individual who has attuned himself to alien cultures over years of stay in foreign lands.

Working At Working Capital . . . Small Is Not Beautiful

Inflation, raw material availability, and the need for advance payments for stocking up the latter, can strain the cash reserves of a firm. Inadequate assessment of working capital requirement, or strain on the same, either due to mismanagement or exogenous factors, can lead to a cash crisis. Fall in market demand and capacity under-utilization of fixed assets may hamper growth over an extended period of time. A relatively low fixed cost base company, like 'Shivam', could survive this. The not so lucky ones may pass into liquidation. Pujari's electronic venture went through the teething phase of getting the product quality right, and adjusting the technical specifications of installed machinery, so as to ensure quality in production. Managing working capital during this phase is of utmost importance, and it continues to remain crucial throughout the life of an enterprise.

The ratio of net sales to total current assets, at the end of a financial year, indicates the efficiency of working capital management, viz., inventory, credit and cash management. Short-term investible funds, to finance the operations of a firm, are crucial for the survival of a business. Any smart entrepreneur, in a manufacturing industry, should strive to reduce the working capital cycle of his operations, either by looking for extended credit periods, by reducing the raw material to work-in-progress, to finished goods conversion period, by reducing the stocking period of inventories, viz., by manufacturing 'just-in-time', and by securing payments from buyers well in advance, or by reducing the period or incidence of credit sales. Working capital management goes haywire in the Indian environment. Managerial skill and expertise will not suffice, as business ethics, or at least market ethics, in many industrial sectors and segments is rather poor. And SSIs are the worst hit. They have empirical evidence, theory, and policy, directly or indirectly oriented against their survival.

Empirical evidence of the weakness of SSIs is suggested by the advice given to Pujari to think in terms of a medium-sized project. The suggestion has a rationale other than that of achieving scale economies, avoiding segments characterized by intense rivalry, or tapping a wider market and catering to consumers with greater financial strength. The SSI sector in India has weak bargaining power, made weaker by unethical business practices. Payments due from debtors are sometimes delayed indefinitely. Powerful customers and suppliers may often use smaller units as sources of their own working capital. An ethically upright RNRI entrepreneur, paying his bills on time, efficiently managing inventories and employing efficient equipment and technology, to reduce the raw material to finished goods conversion period, may still find himself short of cash.

The theoretical rationale regarding the weakness of SSIs is provided by Porter (1984). An SSI invariably suffers from low bargaining power as far as its customers and suppliers are concerned. It's customer is king, but so are its suppliers. An industry comprising of a large number of firms, with relatively low purchasing volumes, combined with intense rivalry, invariably reduces their bargaining power. And policy? The Tandon Committee norms, in 1975, laid down guidelines for short-term bank lending, assessing the levels of working capital requirement and extent of related bank finance. Norms for holding raw materials, stock in process, finished goods and receivables, and eligibility criteria for borrowing working capital from banks, were prescribed. Since then, inventory norms have been given up and the lending banker appraises the desired levels. Subsequently, the Naik Committee recommendations of early 1991, ensured (guidelines) that minimum 20 per cent of the projected annual turnover would be contributed by banks, while five per cent of the annual turnover would be contributed as margin money by promoters. The evaluation of projected annual turnover and enhancement of bank contribution was to be decided at the time of credit appraisal. But how many institutions follow Naik's norms, is anybody's guess. Collateral requirements for working capital may be the decisive factor.

What do large firms do, with statutory regulations regarding institutional support for working capital? As they could have in Kiran Shah's case, powerful, large volume entrepreneurs often employ vendors and employ small firms, as sources of their own working capital, delay payments, or seek large cash advance payments. In the Indian business environment, the severity of the problem affecting SSIs is heightened, as typically, small firms, by reducing booked turnover, to avoid tax, reduce their own access to working capital. The vicious cycle affects the liquidity position, growth and capacity utilization of the small firm. The ethical RNRI entrepreneur in the SSI sector may avoid the latter, but he can hardly reduce the bargaining power of a larger enterprise.

Business ethics among buyers and suppliers may be criticized, but to what effect? The fact remains, that in a strong market, where the product is not in the declining phase of its life cycle and not characterized by bitter rivalry in the market, the bargaining power of buyers and sellers is lower, and one can, at least, afford to be harsh to exploiters. Shama Bhat, whose case follows, has a new and highly competitive product and technology, in the smaller medium-scale sector, and has a countrywide market scope and reach. He can perhaps afford to be as 'American' or as 'English' as he wants.

There are also other limitations of the typical SSI. For example, a 'keenly' competitive market, such as the one in which Hemrajani and Sudhir Parikh operated, and that Pujari had initially considered, the automobile accessories and the plastic bucket manufacturing sectors, are operations requiring relatively large sums of working capital. Stocks of finished goods may have to be kept in reserve, so as to promptly serve customers, discouraging them from moving over to competitors, and liberal credit terms may have to be offered to attract and keep customers. A small firm may be just able to cope.

In some cases, absolute levels of fixed investment may be low, encouraging one to invest in that specific sector. But working capital requirements may be commensurately higher. Small, fixed investments need not imply relatively lower levels of financial commitments. Moreover, the larger the investment option considered by an RNRI, the more is his commitment and credibility, in the eyes of lending and support institutions, and relatively more, perhaps is the viability of the unit, in terms of scale economies and market reach. The latter is by no means the norm, but merely indicative of greater financial strength and resilience. It does, however, seem to help convince appraisal officers and secure institutional incentives and support with relative ease.

Bhat Bio-Tech

From Academia To The Market Place

In 1993, Dr Shama C. Bhat, senior research scientist of the University of Pennsylvania School of Medicine, Philadelphia, USA, discovered a molecule present in brain cells, that was an alternate receptor for the human immune deficiency, the HIV/AIDS virus. Described as a seminal discovery in AIDS research, it paved the path for a new understanding of the pathogenesis of HIV. 'Now, this distinguished scientist, who has bagged the Ranbaxy Research Award, is in Bangalore,' screamed *The Indian Express*, a leading daily in Bangalore. What was he busy with? Setting up Bhat Bio-Tech India Pvt. Ltd., to manufacture diagnostic kits for testing pregnancy, AIDS and other diseases.

Bhat's major rationale for doing business in India was an outcome of his decision to settle here. He had ample savings abroad and was highly qualified technically. A chief minister-led delegation from the state of Karnataka to the United States, with their brochures, flow-charts about what to do, and how to go about doing business in India, and regarding contacts for procuring information about the relevant aspects of the business environment was the key. It encouraged him to give serious consideration to the prospect of doing business in India.

Employment, Home . . . A Bad Joke, And Merit, Returns And Independence

Before focussing on doing business in India, Bhat had explored the option of teaching in India. A professorial tenure in an accredited institution of teaching or research, was an option considered by him. But he realized, from the experiences of colleagues from abroad who had tried these options, that local institutions, and even most top academic institutions, largely seemed to absorb personnel only at lower levels. Competition at the upper echelons was very 'stiff,' and seemed to be based on factors other than pure academic merit. 'Beyond the age of 40, it is very difficult to get into one of these institutions, with a respectable designation,' he observes. Bhat also believes that most NRIs like himself, who return to India, invariably return to the region they have always considered 'home.' There they immediately realize that options for respectable and deserving employment are limited. The income earned through employment in this country is perceived as insufficient to maintain the standard of living they had become accustomed to abroad. Doing business is, therefore, but a logical outcome.

Even while diligently steering his new venture into take off, he continues his research. It is just that he now operates from Bangalore. With available information technology communication, on-line with his research collaborators abroad is not a problem. This academician was doing very well in the West, and he has over 45 publications in reputed journals abroad. He was awarded the Ranbaxy Award for his research work, and his research and findings are considered pioneering work in his field. But his desire to come home somewhat shadowed his desire to focus exclusively and build on his achievements. Moreover, his wife gave him her full support in his decision to do business in India. She maintained a positive attitude throughout the sometimes frustrating and traumatic pre-initiation stages of setting up the business. 'I decided, with her consent, to go ahead and do business, be my own boss, and not lose the complete independence that I was used to while working as a Professor abroad.' He discovered, that in India, to achieve any degree of independence, one should do business.

Children Are Bad Company, Seek Advice And Stay Wise

Bhat, at the age of 44, returned to India in 1994. He believes that he was lucky that he had no children. Children into and beyond their teens often find it difficult to adapt themselves to the Indian environment. It would have been really difficult to come back and settle in India with his family. Bhat, who belongs to Kasargod, in the Kerala–Karnataka border area, decided to settle in Bangalore. His brother does business in pharmaceuticals in Kasargod, and his family did not have the time to work on Bhat's project in Bangalore.

Fortunately, however, he had close acquaintances in the city, who directed him to consultants and officials, to ensure the speedy initiation of his business venture and provision of sound advice.

Bhat is confident of the market for diagnostic kits and immunological reagents. The company will also manufacture biotechnology-based therapeutic agents, and provide advanced technological services to the biotechnology community in India and abroad. The venture was set up at an initial project cost of Rs 13.9 million, with a term loan amounting to about half this sum. This academician may be a novice in business, but he is by no means, worldly 'unwise'. He has constantly sought advice from direct or indirect acquaintances in the business world and the bureaucracy. Bhat had heard of other businesses failing, even at the initiation stage in the region. He cites the example of a firm that also wanted to manufacture diagnostic kits. However, term loans were not disbursed by financial institutions, due to the fact that sanction from the Drug Control Department was not provided in time. What was the problem? The firm was registered as a drug manufacturing company, and not as a diagnostic kit-manufacturing unit. Time lags and simple procedural hindrances killed the venture, even at the pre-initiation stage. Bhat is careful at every opportunity, he tries to learn as much as he can about the business environment.

Ethics, Shortcuts And Professionalism . . . Watch Out!

Bhat, a technocrat in the field of biochemics, decided to work on a project related to his competence. During his visit to the sub-continent, prior to project initiation, he had been worried about the widely perceived corruption in India, and as to whether he could handle it. 'For 17 years, I had not done anything like it, and it is very difficult to do it even if I know how and where to do it,' he says. Sometimes, he also wondered if he should risk investing money and get a 5–10 times return on his investment in a few years time, or instead go in for risk-free options, such as, undertaking research in India, and perhaps dabbling in gilt-edged securities and stocks. Bhat was, and is still worried about the business and social attitudes in India. He feels there is a dearth of professionalism in the business community. If a supplier of raw material, or a provider of household services says he will meet you at 9.00 am, you may rest assured that, at best, the person will turn up at 10.00 am, if at all. He has also come to the conclusion, that in India there is always a shortcut for everything, at a price. In the US, and in most countries in the West, there are also options and scope for undue exploitation, but these are minimal and are not evident in day-to-day life.

He has learnt not to trust-his fellow Indians too much. 'One has to be very careful when dealing with others,' he says. He has been warned by well-wishers to 'keep a watch,' and not to have *prima facie* trust in people, business associates or employees. He has started his maiden business venture, and it is only one month old, but he feels that 'employees are all okay.' He believes in a democratic style of management. 'I listen to advice from my staff, but do not allow them to make decisions for me. I do seriously consider their advice nevertheless'. He now understands better the misgivings of some NRIs abroad. He has realised that, in fact, it is not just corruption, but the lack of business and social ethics that worries the RNRI. For many NRIs returning home, the 'uncivilized' behaviour of those around them seems shocking. Day-to-day life in India is seen by them as one with no traffic rules, little civic sense and callous authorities!

Self-Righteousness And Market Confidence

In the last one year, Bhat's self-confidence has been boosted. Persistence in handling problems, and his firm stand against incompetence, has, he believes, stood him in good stead. 'There was this AC guy whom I used to call every day to come and fix the AC. Nothing happened. After a while, I blasted him and told him that if he did not come in immediately, I'd cancel the order, regardless of the consequences. It worked!' He smiles, 'Many people around me, and my friends and relatives say that my accomplishments are better than that of anybody else (of RNRI status) who has tried doing business in the area.'

Number one on his agenda are quality and professionalism. He does not believe in attempting to strengthen marketing tie-ups for his products, until production has started in his unit. 'Unless I show my product to potential buyers, my credibility will not be established,' he elaborates, 'I will show sample products manufactured in my unit in India, and say, this is my kit, tell me what you think of it.' There are other diagnostic kit-manufacturing units in the country, but Bhat does not expect competition in his field. He is exploring the possibility of diversifying into manufacturing diagnostic kits for veterinarians also, as to establish a good market-mix for his product. An MOU with a company, with expertise in the veterinary field, and competence in marketing in India, is on the anvil.

Product Competition And Indianization . . . A Recipe For Success

Bhat realizes that he would have to work at 65 per cent capacity of plant and machinery to break even. He is, however, as confident of his product and technology as he is about managing his plant operations in the Indian environment. The products of his competitors, viz., other diagnostic testing kits, are outdated and complicated. The 'elaisa test' takes one day, his product will give the result in just a couple of minutes. Also, his products being manufactured in India will be economical, compared to similar products which are largely manufactured and imported from abroad. While he has established tie-ups for raw material supplies from abroad, he is confident that in the next two years he will have established backward integration facilities for 95 per cent of his raw material requirement. Bhat is bullish about his business initiative. He is also sure that he can successfully cope with the initial culture shock that he has to face, specially in the business arena, and also that he will become considerably 'Indianized', in every sense of the term, in a short time. He is, nevertheless, wary about the requirements of becoming a successful entrepreneur in this country. Institutional limitations may force most entrepreneurs to build up a network of connections, and political and bureaucratic support, and ignore the 'black or white' colour of money! 'The environment will one day change for the better', he declares adamantly. He remains confident of eventual change!

An Aeon In Project Appraisal

Not everybody can start off with only his own and his family funds, even at a relatively low scale of investment (which in itself could put one in trouble), and start doing business immediately. Seeking and using term loans is crucial, as it is generally used for the acquisition of capital assets. The surplus generated out of the production operation of these assets is used to pay off the interest and the principal of the loan, during a period generally ranging from one to about five to seven years.

While Dhirubhai Desai, who presented an excellent image and proposal, had his formalities completed in just three months, many entrepreneurs in manufacturing in the small category, complain about the gestation lag involved in the sanctioning of term loans from the time of submission of a report. But they ignore the complexities involved in the appraisal of a project by a financial institution, and the necessity of scrutinizing the entrepreneur's commitment, competence and credibility at this stage. Delays occur due to the questions asked by appraisal officers regarding the technical feasibility of the project, its legal aspects, market feasibility and financial viability. The financial institution has a stake in the project, and they obviously have to be careful!

The liquidity of the term loan, indicating the repayment capacity of the promoters, also depends on managerial competence and other exogenous factors. Appraisal officers of term-lending institutions have very little experience in assessing the managerial competence of the first-generation first-time RNRI would-be entrepreneur. How serious is he about staying and fighting it out in the Indian business environment? Does he possess entrepreneurial competence? If the RNRI has come in with new technology, is it appropriate, given the infrastructure and the market? While the qualifications and experience of the RNRI may indicate his technical ability as far as handling a project is concerned, his managerial skills or ability to procure people, who will make up for his entrepreneurial or managerial deficiencies, is anybody's guess, unless a thorough scrutiny is made. Nobody will question Bhat's technical capability in terms of the knowledge and 'know how' required in handling the manufacturing function of an aids test or a pregnancy test kit. But the technical feasibility of a project also involves analysis regarding project size, giving consideration to scale economies, market potential, potential for technological change and the promoter's contribution.

Bringing in new technology, which sometimes increases viability from the market point of view, throws up questions regarding the availability of reference cases for evaluating its adaptability to the environment, given infrastructural availability regarding choice of location, and the adequacy of utilities, labour and raw materials, for the operation of equipment and process. The implementation schedule, and arrangements to procure raw material, plant, machinery, land and buildings have to be scrutinized. The clearance of legal aspects, such as approvals under the Urban Land Ceilings Act, all need be scrutinized—and it takes time.

Shama Bhat has been lucky in acquiring the services of a consultant, and he feels that it ensured the speedy approval and dispersal of term loans. He had the press on his side, and his own accomplishments, to give him technical credibility, and a good consultant to present him and the project in an impressive manner. His project, in the medium-scale category, provided sufficient resources to employ qualified professionals in those functional areas of management in which he had no qualifications or experience.

With little knowledge regarding the preparation of financial projections, lending norms and guidelines, or about project report preparation, a technically qualified and experienced entrepreneur would obviously find it difficult to prepare and submit a thorough proposal for funding. A consultant does this work. Investing in a good consultant does not necessarily mean that he is just a person who liaises and pays graft, as is believed by some. A well-prepared report can pass muster, with little trouble, but one cannot jump the queue officially, and the entire process takes time. In many cases, it may be possible to employ unethical means to hasten the process, or to get a defective proposal through. In such circumstances, it is the entrepreneur who is exploiting the environment, and hardly the other way round!

13

A 'Safe' Entry Stratagem

Strategic philosophy tells us that entry barriers may emanate from economies of scale, brand dominance, cost advantage independent of scale, controlled channels and government policies relating to industry. The RNRI's entry barrier is his worry about his idea not taking off. The problem is not due to the facts mentioned above, but simply in terms of support in India, to follow up on his idea, and the lag in securing statutory clearances and supporting incentives. If you do not require the latter, it is a lot easier.

—Anonymous

The market entry stratagem of most NRIs is to initially let an India-based associate initiate the business and carry it on for some time. The NRIs later return to directly involve themselves in management. This is perceived as a relatively low-risk approach, ensuring that they do not give up their lucrative options abroad, if they find that their business in India is not taking off in the way that it should. Some, like Basant, whom we shall now consider, have a long-term plan, and set off on their entrepreneurial initiative through a representative in India. On their 'eventual' return, they can always involve themselves in or directly take over the reins of business.

Potential Entrants: One Sleeps While The Other Plans To Rise

Rohit Basant is an NRI entrepreneur exploring final bag and baggage resettlement back in India, along with his wife and children. Basant and an NRI friend of his, Padmanabhan, provided financial backing to Indi Pharmaceuticals, a firm in India. The NRI has a 51 per cent stake, and Mr Basant, the balance. Both were room partners for some time abroad. Until today, Basant's role has been mere financial partnership in the enterprise. However, at the fag end of 1995, he was in India for two-three months, when he involved himself seriously in the business, as a precursor to his final return and direct management of the enterprise. Padmanabhan is expected to continue as a sleeping partner. Basant had migrated from India in 1974 and hopes to return with his family in the near future. He is in a bit of a hurry to do so!

Planned Entry

Basant, a Certified Public Accountant (CPA) from the US, possesses state licenses for provision of financial services to clients in that country. A New Yorker, he is currently employed as an independent consultant, selling financial service products, viz., insurance, oil and gas stocks and mutual funds. His business idea in India was decided upon and selected by his Indian managing partner, his elder brother, who has technical experience in chemistry. His brother was a production engineer in an established MNC in India, and has set up several pharmaceutical plants. Basant and Padmanabhan merely contributed towards the initial investment and periodic working capital requirements, all totalling about US $600,000. Padmanabhan, today, leads a retired life in Kerala, and has no direct involvement in the management of the firm, nor does he desire any active participation, but Basant does.

While abroad, Basant was confident of his elder brother Nikhilesh's abilities to handle business. However, poor performance of the unit required that he plough in considerable amounts of working capital funds from abroad to keep the business afloat. This, and the fact that his pre-planned decision has always been to return to India, with adequate savings, have strengthened his resolve to return and turn around his business.

He has got his return all planned. As he sees it, his major motivation for directly managing business in India is his family background in the subcontinent. An established, though ailing firm, his adequate financial resources (he lives in long Island, and is worth millions of dollars), and his decision to return 'home' at any cost, served as strong positive pull factors. Indian culture and tradition are still strictly adhered to by his wife and mature children abroad. There are no hitches!

Business In The Doldrums And A Turnaround Stratagem

The firm in Halol, India 'Indi Pharmaceuticals', manufactures about 60 prescription drugs. Consequently, the brand image of the company is of vital importance, but it has yet to entrench itself in the market. Basant, who comes across as a highly idealistic and service-oriented persona, had left the reins of initiation and management to his brother, in view of the latter's exposure to production engineering and plant commissioning. Though no loans or interest remain overdue, the performance of the firm is poor. Basant, who was selling financial services across the East Coast of the USA, is supremely confident of his capabilities, in marketing in particular. He realizes that the problem with his firm is ineffective marketing. The problem, he also realizes, is the absence of the company's focus on a narrow product line, and poor labour productivity. His products being prescription drugs, market development is crucial, but has been given scant attention. A turnaround, Basant believes, can be achieved by specialization in a few products, and by building up a brand/company image for specific bulk drugs . . . and training his sales personnel.

His own experience in marketing abroad, could, he feels, give him an edge in handling and reviving the firm. His brother, acting currently as MD, could handle the production aspect of the business. Both could work as a team. During his three months' stay in India in 1995, Basant, for the first time, took keen interest in aspects related to his business.

Labouring with Labour

Running a business in India, and in the developed West, Basant feels, are rather different. The crucial factor is labour. Indian employees, largely, do not think of their responsibility to the organization—'that they should contribute a little more than their salary to their business. Basant believes that he can harness labour potential effectively by means of incentives. In India, labour has to be motivated with extra care. Work ethos should be nurtured and developed. The work environment is bureaucratic, with no incentive mechanism other than the possibility of being thrown out if caught shirking or napping on the job. The extreme penalty is also possible only if the employee is employed on a part-time basis. In larger SSIs, labour laws and unionism plague potentially efficient units. 'Labour laws in India are foolish,' he declares vehemently, 'Compulsory distribution of bonus without profit! This is unheard of in the West. But here this has to be given before every other religious festival.' And often, Basant emphasizes, this is claimed as a matter of right. Also amongst employees, he observes, there is no affinity, personal or professional, with the organization. All this can be changed only by dynamic leadership. In order to ensure a successful turnaround, he feels the unit must have a democratic style of leadership. He feels that this alone will work. The word 'Sir' needs to be removed from the organization. A competitive wage must be paid to ensure motivation and reduce labour turnover. 'Management and motivation are very crucial elements for successful entrepreneurship in India,' he declares. And he hopes to do something about it!

Serving The Nation Sans Relatives And . . . And Hindu Philosophy In Business Entrepreneurship

Basant believes in living idealistically and performing one's work or duty for today. The possibility of extraneous factors affecting outcome, he feels, must not worry an individual or an entrepreneur. His business venture, he believes, is an attempt to serve the nation by producing bulk drugs. Until his visit in mid/late 1995, he was not very familiar with the Indian business environment. Nor did he want to be. But now, he feels that it is time to return—he has made his millions in dollars, abroad!

He urges potential NRI entrepreneurs to avoid getting into a business venture with close relatives. He had followed the time-honoured tradition of NRIs planning eventual return to India, had invested funds, and let his trustworthy brother handle operations and set things rolling before his return. He observes that Indian social values create problems. So long as one's close relative is younger than one, it is easier to give suggestions and get them accepted. A local person, who is a friend or a colleague, and bound by contractual agreement, is ideal, as one can make suggestions, without it sounding like 'hurting or intruding orders.' He has been lucky and does not foresee any such complication in his own case. 'But this is a very real possibility,' he insists.

Basant reiterates his conviction that it is necessary to build a strong company image of solidity, with a strong marketing focus on company and product strengths. 'Networks and connections are for weaklings! Total commitment to one's duty, and not worrying excessively about results, will lead to success. This philosophy positively affects the performance of the organization.'

Confidence Of An Idealist And A Self-Righteous Fighter . . . Notwithstanding A Tarnished Image

His children, brought up in the traditional Indian way of life, even abroad, encourage him to return to India and do business. And he is confident that he possesses the requisite skills for doing business in India, particularly as far as creativity and marketing ability are concerned. 'This is as is elsewhere,' he says, and further elaborates, 'and closely linked to the latter is establishing good liaison and public relations with other entrepreneurs and the projection of the right image.'

Negative feedback regarding the Indian business and bureaucratic environment, he believes, has created a stigma, and the lack of professional, bureaucratic, or labour ethos, delays, and the relative absence of basic infrastructure, in several cases, has done a bad job of promoting India and encouraging RNRI entrepreneurship. An RNRI may have to fight against negative impressions, his own apprehensions, and the hindering factors in doing business in India.

Similarly, Basant believes that laws are implemented, or at least framed, for social living. They need to be followed in letter and in spirit, for long-term benefit, as long as they are enforced, that is. It does not mean that one cannot make constructive criticisms, and attempt to try and change laws that are stupid, as he believes some are in India. Fighting for what one believes is right will lead to a positive outcome, he is sure.

Costs In Business

As amply indicated in Basant's case, as in most others discussed earlier, the marketing and sales function may make or break a business opportunity. But linked to these is another important variable that affects profits and viability—costs. This variable is more under the control of an entrepreneur. Cost is influenced by the volume of activities, the product mix, the method of production, and productivity of labour. To plan for and achieve profits, it is necessary to analyze the specific relationship in the firm between cost, profits and volume. Variable costs and hence profits are affected by changes in the level of activity, selling price, variable cost per unit and changes in fixed cost. A business attains a break-even stage when its contribution, shown by the surplus of sales over variable cost, meets its fixed cost expenses. A simple contribution analysis indicates product pricing in product and sales mix strategies. Some products at least contribute towards their variable costs in production, and a bit to meet fixed costs. But some hardly even meet their variable cost of manufacture. They are a burden to any multi-product enterprise. All a finance professional like Basant would obviously do is a simple contribution analysis, and decide on the ideal product line in India. He plans to improve labour efficiency in manufacturing by motivation and incentives, and volume of activity and sales, by training the sales personnel himself. Selling financial services or bulk drugs, the concepts are the same!

14

RNRI Proposed By NRIs

> The advantage of cheap labour, institutional sup-
> port and incentives, are affected by a poor infra-
> structure and implementation record. India ranks
> far behind even newly industrializing countries in
> terms of international competitiveness. Areas where
> India has a competitive advantage are reserved for
> the SSI, which do not possess the resources for glo-
> bal marketing and for forming strategic alliances.
>
> —Anonymous

After liberalization, the cap on foreign equity holding is being
removed. This has enabled NRI investors to collaborate with Indian
companies. Such collaborations may take the form of partnership
alliances, sell-outs or acquisitions, take-overs or increasing equity
holding, or direct entry into the market. Some collaborations take
the form of a typical outsourcing arrangement, as in the case of
RNRI Lalwani's venture into business, at the request of NRI
colleagues abroad.

An Offer Out Of The Blue

Several decades earlier, L.N. Lalwani's parents, of Sindhi stock, moved to Gujarat from Sakhar in Pakistan. An immigrant in Gujarat, he was raised and educated in the state before proceeding to the USA for higher education in 1972. Lalwani, aged 47, returned to India on completing his education abroad. He worked in Bangalore for some time, before tying-up with NRIs in the USA, to initiate and manage a business in India. The business idea and offer of funds, in terms of financial collaboration, came from these NRIs. One of them was a former college mate who had experience in the micro-surgical blade industry abroad. A unit was required to be set up in India under Lalwani's charge, as a typical outsourcing arrangement of inputs, so as to reduce the cost of manufacture. The product was to be sent to the US for value addition, and then exported all over the globe. Lalwani assumed the role of Managing Director, with three other NRIs as his financial partners. Simultaneously, 'Hirel Circuit' was also initiated, as the perceived market potential abroad for Printed Circuit Boards (PCBs) was high. Lalwani's entrepreneurial adventure, hence, started off with the manufacture of micro-surgical blades, and later included Printed Circuit Boards. Of the micro-surgical blades, 90 per cent went into the export market, the balance was tailormade for the local market. For PCBs, the market is the whole electronic equipment market. The domestic market for Lalwani's products extends up to a few dozen kilometers' radius from the GIDC electronic estate, where the plant is located. The micro-surgical project was small, and was wholly promoted by owners' equity capital, while Hirel was promoted by both loans from financial institutions and promoter's equity. For Hirel Circuit, the larger size of the project, equivalent to that of a middle-sized SSI, a systematic methodology was followed for project implementation. A project consultant was recruited to finalize the financial requirements of the project and mobilise funding from institutions.

Economic Rationale For One . . . And, Pushes And Pulls For The Other

The rationale for his colleagues to set up business in India, was the low cost of manufacture and the presence of Lalwani, and not any specific advantages or incentives offered to NRI firms. Lalwani, in fact, feels that a firm registered as an NRI firm, should get some priorities here and there, for example, priority in land allotment—nothing more. Lalwani's major reason for getting into entrepreneurship with a vengeance was a negative push from his job, which was not challenging enough, and also due to professional differences with his boss. The major pull factors were encouragement from abroad, in terms of a captive market, funds from NRIs, and his own technical knowledge. He emerged as a technocrat-entrepreneur, armed and confident, with his years of experience in a leading Public Sector electrical/electronics unit in India, and a business idea from his ex-collegemate abroad.

Entrepreneurship . . . A Piece Of Cake For RNRIs With Contacts Abroad

Both firms have been doing very well, and Lalwani has now proposed a massive expansion in the PCB project, to his NRI partners based abroad. The entrepreneur, who believes in being professional in his style of management, feels that NRIs abroad and RNRIs have one distinct advantage over local Indian entrepreneurs in that they invariably have useful personal contacts abroad and the capability to mobilize funds to set up an SSI or medium-scale unit. Either independently, or together with a local partner, an RNRI can take advantage of the relatively lower level of competition in several sectors, before others or outside competition, enter the market. In the context of a liberalizing, opening and growing Indian economy, the possibility of immense profit from early business perception and innovation exists. However, NRI entrepreneurs must not confuse this with a 'quick-buck' speculative option, which is not always possible in business.

Lalwani, like most other NRIs, has always focussed on providing better quality and after-sales service, and on meeting his obligations to sellers, buyers and institutions on time. Maintaining a solid image automatically leads to the building of networks and connections, which may initially not seem of much use to some entrepreneurs, but is vital for a growing company.

Lalwani believes that success does not come automatically to a first-generation, technically specialized entrepreneur like himself, merely due to access to resources of all sorts. Information regarding the financial aspects of management, about new business opportunities, on means of finance, and financial structuring of projects, and concerning institutional and market norms, rules and regulations, has to be maintained, as a sort of inventory, throughout the life cycle of an enterprise.

A Systematic Methodology

Lalwani claims to have followed a systematic methodology to initiate his commercial venture. Simple words, but with a wealth of implications. When conducting a feasibility study for a project, the technical feasibility of a project is given utmost importance. Specifications regarding the product, and the process of manufacture, may be the forte of a technically qualified professional, or it may come from a consultant. Some financially qualified professionals, with little technical expertise, rather than going in for a short- or long-term technical training, perhaps at an industrial training institute, or a Small Industries Service Institute, may look for a business where the manufacturing process is automated, or which does not require much technical expertise on the part of the promoter.

Dr G.R. Patel, or Dr Shama Bhat may be masters in technology and have immense knowledge about the product . . . in a laboratory. The technical aspects of the feasibility study however goes far beyond. It looks into the commercial viability of the product, optimal plant capacities and scale economies, and the compatibility of equipment with available infrastructure. The whole manufacturing process has to be scrutinized. Suppliers of equipment and inputs have to be identified. Suppliers have to be selected on the basis of compatibility, quality and price. Price has to be determined, based on market characteristics (not upwards from costs). And, infrastructure and technology absorption and adoption requirements have to be specified, amongst other things.

Ideally, location of the unit needs be tailored to markets, raw material sources, labour availability and commercial infrastructure. It should not be oriented largely towards tapping maximum investment subsidy, income-tax concessions, sales tax exemptions, reduced promoters' contribution, and exemption from octroi and other levies, and neglect the imperatives mentioned above. Information sources include officials of support institutions and existing entrepreneurs in the area.

Also, it is not merely by keeping one's process proprietary, as Dr G.R. Patel and Chandresh Parikh could and did, that one can maintain a competitive advantage. Everybody is not that lucky. The major objective in business management is to operate at an optimum capacity level. This can also be ensured by planning for the strict monitoring of schedules at the pre-initiation stages, and subsequently.

Similarly, simulation exercises must be undertaken, so as to ensure that the strain on working capital is not too much during adverse business conditions. Investment in raw material and finished goods stock must be reasonable, due consideration must be given to aspects, like the cost of ordering raw material and inventory, the interest on working capital and the cost of storing material. The 80–20 rule, indicating that 20 per cent of items often carry about 80 per cent of the total value of stores, indicates the necessity of focussing on the strict control of these 20 per cent items, or a conventional Economic Order Quantity methodology. It should be noted that low inventory-carrying options may be more feasible for large firms, which are large-volume buyers, and whose suppliers have relatively low bargaining power. Small firms, with a large import component, or those hedging against price fluctuations, or availability, may have to order products sufficiently in advance, and stock them up. Circumstances and options would, of course, be sector and industry specific.

Further, manpower planning, personnel selection, job analysis and placing the right person for the right job, is a crucial imperative. The sources of manpower, based on job description, may include the employment exchange, industrial training institutions, and polytechnics. Problems of absenteeism, shirking work and low motivation must be targeted, to be curbed by designing adequate incentive and penalty systems. Systems must be planned, so as to ensure job satisfaction, effective supervision, efficient performance appraisal systems and effective training.

A systematic methodology in project initiation and management is hence a crucial parameter for project viability. Similarly, the means of financing a project is to be decided upon once the total cost of the project is determined. A maximum permissible debt-equity ratio of 3:1 is permissible for small projects, and 1.75:1 for medium-scale industries. Financial institutions may like to keep this ratio at .5:1 and 2:1 for medium and small industries respectively. Levels may be reduced for experienced or technically qualified entrepreneurs. The fixation of debt-equity ratio is also governed by the Debt Service Coverage Ratio (DSCR). The cash flow of the project prepared on the basis of the assumed repayment schedule, helps establish the DSCR. If DSCR is high, the repayment span of the loan may be reduced, and if it is low, either the loan component may be reduced, or the repayment schedule to lenders attempted to be increased.

15

The Lucre Of Business

Some of our boys come in from abroad, walk into a convenient nodal agency as one would into a fast food joint, and ask for business ideas. After days of discussions, when asked as to whether they have decided on how much they would like to invest, the answer comes innocently, $10,000! $20,000, maybe! No wonder the rest of us are not taken seriously.

—Anonymous

The Lure Of Greenbacks

A guru in the field of entrepreneurship, David McClelland, believed that entrepreneurs were motivated by a high need for achievement rather than by money. The need for achievement is defined as a desire to do well, not so much for the sake of social recognition or prestige, but for an inner feeling of personal accomplishment. Similarly, Schumpeter attributed entrepreneurial motivation to the need for succeeding for the sake of success itself. This corresponds with the 'need for achievement'. Simply put in words by Bhaskar, 'to become a super rich Indian for the sake of being one.'

NRI Lured by the SRI . . . Banking On Entrepreneurship

V. Bhaskar is the son of a first-generation entrepreneur. His father was a pharmacist trading in pharmaceutical products in India. Bhaskar returned 'home' from South East Asia, attracted by the prospect of doing business in India. He was confident of the advantages, that business in general, and doing business in India in particular, would provide in terms of a reward for himself, by virtue of successfully taking a risk . . . the creation of another super rich Indian businessman!

A highly qualified and accomplished professional, Bhaskar, after university in Bangalore, completed his education in business administration from Delhi and worked for an Indian nationalized bank for over 13 years, from 1977 onwards. In 1987, the bank decided to send him to Singapore to work as a consultant to a bank under a government scheme. In Singapore, lending is mostly ethnic. The Chinese never came to an Indian bank, as deposit rates were lower and lending rates were higher. And given the fact that most Indians in Singapore were involved in trading, the banks portfolio was focussed on trading accounts. Combined with the dearth of a clientele, there was an acute dearth of project consultants. Bank officials easily establish a wide network among businessmen. Hence, when it was time for him to return to India, 'someone' required an engineer, with a background in finance, to take care of their operations in Singapore for project streamlining, funding and banking. Bhaskar fit the bill and he was approached.

The 'someone', an Indian businessman settled in Singapore, had a plant in South India, to take advantage of lower labour costs there. However, 'the firm was just not going', explains Bhaskar. Cash-flow management and troubleshooting teething problems was what was expected of Bhaskar in this operation. He handled the project well, ensuring receipt of raw material on time, streamlining customs-related formalities and other such activities. They were all accomplished as per schedule and completed in a down-time of about six months. While officially residing in Singapore, he was largely based in India, ensuring that the project kept moving. With the success of his troubleshooting activities, he was invited by yet another firm to set up a project in Singapore. 'Following my first assignment, several more came through,' he says, rather humbly, 'a 2-year contract to set up an operation in Indonesia was completed in 18 months.'

Private Entrepreneurship Came Easily

While offering himself for private troubleshooting services, he also ventured into entrepreneurship. Just after he quit the Indian bank in 1990, Bhaskar and some NRI friends of his also set up a small unit in Singapore. It was an electronic sub-assembly manufacturing unit for disc drives and optical sensors. The group of friends and acquaintances set up the enterprise with Bhaskar, having a minor stake in the total promoter's equity of about half a million dollars. Later, a US branch was set up, with a unit in Bangalore. Then a second unit was established—this was 'Altron'. The basic idea behind the unit, intended it to be a subcontracting firm for those who offer buy-back arrangements. 'Other companies', where he was a member of the board of directors, also wanted someone in India to broadly oversee their operations. Everything came together perfectly, and he was back in India!

Economics Is Rarely The Only Rationale, While Consultants And Competitive Cost Advantages Lend Confidence

While working on a private basis, Bhaskar had ample exposure to supervising hundreds of personnel, skilled and unskilled, and reported directly to the Chairman, in his capacity as project manager. He had all the necessary experience for successful entrepreneurship. While he had an economic rationale for business, the major motivation to return to India was the fact that his children had reached a 'learning age'—one was ten years old and the other six. 'Singapore is okay, but cultural problems remain. And I wanted them to imbibe Indian cultural values,' claims Bhaskar. The electronics estate in Bangalore, with the subsidy given for setting up a unit amounting to about 30 per cent, served as an added incentive. Hence, at a project cost of over Rs 5 million, 'Altron', manufacturing optical sensor sub-assemblies, was set up. The product was oriented towards exports to Singapore and the US. Bhaskar had known all his partners based abroad for close to a decade, and trusted them explicitly. Production commenced in July, 1994. The unit employs 35 employees, and the State Industrial Developmental Corporation offered a term loan. 'Everything is as smooth as silk,' claims Bhaskar, 'We are an export-oriented unit, and license procurement took not more than three months.' Certain 'problems' regarding licensing and financial support from funding institutions did crop up. However, an established and reputed local consultant was gainfully employed in streamlining pre-initiation support and liaison activities. And, all was well. Bhaskar, today believes the firm has a definite competitive advantage in terms of quality and price. Competition comes from China, the Philippines, Indonesia and Mexico, basically low-manufacturing cost-based economies. His major competitive advantage over possible new entrants within the country are his contacts with buyers. He keeps it a closely guarded secret. This advantage, especially when coupled with the 10–15 per cent relative cheapness of his product in comparison with his international competitors, gives him confidence in rapid firm-level growth.

An Assessment Of Motives

Setting up an SME may require an RNRI to be a jack of several trades regarding the functional aspects of management in connection with the necessary entrepreneurial competencies. Entrepreneurship, in its strictest sense, is not for those who wish to lead a retired life, or just a way of keeping oneself occupied. The retired NRI, with business in his blood, may well be extremely successful in business. But the spark is low. It is often the 18 hours of work a day that some RNRIs are used to while abroad that ensures sustainable and rapid business growth.

Also, money-making can never be the only motive or goal for entrepreneurship and for success in it, though most RNRIs indicate that their business decision was to also help maintain the standard of living they were used to while abroad. As Bhaskar so casually implies, it is the need for creating an impact on society, the sense of achievement of being a super rich Indian, for the sake of being one, and the desire for independence, that propels and sustains the entrepreneurial urge.

Academicians like Shama Bhat or a G.R. Patel are used to certain levels of independence that being one's own boss can ensure in the Indian environment. This is an underpinning characteristic of the true entrepreneurial breed.

16

Starting Crises

*Corruption at the grassroots is something one can
think of as tips to a waiter at a restaurant. In some
countries, say France, the norm for tipping is 10
per cent of the food bill. So long as one is not fleeced
out of one's skin, doling out the equivalent of a few
dollars or more to keep the underling at the utilities
department happy will not take an enterprise towards bankruptcy. It may, at least, avoid pin-pricks.
An Indian would not think twice before giving it,
and a large number may not think twice before receiving it. But for the RNRI the same could seem
demeaning and be perceived as buckling down to
exploitation.*

—Anonymous

Teething Problems

The starting crisis, which comes in the first two or three years of an
RNRI starting an enterprise, is often the biggest killer. Several RNRI
entrepreneurs pack up and leave at the teething stage. Often the
culprit could well be the environment, the value systems and

attitudes, that they cannot attune themselves to, in spite of their trying hard to do so. But crises may also arise due to incorrect market assessment, affecting projected cashflows and capital investment decisions. However, those who are committed to their endeavour look for options, do not give up, and generally make it. They may be relatively inexperienced, they may not have contacts in the business world or with bureaucrats, but they possess or develop entrepreneurial qualities, the major one being persistence.

A Dilemma In The Shift From Cracking Naphtha To Cracking Business

'Through the last couple of decades,' Kuldip Arora says, 'There were two major occupation-related dilemmas that faced me. The first was after graduation. I took up a production-line job in India rather than turn into a medical representative.' The relative social stigma attached to the job, and the lack of professional value addition in it, rationalized his decision. The second dilemma he faced was when he first returned to India in 1988. 'I was offered the post of Deputy Manager at a leading national petrochemical unit. However, I had to stay in Lucknow, where, unlike in my hometown Gorakhpur, I did not have a house of my own. Also 30–40 per cent of my salary would have disappeared in tax. The low salary, nothing in comparison to potential earnings in the Middle East, psychologically rationalized his decision to do business. He wondered, 'Should I just buy and sell land and property, or should I take up the business of a building contractor? Should I buy land, build houses and flats and sell them?' Finally, he felt that his interests and potential were more suited for a manufacturing business.

Partnerships And 'Genuine' Consultants Smoothen Initiation

On his final return to India in 1990, he and two of his partners shared the burden of the pre-initiation running around, after narrowing down on a business idea. A consultant, currently in the USA, had prescribed the formula, which was adopted in the manufacturing process. The formula indicated temperature and other parameters related to technical criteria. Arora decided to manufacture 'accelerator thirum', used in the process stage by chemical units manufacturing fungicide. Registered consultants prepared the project report, including a broad market study, and got it approved. The business idea was honed after his return to India, so were aspects relating to technology and finance. Locating the unit in the state of Uttar Pradesh, and Gorakhpur in particular, was a foregone decision. He had his own property in Gorakhpur, and the decision to set up business in its environs was a logical one. The firm, a small-scale unit, which employs about 10 persons, was just into production in 1996. The partners shared the burden and responsibility of pre-initiation formalities. They employed another resourceful, local and reputed consultant to hurry up bureaucratic formalities, with regard to project appraisal and financing.

Negative Pushes From Abroad And All Set At Home

Kuldip Arora first returned to India after about eight years in Saudi Arabia, after having resigned from his job in disgust. The promotion of Americans to senior positions in his firm in Saudi Arabia, overriding his genuine and accredited potential, led to his return to Gorakhpur in righteous indignation. Within a few months of his return, he headed for Kuwait, but returned just before the Kuwaiti invasion. He decided to stay put in India. He had left the Hindustan Petrochemical Corporation Ltd, to accept a lucrative offer in Saudi Arabia in 1980. There, he supervised engineers and field operators, and served in a key position in an explosion-prone unit. Handling labour was an acumen he developed over the years. He had some savings, amounting to a few 100,000 rupees. He decided to resettle and do business in India.

Teething Problems: The Bureaucracy, Overheads And The Market

Arora realizes that certain aspects of initiating business, such as handling bureaucratic problems, and the necessity of establishing contacts with support institutions, were matters he did not give due consideration to. Also, being a technically qualified person, he concedes that money management has been rather problematic, and that overheads are not being managed well. Consultants solved his first problem and unique measures are being employed to target the second one. For example, the three partners being close acquaintances, often travelled together to their factory site in the same car from their respective homes, in order to conserve on fuel expenses. Arora realizes that little things like these are basically an overhead minimizing management style that will avoid project cost overruns. The partners ran into yet another problem at the teething stage. Arora wonders, 'I should have tied up marketing, or explored job work or sub-contracting options, in order to ensure sales the first few months, before stability in production was achieved and I could confidentially tackle the market. However, I feel marketing may be just a teething problem.' He acknowledges that there is a heavy stockpiling of inventory and that something has to be done about it in haste.

Clinching Entrepreneurship With A Human Touch As Far As The Market And The Bureaucracy Is Concerned

Arora believes that quality in management, product and service is essential for survival in business, and credibility counts. Hence, business obligations of all sorts must be met, regardless of legal enforceability of obligations by aggrieved parties. This first-generation entrepreneur believes that focussing on these two aspects, and with a sincere mix of personal–business relationships with one's partners and close friends, entrepreneurship should be a cinch. Arora also believes, that in India, as elsewhere, it is crucial to treat labour well and sympathetically, try to adjust to their requirements, solve their problems and get them emotionally attached to the firm. If an employee is doing overtime, Arora makes available his own car to get refreshments for him. Informal networking is crucial, he feels, as information of all kinds, are not readily available and, 'networking was what had led us to achieve good product and project consultancy services.' However, he is exploring the possibility of entering into a marketing tie-up, a five-year pact, with his firm offering the output to marketing middlemen, at a relatively low price margin.

On a general note, Arora advises that informal contacts with the administrative and support machinery will help speed up initiation hurdles, for example, with regard to the allotment of infrastructure facilities and utilities. He observes that Indian bureaucracy needs some pep, but 'they may also have their own infrastructural and resource constraints.' A straightforward individual, he believes that profit must come from hard work, and not by cheating the government of its revenues by tax evasion or avoidance. Being completely 'Indianized', or so he believes, Arora perceives that the information most needed to ensure successful entrepreneurship for the RNRI is with regard to the marketing environment, marketing management and market assessment of a specific business. The technical, financial and institutional aspects come in later!

Cash Is King (?)

Let us look at Arora's predicament in terms of a balance sheet. Sundry debtors and inventory are crucial elements influencing the liquidity position of a firm. Speed of turnover, volume of working capital and structure of financing influences the liquidity of a business unit. Liquidity depends on current assets, which can be converted into cash within a year (which is normally taken as short-run) and, on current liability, such as accrued expenses, trade creditors and provisions. Current assets get converted into cash in the operational cycle of the business. Usually a high proportion of sundry debtors is indicative of more liquidity than is a business unit strapped with a high proportion of inventories. The ratio of current assets to current liabilities may seem adequate, but the composition of current assets may be adversely skewed in favour of unsold or excess inventory. Quick current assets may be low in proportion. Arora, like Kiran Shah, faced this crisis at the teething stage of his enterprise. Inventory is being stockpiled, but the market is playing truant. Arora faces symptoms of a liquidity crunch and is realizing that it is cash that is the most crucial component of running a business. But the cash crisis, as he realizes, is but an indicator reflecting problems in the marketing function. Market information, reliable, authentic, product and market segment specific, is by no means available on a platter. A chartered accountant may get you your term loans, and a technical consultant may give you product and process and specific information. But they cannot be a substitute for professional market research. As indicated earlier, few RNRI entrepreneurs in the SME sector have invested in professional services. They may be expensive, but if one has not got the time or the competence, as is the case with most RNRIs, professional services may be worth the investment.

A thorough market study helps in projecting demand for a firm's output, on the capacity decision, and on the ideal marketing strategy and programme. Marketing decisions depend on evaluation of the demand-supply gap and on formulating an efficient market programme regarding the product features, price, promotion methods and placement. Considering any of these elements in isolation could lead to major problems in project viability. Several NRIs have complained about the absence of adequate information or about the access to it. The imperative need, nevertheless, is not the mere collection of information on an ad hoc basis, but on determining ideal information needs and analyzing collected information regarding a specific project. Critical information needs for the typical SME includes information about market segments, about demand determinants and about geographical boundaries. This would also indirectly help in deciding about the competitive strategy to be adopted. This strategy may vary with different market segments. An analysis of specific market characteristics is essential while formulating the marketing strategy. The nature of competition and potential competition within the sector, in related, up-stream and down-stream sectors, and in the business style and practices in the industry is essential information. Sudhir Parikh was very uncomfortable with his industry and trade practices. His product could not be pushed on product quality and price alone. An analysis of existing and potential government policy that may affect market entry and exit is also a crucial element that need be considered. A specific financial institution's decision not to encourage installation of firms related to powerlooms or woven sacks, in selected areas, may serve as an entry barrier. Fiscal and monetary incentives have to be scrutinized.

So where does one go for information? Sources of information include end-users, existing and potential buyers, trade associations, manufacturers and suppliers of equipment, middlemen, support institutions, private consultants, technical institutions, and private and government databases. Many of the RNRIs have used some of these sources, but often the focus seems to be on desk research, by studying publications, having cursory discussions with potential buyers, and through correspondence with support institutions. Most in the smaller sector seem to prefer a scanty exploratory or desk research option to a detailed market survey. This is a harbinger of a crisis.

How does one analyze information? The analysis of information may be conducted employing simple statistical tools such as correlation and frequency distribution, trend analysis and time-series forecasting. Qualitative data are also as crucial as quantitative information. Governmental sources of information and databases available with support institutions may be outdated, and several factors progressively influence demand. Hence only a thorough study can significantly capture the various complex factors affecting market characteristics. The technical co-efficients adopted by consultants can only indicate broad approximations. Existing demand characteristics of a new product, and products for which a demand has to be created, is all the more cumbersome, and uncertainty of cent per cent validity of findings remain. That is the risk-return trade-off in business, and there is no alternative to thorough information-seeking analysis. The latter is all the more crucial, as the supply position and market entry of new competitors from within and abroad is something that is even more difficult to anticipate, and it could upset the applecart even before initiation. Under the circumstances, strangely, while most RNRIs invest in a chartered accountant or consultants to get projects prepared and cleared, and most realize that it is the market that is the de facto determinant of success, few have invested specifically in a market research professional. Maybe they realized it too late, or did not look hard enough for good, though expensive expertise!

17

Back To One's Hearth

The cows on the roads, the unfed and sickly looking beggars on the streets, the crowds of people, are all eyesores. One can go on and on about the trivialities that NRIs abroad sometimes worry about rationalizing their decision not to return and do business in India! This is mere escapism.

—Anonymous

Back To Family Business

Negative pushes from abroad combined with positive 'emotional blackmail' from home often serve to ensure the move towards business entrepreneurship. This is amply highlighted in Prabhakar's case.

Sesha

Striking Out On One's Own For Well-Rounded Experience

Prabhakar, the son of a businessman selling stationery items in Bangalore, had his marketing skills honed while working with his father. He then decided to go out into the world on his own. He had come across a job advertisement from a leading Indian firm manufacturing machine tools, applied for it and got it. The firm had offices worldwide in America, Australia and in Africa. In 1977, an office was opened in Nairobi, East Africa, and in Lagos, West Africa. A person was needed to head the office in Nairobi. Prabhakar had been working on the Africa desk in India. Over a period of time, he had come to know the country, the customers, and details regarding the varieties of machine tools sold. Lathes, milling machines, drilling machines, and pedestal grinders were his forte. He was selected. The market for the machine tools manufactured by the firm was much more suitable for developing countries like those in Africa, as absorption of technology was simpler. The firm did well against competition from Western manufacturers and focussed on product marketing. Prabhakar worked in the firm from 1976 to 1982. Then came an offer from a multinational firm run by people of Indian origin and based in Africa, with diversified interests. A 300 million dollar group then, and today worth about two billion dollars, the organization had 48 manufacturing companies throughout the globe. Prabhakar left his machine tools firm to take up this offer in Kenya, and operated as a one-man show, reporting directly to no one, with total independence, and handling business worth Rs 25 million. He independently handled accounts, its reconciliation, collection and delivery of funds. He also developed an accounting system that was later adopted by all other offices of the organization.

Back To One's Roots And To Business, Due To Disillusionment Abroad

While Prabhakar was with the machine tools firm, he had problems with his supervisors, and particularly with his immediate boss. Often, he felt like a fish out of water, especially when his boss tried to sabotage everything he attempted. 'It basically put a spoke in a running wheel, and frustrated my desire to stick to the organization,' he says sadly. It was then that he met the MD of the large business group based in Africa. They were setting up a project in Nairobi. He moved over. However, differences with this organization over his posting cropped up. He was transferred to India, where things were not challenging enough. He was disillusioned and returned to Bangalore in accordance with his father's request, imploring him to join the family business and assume his rightful place in it.

If You Got It, Show It!

Prabhakar's entrepreneurial competencies were honed by virtue of his experience and independent responsibility in diverse markets abroad. He took over the mantle of family business with a flourish. Neither the environment nor the business was new to him.

His Sierra and Sumo, flashy and expensive cars in the Indian domestic market, have spread the word of his success around. Earlier, in fact, he was in touch with his customers personally, on his Sumo, and the vehicle not only helped carry his goods, but also helped lend credence to his success, in turn, getting him more customers. Appearances are important in India to prove one's success in business. This hold for those in the trading and services sector. Prabhakar's opinion of the Indian market is bullish. In fact, he believes that India is a big country and has a market for everything, and even if one focusses one's product at the smallest market segment, scale or production level, the gods of business will smile with benevolence. He does not yet consider himself amongst those who are successful in business. He corrects himself, but 'others' in town count him as a successful RNRI!

Deliver Your Goods And Remain Wary

He believes that the major factor for success in business in India is not merely the appearance of being successful, though it does count. An absolute requirement for successful business entrepreneurship, Prabhakar believes, is to provide and deliver the goods promised. In his case, he often does it literally. He personally goes to top companies and business houses in the region to offer his services. He offers door-to-door delivery, free of charge, and has developed several new concepts in stationery trade. He has transparency sheets stamped with customer organizations' logos, which serve as a unique selling proposition. He offers to accept rejects without any qualms if the customers so desire, he maintains an excellent filing system and ensures quality service and personal attention to all his customers, regardless of their being big or small purchasers. However, he explains all these alone will not guarantee success in business. While success in business may arise from the desire to excel in what one delivers, he has experienced several problems related to business ethics while doing business in India. For example, a private limited company has not paid his dues for over a year. But he has no time to chase customers. He has a simple logic. He does business worth Rs 250,000 in 25 days in a month. Breaking it down to eight hours a day, his manday cost works out to about Rs 10,000. There was another case of a firm marketing a new packaging system, requiring an advance payment before delivery. However, despite the advance payment, delivery was not made for over a year. 'They kept telling stories and I kept writing letters,' he explains. He then gave them an ultimatum and things did move finally. But these instances just go to prove that one should not necessarily or always expect the same ethical and moral standards as one's own from other people associated with the enterprise.

As a cautionary note to returning NRIs, Prabhakar suggests that it is necessary to verify the credentials of consultants and potential partners, and also bureaucratic rules and regulations very carefully before setting up business. One cannot be too careful. Prabhakar is now exploring the option of getting into manufacturing. He will take over the managerial function of a company, with separate divisional heads overseeing various aspects of functional management, to produce carbon paper. Given his success (though in a non-manufacturing sector), he is confident that the proposed project will take off!

18

Innovation Is The Name Of The Game

*Indian bureaucracy is slow and lacks enthusiasm.
Pronouncements and promises are often made in
hot air. The 'single window' has yet to open, for example.*

—Anonymous

Strategic literature tells us that introducing a significant technological
innovation may allow a firm to lower costs and enhance differentiation at the same time. An example is the introduction of a new
information, advertisement or promotion system, which is relatively
low on absolute cost to the buyer, overhead costs to the seller, and
is differentiated from other conventional systems—the Yellow Pages,
pioneered by Bijahalli. Further, Bijahalli, did not, in his pursuit of
both low costs and differentiation aspects, ignore the possibility of
imitation. Constant innovation, such as by printing his Yellow Pages
in colour, and in bringing it out as CD-ROMs, will but ensure
sustained success and help him be one up on his competitors.

Deccan Yellow Pages: A Conservative Entrepreneur Of Conservative Upbringing

Incredible Successes: A Concept, Little Money, But Overflowing Zeal

For four years, 1982–86, Bijahalli was a student of computer engineering in the USA. He worked for some time in that country and returned to India in 1986 at the relatively young age of 36 years. He had no family background in business, and had meagre savings, but he developed an idea.

Manjunath Bijahalli, a pioneer in the services sector, brought the Yellow Pages to the subcontinent. On his return to India, he refused to explore the option of working as an employee and explored various business options with friends as partners. And then, with an investment of only Rs 40,000 he got into the Yellow Pages business. His idea came into being before the Yellow Pages telephone directory services were offered by others in India.

Bijahalli has personally developed the market, like a salesman almost, in order to promote the new concept amongst the local populace. Establishing the concept in his market was possible only by his making 20–30 calls per day on his own. This reduced overheads, while he sold space for advertisements. Initially, he focussed on Bangalore and its environs alone. He now has an employee strength of 50 personnel, and has since 1993, for the first time in the country, introduced three editions of a colour directory for Bangalore. Looking back at his phenomenal success, Bijahalli observes that he does not look upon the Tata Yellow Pages or the Get-It Yellow Pages as competitors, nor does he feel he has competition in South Asia.

His first publication was out in July 1987, and he has never looked back since then. From a total investment of a mere Rs 40,000 in the project in 1987, his current office alone is worth Rs 10 million.

Why Business And Why Go Yellow?

His initial motivation to start business was the relatively low scale of investment initially required for his project idea. The second major reason was that business was an option that could help him maintain the standard of living that he was used to while abroad. There was then no comparison between salaries received by even top professionals in India with the kind of salary he had received abroad. The third major reason was his desire to return to India, to his home town Bangalore, at any cost. Bijahalli's initial attempt at business in India was linked to his direct area of training and competence. However, the computer software firm which was initiated, with partners, collapsed. 'The partners, or at least most of them, were not reliable, and I was too busy to personally oversee operations, since I simultaneously (also) got into the Yellow Pages industry. It was obvious that the computer software firm would not last.'

He had seen the Yellow Pages abroad and introduced it in Bangalore as a new product and concept. The business idea, scope of operations and means of finance were all developed and decided upon only after his return.

Conservative In His Heart . . . Hearth?

Business norms in India were 'somewhat' different to what he was used to in the USA. However, he believed and continues to believe, that regardless of the environment, ethics and hardwork go together, leading to success. His educational and family background shaped his beliefs. 'If a buyer comes to me and asks for credit, I will give it. If a supplier gives me credit for 15 days, he may expect it in three weeks to two months, as is normally the case in Indian business. But no, I pay up exactly on the date due,' he declares vehemently. He has an aversion to seeking funds from support institutions and other private sources of funding, and believes this is due to a psychological aversion linked to his conservative 'service class' family upbringing, against playing with other people's money. This may not sound very business-like, but he finds it difficult to change his perception. He believes that it is a conservative and solid image that results in successful business. Bijahalli also believes that expansion beyond the stage where one cannot personally control activity levels ensuring quality is unwarranted. He has hence expanded operations so as to include only three states, including

Gujarat. Bijahalli is satisfied that his beliefs and style of business have ensured his success in business.

Style, Principles, Trust And Perspiration— A Winning Combination

With regard to labour ethos, he believes that he has managed to motivate his employees and salesmen by virtue of his courteous behaviour and display of confidence in them. He advises, 'Drink with your employees and dine with them, but don't bed them.' This is the American philosophy of employer–employee relationship and equality. He follows it in India and tells his employees to work, giving due respect to their conscience—'You may go to a movie and place on record several phone sale calls made during the period. I have no means or interest in verifying your claims. However, it is you who should listen to your conscience and contribute your mite to the organization.' His style has worked! His business assets were worth Rs 40,000 when he started. Today, a decade later, he values it at Rs 30 million at least.

He believes that business and the external environment should be handled with professionalism. A businessman should adopt the right approach to human beings, labour or business associates, based on mutual respect and always backed by strong ethical principles and values. His niche in the market remains intact, in spite of the rise of several 'potential' competitors. 'Potential' because they have all failed to meet his challenge. His goodwill remains strong and he is always one up on competitors as far as ideas are concerned. For example, other than a colour directory, which is a first in India, he has put his directory on the internet. And will be putting Bangalore business and its history, tourism, industry, etc., on a CD-ROM. His long-run objective is a focussed state market— in Hyderabad, Gujarat and Bangalore. He believes that everything in most businesses like his is on trust, 'I can't do business without it. One can't do everything by oneself. My customer trusts me. My manager and attendant keep the keys to the office.' While there had been some attempts earlier to pilfer official documents concerning business contacts and plans, by potential competitors, he continues to repose trust and confidence in his employees. 'The rotten apple will always reform or will leave on his own in our office environment of bonhomie, cameraderie and committed hard work,' he emphasizes. He never attempts to hold back employees leaving for better options. An employee is always free to leave and come up in life. His democratic style of functioning, with no compromise on quality, seems to have worked miracles. Goodwill, image and networking all developed steadily over the years.

Success in business came to Bijahalli from a new business idea, which developed within himself, putting to shame his family's and well-wishers' apprehensions about his attempt to do business on his return to India. His kith and kin in India were not supportive, and friends and relatives had mocked his attempts, as he did not have any experience in business, and he had no family background in business to fall back on. With his return, after a few years' stay abroad, at a relatively young age, he had to work harder and perform better to prove that his return did not mean a failure abroad. It was creativity and sheer perseverance of this committed entrepreneur that guaranteed his success in doing business in India.

The Service Option Through Perspiration

Bijahalli's initial business decision 'consciously' or otherwise turned out to be smart. This is specifically with regard to his strategy on the initial outlay of fixed investment and overheads, and his approach of not seeking term finance. He did not have much by way of savings from his short stint abroad. The Rs 40,000 that he ploughed into his 'Yellow Pages' industry was largely for a small office space. Initially Bijahalli did not do the printing himself, but had it done by others. He thus had relatively low fixed costs when he started off. This is an advantage one can avail of with relative ease if one gets into the service industry rather than into manufacturing. Bijahalli had a fleet of marketing personnel, who brought him orders, and salarie were largely linked to the business generated by an individual. This too served to reduce fixed overheads. He thus had a low operating leverage, as the proportion of fixed costs in relation to total costs was low. His profit before interest and taxes (PBIT), as a proportion of percentage of sales, increased at a rate lower than sales. But given the fact that he was trying to sell a new concept, with relatively high sales uncertainty, the initial rate of risk to the firm was reduced accordingly.

By not trading on equity or gearing up his investment, by not seeking debt from outside sources, his earnings per share would have changed in the same proportion as PBIT—an excessively conservative financial policy. But then, he is of a typical 'conservative South Indian middle-class family background! But it made sound business sense at the initial stages.

A person of technical background, Bijahalli did not really understand that net profits accrued post interest and tax, as a ratio of worth of the business, or that the owner's funds in a business of the promoter's equity investment in the firm indicating the profitability and return on equity investment. This ratio is affected by the firm's return on investment, the average cost of capital, the debt-equity ratio of the firm and the rate of income or corporate tax. While the unscrupulous entrepreneur ensures that tax incidence is reduced, avoided or evaded, by employing competent tax consultants. For most businessmen, and their trustworthy counsellors, selection of an ideal debt-equity mix in the firm's capital structure, are the result of a conscious decision by both. The more the promoter's equity contribution, the more the solvency, safety and structural strength of a firm, but some entrepreneurs, like Bijahalli, do not adequately appreciate the potential for higher return on net worth, due to trading, on equity—particularly for an established and rapidly growing firm. He, like some other RNRIs, has picked a low financial risk, a low investment, low fixed cost and low overhead business option in the service sector. Bijahalli merely adapted an idea from abroad and pushed it through with his grit and determination, ignoring support, financial or otherwise, from the support system.

Acid Tests For Project Viability . . . For Free

But one wonders at the excessively 'conservative' attitude of some RNRI entrepreneurs. State level financial institutions provide funds for projects up to a few million, while the national ones offer larger funds. The advantage of these sources of funding to the entrepreneur is that the repayment period of the loan is quite long. There is also a moratorium period in the beginning which helps. Temporary routine capital financial requirements may also be met with. It is not just funds that proposals submitted to these term-lending institutions provide. The project's viability is scrutinized and verified, and this serves as an acid test for project feasibility. Some entrepreneurs and RNRIs employ unethical influence mechanisms on appraisal officers to push through their project ideas. Often, in such cases, it is not the official who delays approval or rejects the proposal, but the entrepreneur who tries to push through a defective project or proposal.

Commercial banks provide working capital finance, but not for fixed assets. However, they may also do the same, in specific circumstances, for a shorter repayment period of five to six years. They too could serve as objective analyzers of a project's viability.

Simply put, finance from suppliers and distributors may be procured in the form of trade credit. Lease finance from companies may serve as a means of reducing initial investment. This latter option helps avoid being stuck with obsolete machinery, and has the advantage that often only relevant equipment has to be hypothecated, leaving other fixed assets free to be mortgaged for raising funds from other sources. Venture capital funding schemes could serve as an alternative method of reducing the financial risk of an entrepreneur. Adapting imported technology so as to widen domestic applications and projects, and encouraging commercial application of indigenously developed technology, are encouraged under such schemes.

The sources of finance are many and useful, and while raising funds, an entrepreneur should consider the cost of raising funds, the time lags involved, the terms and conditions, and the tax implications.

All these sources of finance have their own mechanism of evaluating the viability of a project and the repayment potential of an enterprise. As important as their money is, they basically serve as acid tests to cross-check a business plan and project report.

19

Business In India: A Piece Of Cake For The Second-Generation Entrepreneur

Corruption is almost all-pervasive in Indian society. Everyday you see top politicians, de facto rulers of our country, being hauled up. Newspapers bring it out everyday. There are a whole lot of books written about this cancer in Indian society.

—Anonymous

Grahi Constructions And Finance: Retiring To Real Estate

Ratan Thakore practised dentistry in Chandigarh for over two years before he left for the USA in 1972. Abroad, even while practising as a dentist, he also bought, developed and sold property and generally dabbled in real estate. Two decades later in 1992, he returned and permanently resettled in India, 'just to have peace and relax'. But things are not all as uninteresting as Thakore makes them out to be. Thakore's family (his father) was in the construction business in Chandigarh. Even during his schooldays, specially over vacations, Thakore was regularly involved with the family property development activities. He returned to India, and his only link with his area of professional specialization is the part-time couple of surgeries that he performs in his family-run hospital, 'Just to keep in touch and ensure that skills don't decay'. In 1993, Thakore returned to plunge into real estate development, while also promoting a finance company. He put in about Rs 5 million initially into the construction business, and immediately after, ploughed in Rs 2 million into a finance business, as part of promoter's equity. In a local hospital funded by NRI equity, Thakore even while abroad had a stable of about a third of the total equity contribution of 30 per cent in the project investment of about Rs 110 million. The hospital project was not doing well due to poor management, and hence Thakore, on his return, decided to go in on his own into real estate and finance. His finance and real estate projects are doing quite well, with a post tax return on investment of 22 per cent.

'Enough Was Enough . . . But Enough To Take Up Business?'

Thakore was in his mid-40s when he decided that 'enough was enough', and came to India, psychologically burning his bridges (abroad) behind him. Between 1987 and 1992, he moved back and forth several times between India and the US. He mobilized finance for investment in India by increasing his business activity abroad and from his family in India.

At this point of time, he was disturbed by the general mentality of Indian society, the woeful business ethics and the widely perceived corruption in day-to-day life in the sub-continent. However, the going was rather smooth on his return. His personal and family financial backing gave him the strength to start off well.

The real estate development industry in India, he observes, operated in a different environment to what he was used to in the USA— buyers negotiated the price and documentation proceedings were longwinded and unnecessarily difficult. In America, funding from financial institutions was easily available for the construction industry. In India, builders had to mobilize their own resources.

A man of strict ethical standards, Thakore found himself in an Indian industry which is particularly notorious for its unethical practices, the word 'builder' often throwing up images of a 'shady' businessman. Even while operating in such an environment, Thakore declares, 'The industry one is in does not matter. One should be straightforward and clean,' he continues, 'I may not be making a lot of money, but I am comfortable.' In India, the industry is in personal value-terms difficult to enter and do business in. The 'black' component of investment and revenues is significant. In the USA it is all above board, but here 'it is very hard', says Thakore, 'Business ethics in India on the whole is rather poor. In construction it is worse!'

Economic reforms are changing the environment to some extent. In fact, Thakore felt that the rigid, closed environment was not sustainable, and 'things are going to change'. It happened exactly as he had predicted, he believes. However, ethical values which develop from within society may require a sort of radical mental revolution to change. Nevertheless, Thakore thrived in this environment, without having to compromise on his principles and values.

Ethics, Planning And Delivery—'Above Board' Is Priority Uno

Thakore returned and built a nice house, his wife started a nursery school. Practising dentistry in India was not worth his while. 'I earned a day in the US what I could earn in a year in India,' Thakore explains. He therefore invested in property development, and then converted it into a company, Lisa Finance, two different entities under one banner, with joint synergies. Thakore had been worried about getting acclimatized to the general mentality of the society, business and the bureaucracy in India. But with his 'nice' professional ethics, honesty, straightforwardness, and his emphasis on quality, safety and delivery, Thakore manages to do pretty well. As in the USA, he had kept to these values as priority number one. This is in spite of the fact that in India it is price-based competition that largely prevails. Thakore handles two diverse projects with a handful of staff. With a real estate business, warranting long-term planning and investment, and the second a financial company, necessarily requiring adequate short-term strategies and planning, doing well in business in India has much to do with his accepting the philosophy that business is business, combined with sound planning and stringent ethics. Thakore smiles, 'I display no unwarranted ego. If my clients disagree with my proposal, I ask them for a chance to prove that I am right and deliver.' While the average entrepreneur may prefer to be flexible to please his customers, hard nuts like Thakore get away with the quality of their services. At times, he shows his plans and designs to potential buyers of his property. 'I show what I have done and they buy it. No hardsell is necessary.' For this quality, customers are convinced, the price is low. His transactions are above board, unlike those of most other builders. His clients like that too. Similar is the case with his finance company, 'They say a lot of things go on in finance companies,' says Thakore, 'Mine is clear.' This in itself attracts customers. Thakore sets goals and works hard to meet them with persistence—not exactly a retired lifestyle!

Retirement Need Not Necessarily Lead To Entrepreneurship

Thakore finds it difficult to change the ethical values he has imbibed. He also likes his daily golf after four hours of work. But this does not mean he is either unprofessional or does not take his entrepreneurial adventure seriously. Thakore perceives that a market exists for entrepreneurship in India. In construction, even small entrepreneurs like himself do well. Hence his business idea was not a gamble. Risk is less in this industry, and he had earlier exposure to it before he went to the US. In the US business environment corruption is not high as the system is strong. Ill-begotten gains cannot be shielded from public authorities easily. In his 20 years of stay in the USA, Thakore also observed that Indians there exercise their rights like anybody else, and are quite contented. However, in India, liberalization and reform is institutionally and mindset-wise largely on paper. Red tape is by no means absent. There is a difference between environments.

Thakore observes, 'Indians in India, including some RNRI entrepreneurs, or some of their Indian workforce, do not work hard, while those abroad drive themselves to limits, given the potential for returns and a competitive environment.' Hence, RNRIs need not necessarily opt for the hard work and risky option of doing business in India. Their knowledge and services can be contributed by means other than entrepreneurship. And, given the fact that earning a 'quick buck' is not often the reason for returning to India, particularly for retiring NRIs, why should they do business at all? Retirement and searching for some work to keep oneself meaningfully occupied at 'home' had taken him to business, others need not necessarily do so.

A Contradictory Retiree?

In Narain, whom we shall meet in the following section, we have a thoroughbred businessman who concedes the prevalence of a scenario of dismal business ethics and several environmental limitations in India. He nevertheless specifically highlights the excellent performance of serious and 'staunch' businessmen, who have experience of doing business in India and abroad. In this context, do we have something of a contradiction in Thakore's claim of retiring . . . to business in India, and being very successful at the same time? Not really. The fact remains that while Thakore makes his business option look like a semi-retirement stage pastime, he was neither a first-generation businessman nor inexperienced. Real estate development was in his blood, so to say. His father had been in the line, and Thakore himself had ventured into property development in the USA and done well. He may work only four hours a day on his venture, but he takes his job very seriously, as his experiences and impressions indicate. And, he has the skills and competencies to do it successfully without unwarranted exertion. Hence, successfully doing business in India does not necessitate a do or die approach, nor does one have to be a fiercely competitive businessman, always trying to be one up on competitors by all means at his disposal. Skills and competencies of an entrepreneur related to one's project lead to success, and a market exists in several sectors which allows easy entry.

Project And Product Decisions

The project and product decision of a Bijahalli may seem curious, as must that of a Thakore's, to a casual observer. It is not! Perceived competence and opportunity are the determining criteria. The project and product decision is crucial, especially since asset specificity may prevail and the flexible manufacturing option cannot be easily applied in several industrial sectors. The project and product decision remains very crucial at the planning stage of the 'doing business in India' option. For example, in industries where the value addition to input is low, the make or buy decision affecting project decisions is crucial. In a small firm, where backward vertical integration may not be economically feasible, the input components are sourced from outside the firm and value added to them. Hence, but a reduction in import tariffs made the final products coming in from outside more competitive destabilizing market potential for Kiran and Haren Shah's computer-related options.

Similarly, RNRI first-generation entrepreneurs, or those unfamiliar or uncomfortable, at least initially, with the Indian environment, should decide about capacity and investment limits in a manner so as to reduce financial risk. Starting small, gaining exposure to the environment and to 'doing business', before expanding or investing larger sums of personal equity in the form of promoter's contribution and institutional loans could well be a rational decision. The 'how much to invest?' decision may be based on the extent of an RNRI's net worth or disposable savings that he is willing to invest in business. It may be 30 per cent or 50 per cent, based on his risk-return trade off. He would not want to watch all the hard-earned dollars from years of working abroad going down the drain, especially when he is not absolutely confident about himself or the environment. Regardless of professional experience, some RNRIs like to choose a project they are comfortable with. Suganarthy did just that.

It is by no means only at the initiation stage that the decision is crucial. Even at the stage of the growth of an enterprise, it continues to remain so. Dhirubhai Desai diversified into a wide range of projects and services, while Chandresh Parikh stuck to his core product of micronized minerals. The product range decision and the extent of its diversity cannot be based only on a product mix or contribution analysis at the post or pre-initiation stage. Market prospects and analysis of the same, on a regular basis, could progressively play a crucial role in estimating risk reducing options. Acceptably, the technical capabilities of equipment, the entrepreneur and the financial resources available at his disposal, are essential determinants. Technology choice and quality of product should be based on the market requirements of the final products, plant capacity, financial and technical competence, and manpower and equipment availability. But regardless of the indicative criteria specified above, the crucial decision-making criteria need consider the market requirement and the resources available and mobilizable, viz., both the environment, and hard and soft skills of the entrepreneur.

20

Business In The Blood

There certainly is bureaucratic corruption. And, it may, in some cases, be amply evident at the project initiation stage of an SME. But only if you allow it! Hovering around a newly returned NRI like us, 'they' eye us as one would the proverbial 'golden goose'. But when you 'holler' in indignation, they buckle down and scamper away. But, what there is of corruption is largely at the grassroots. A relief!

—Anonymous

Coolsip

Closely Held Concerns Back Home

R.G. Narain's father had migrated to Zimbabwe to work at Rs 30 a month in a town a 100 miles from Nairobi. Two years later, he procured credit from trade, 'and a little from a bank', and started business in Zimbabwe, trading in tea. Narain trained under his father. Political and some economic instability in Zimbabwe rationalized Narain's decision to return to India. The family-run businesses include cinemas in Mumbai and a soft drink manufacturing base in Pune. Narain has been managing his firms, including the tea estates in India, quite successfully. After all, be it London, Africa or India, wherever in the world, it is the same thing, 'Business, is business', vouches Narain.

From Collaborator To Competitor

From his base at Pune, Narain manufactures 'Coolsip', a soft drink that is sold largely in Maharashtra. Earlier, he bottled coke. Today, he has several plants in the environs of Pune, and manufactures and distributes his own soft drinks. While there is a market growth of 10–15 per cent every year, competition from multinationals, like Coke and Pepsi, is today, giving 'Coolsip' a hard time. But Narain with his family-controlled enterprises, with a diversified portfolio in several sectors, maintains the 'success' stature of his businesses in industry.

An Idea Over A Cup Of Tea

While in London, Narain had met a colleague. Over a cup of tea, Narain's colleague enquired, 'So what are you doing now, Narain?' Narain elaborated on his estates and trading in the tea business in India. The colleague suggested, 'Why don't you get into bottling and distributing a cola drink in India?' It struck a chord. Narain heeded his advice and took over an MNC's operations in Maharashtra.

At 72 years of age and still young, Narain reports to work at 10.00 hours in the morning, and is at his desk till 5.00 in the evening, six days a week. Hale and hearty, 'with no diabetes', Narain likes his Scotch . . . once a fortnight, at a Pune club. He choose Pune for its climate and also because of it being a beautiful city with a good market and infrastructure. 'I like the people here, my class of people at the club, that is,' says Narain.

A 'Risk Taker' And An Innovator

Back in India, when he started bottling Coke, Narain says, 'All my friends at the club said I was making a mistake. Nobody in Pune drinks Coke, they are all coffee drinkers!' But he rationalized his business decision to himself. People in England drink Coke, regardless of the almost perpetual cold weather, so why not in India? He was almost wrong! He had three or four trucks going around Pune the whole day, but selling a maximum of only 10 crates of the bottled cola a day. An idea struck him. For a whole year, he distributed Coca-Cola during film intervals, free of charge. The cinema is a big business in Maharashtra, he believed, and tried to institutionalize his new concept into his customers' psyche by this innovative, if expensive, strategy. The MNC cola manufacturer and Narain bore the burden of expense equally. It worked! In three years' time, sales increased from an average of five cases a day to one million cases a year.

Institutional Networks . . . Pah! Union Networks . . . Sigh

In India, Narain observes, an entrepreneur has to work much harder at marketing his products than in other developing economies, like Zimbabwe. Competition is stiff. Of course, the closed economy that India was in the 70s and 80s lent opportunities to entrepreneurs, without them having to worry about the threat of multinationals. But the scenario is changing fast today. What about the institutional environment? Being a second-generation entrepreneur, with exposure to doing business throughout the globe, he does not believe that institutional networking with support institutions and 'connections' with the bureaucracy are necessary to do business. 'No politician comes into my factory,' he declares with some vehemence. However, politician or no politician, the policy in India is not very kind to the entrepreneur, he observes. Government taxes in India are much higher than in many developing economies,' he observes. For every case of drink that he sells for Rs 128, Rs 90 goes to the government as tax.

Labour ethics? Narain has never been a hard taskmaster, and he has his loyal confidantes who have stuck by him since his business days abroad. His personal secretary has been with him for decades, since he started his business in tea estates. But labour in India for a medium-scale enterprise can be rather problematic, he explains.

One of his plants that today seconds as his administrative headquarters, has the potential to produce 5,000 cases a day, but has been closed for the last eight years due to labour problems. 'They wanted more money, I wanted more productivity,' Narain recollects 'Labourers coming in from other states are better than the locals. It is labour unions and not necessarily labour laws that are problematic—it is the human factor. But policy helped the unit where I worked in Africa. In Kenya one cannot go on strike.'

Do Unto Others What They Do Unto You!

While competition, policy and labour adversely affect the attractiveness of the environment, so does business ethics, feels Narain. Some smaller entrepreneurs often fill our bottles with their soft drinks and sell them. Other competitors buy up Coolsip bottles from the market, just before peak season in summer, and replace them with theirs. Unhealthy competition can be tackled by retaliation. 'If they do it, we do it,' says Narain in a harsh tone. Dismal ethical values are percolating deeper down into society. Several students doing their Masters in Business Administration have utilised Coolsip's hospitality for their project work or case studies and given away information that Narain had quite innocently and trustingly provided them with. In fact, a whole project report was given to a competitor. The combination of relatively poor standards of business ethics, relatively higher taxation, labour-related problems, and the increasing levels of entry of MNCs, with progressive reforms and tariff reduction, the Indian environment is not very favourable for the soft, and not very experienced potential RNRI entrepreneur. The impact of competition is seen by the fact that his plants are operating at less than 50 per cent capacity, even at peak season. But the seasoned businessman that he is, Narain is looking at profitable and sustainable diversification options. His family-controlled group of companies, however, have the financial clout, and Coolsip, the brand image to withstand competition in the medium term.

Cash Flows And Born Businessmen

The most crucial factor in business, Narain observes, is finance, financial management and cash-flow. It certainly is. Coolsip faces highly seasonal demand. Capacity utilization falls down to 50 per cent of a peak seasonal production of 1,600 cases a day during off season, in each of his three operational plants. Cash flow and financial investment decisions play a crucial role in his line of business. Narain was not professionally qualified. He learnt the tricks of the trade while doing it. Business was in his blood he believes. 'You have to be a staunch businessman,' declares Narain, 'a born businessman RNRI technocrats and professionals can't do business unless they have at least some training. Look at the failures around you!' Narain underscores his argument, 'So many businessmen from East Africa are in India, and they do very well.' Narain softens, 'RNRI entrepreneurs are welcome to the environment and will survive if they have a business mentality.' Business must yield return—it is not for charitable purposes, or a post or semi-retirement stage pastime!

21

Service, To Avoid Bureaucracy And Reduce Financial Risk

Prior to setting up shop in India, we had apprehen-
sions about getting 'the work done and the quality
we wanted'. Stories of graft float around in plenty.
We were taken aback! No corruption, no unwar-
ranted lags from the support system, no utility sup-
plier blackmailing us for 'speed' money. Nothing!

—Anonymous

A Project Cost of US $300 To A Market Capitalization Of Tens Of Millions Of Dollars

'We compete in the first world with companies there' declares Dheeraj Kapadia, with a complacent smile. Softwings has come a long way since seven employees of a leading Indian software consultancy firm decided to do it on their own. Operating out of a rented office, with an initial project investment of Rs 10,000, the private limited company is today a fast-growing public limited firm, employing hundreds of personnel in an industrial estate in Pune. Softwings is a software company with multiple products, including software development and maintenance for customers. It is not just the cumulative brains, skills and efficiency of hundreds of engineers and advanced computer hardware systems installed in its headquarters that has contributed to sustained phenomenal growth, but the firm's marketing skills in approaching customers, conceptualizing and analyzing their needs and saying, 'Look, these systems could be developed to increase operational efficiency,' that has contributed to its phenomenal success. Customer problems are addressed, models are simulated in the computer, database created, and value delivered to the customer. 'It may be mere accounting systems, for example,' Kapadia says. Almost two-thirds of his products and services are targeted at the American market. India accommodates only a small per cent of his business.

A Different Organizational Model, A Different Mindset

Softwings, set up in 1981, was initiated at the instance of Kapadia, then employed as a systems engineer, and six of his colleagues, in 1981. Kapadia was the valuable employee of a leading consultancy firm in India, and a man of strong personal ethics. He had given 14 months notice when he resigned from his job. He completed his assignments and gave his company sufficient time to find a replacement. In 1982, more than a year after the initiation of Softwings, by his partners, he personally took over the reins of operation. 'It was not a conventional project where large money was invested, in our model we bring together high-quality professionals,' explains Kapadia. The project required a different mindset of management, as the business depends on white collar professionals.

'Traditional management gets firm equity, leverages it with loan, and runs an enterprise,' Kapadia differentiates. But when he started, initially, he focussed on brain, and not on financial muscle. It was a relatively new concept, the market was abroad and investment requirements for their scale of operations low. Hence, the capital structure leaned exclusively on promoters' equity. The different management style warranted in his business kept away 'a Tata, a Birla or a TVS, at a time when India was a closed economy, focussing on self-sustenance, and when our policy makers feared opening up the economy, or removal of the License Raj, and wanted us to discover the atom again! 'A regressive, stagnationist policy!' Kapadia observes. In fact, between 1981–90, the firm grew at a snail's pace, there was no telecommunication structure in the country, and it took him 'six months and 20 trips' to Delhi to get a license to meet a paltry $1,500 business commitment. This was when technological change in the US occurred every six months. The going was tough. But, since economic reform in 1991–92, there has been no looking back.

As in conventional Indian manufacturing businesses, a relatively stringent style of work force management cannot be followed. For example, if an employee is not performing up to the mark, it is only after several subtle warnings that one can say, 'Look here, chap, you had better pull up your socks or you will be in trouble'—very professional, of course, and not a boss–employee dressing down session, but more as one committed organizational employee to the other. It invariably works, observes Kapadia. Labour management and motivation should be 'transaction based', and as long as there is affection underlying it, employees will accept and outperform themselves. Softwings has a canteen, where everybody from the top management executives to the juniormost staff eat together. Roles and responsibilities are allotted to each individual. Kapadia scrutinizes budgets and targets only.

A Reformed Socialist, Disillusioned With Research

'Working in France, everyday I learnt something,' Kapadia declares, 'I was an engineer, and not many engineers can develop operating systems. It was a very advanced, on-the-job training for me. It was a great honour and experience.' After working for four years abroad, he felt he needed a change. He returned. He returned as he wanted to 'be in India', his home. He came back after donating his earnings to a charitable organization called the 'Friends of the Third World'.

After his Masters in Electronics Engineering, he was in fact supposed to go abroad for a PhD, when he got a job offer from France. In France, he was a member of an 18-member team in designing systems. A native of the Kolar district of Karnataka, he was a staunch leftist. But when he went to France, where socialist parties were very strong, he learnt and understood several things. First, the only way to eliminate poverty is by creating more wealth. By saying 'Garibi hatao', it will not go away. You need to create more jobs, more wealth, so that it is shared by employers and employees, to their mutual benefit. Second, that there are only a few good entrepreneurs, just as there are a few good doctors, engineers, lawyers or computer professionals. 'Is it birth, training or circumstances that make them good, I don't know' he confesses. Not everybody is capable of taking risk, of exhorting people to follow them! The third lesson he learnt, was that entrepreneurs are human beings. They need incentives to perform to the best of their ability. His final observation was that the government should create an environment to encourage entrepreneurship.

Earlier, before leaving for France, he had worked at the Indian Institute of Management, Ahmedabad, on projects for big clients, including the ONGC. For two years, he was involved in research in projects, including forecasting oil demand. He, and professors at the IIM, worked day and night on such projects, to complete reports. At the end of it all, he says sadly, 'Invariably some reports and findings land, not in a dustbin, but on a shelf to gather dust.' Hence, on his return, for more job satisfaction, he joined a leading Indian software consultancy firm. Then he realized that once you reach your 40s, 'your children grow up, you need something substantial psychologically and materialistically for yourself and your family'. His wife had a job in Mumbai. 'So it was okay if I didn't earn for a while and tried out business.' He did just that.

A Force In The Global Market From A Base In A 'Problematic' Environment

In 1982, two partners and Kapadia left for the US, and launched a project of installing systems packages in companies there. 'We had the brains and were relatively inexpensive, with low overheads and charges in dollar terms, in comparison with competitors abroad,' Kapadia elaborates. He had returned in 1982 and explored the possibility of setting up a base in Pune. The electronics city seemed promising, and he decided on it. And at a total project cost of Rs 7 million, Softwings set up a large base in Pune and went public in the 90s.

In India and abroad, regardless of his client being the government or the private sector, Kapadia has focussed on quality and on meeting his obligations as per his own stringent professional values. In a country like the US, the economy is more stable, and even during recession, business opportunities from a base in India exist if one is innovative, he observes. He avoided dealing much with the Indian government, bureaucracy or market, and focussed on tapping the potential abroad. Kapadia says, 'Abroad, if one wants to set up a business or tap a market, it is very easy, through incentives and almost dole systems (in several sectors), which are not available in India.' However, he concedes that, in India, the procedures and guidelines, believed by many to be rather frustrating, show promise of greater efficiency through progressive reform.

Indian government authorities, Kapadia sighs, 'have perhaps resource problems in execution.' It is a question of attitude. For 10 years, there has been a power problem in some Indian cities, and authorities have been vehemently exhorting people that, 'we must do something about it,' he says. Yet today, some cities have several hours of power cuts. The less said about many industrial estates the better!

There are changes. Political and administrative support help, and the 'bad old days' are gone, by and large. Earlier, it had taken Kapadia six months at times to get a license for meeting an overseas commitment, while today it takes just a matter of hours.

It is the system that has some lacunae, he feels. Democracy, as is practised in India, is not democracy, 'there is no responsibility, there are only rights'. Democracy, as practised in the West, implies that every individual has some responsibility to society, from which he desires some rights. To Kapadia that is democracy!

The Sky Is The Limit In Quick Shift

Kapadia perceived an opportunity for software services overseas, and observes that the 'industry does not require money, but a few dedicated people.' The government had restrictive policies in the 80s, imports were curbed, socialist and 'silly ideas' against computers existed. The fact that he had a European orientation helped. A socialist himself before he left for France, his exposure to the French system, with strong socialist leanings, but with practical and realistic orientation, sowed seeds of an inclination to entrepreneurship in his psyche. His experience and exposure to the business of providing software services in India, the contacts he nurtured abroad, and his ability to mobilize and motivate a strong team, took Kapadia, in slightly over a decade, to the pinnacle of his industry in the Indian sub-continent. He realized, that in India, 'everything takes time, and the government plays a much larger role in your life than it does in the West.' However, patience, technical expertise, managerial and commercial acumen, and identification of a niche in the field of information technology, ensured the growth of Softwings into a market force to reckon with. Kapadia realized his strengths, had realistic 'but slightly ambitious' targets, planned and allocated time and resources, and backed it all with hard work. RNRI entrepreneurs, he observes, may have to put in not eight hours of work a day, as they may have abroad, but 18 hours, when doing business in India. But, as long as they don't stop, or mentally throw in the towel, success is ensured.

Quality And Vision

Kapadia harps upon the fact that management styles in business organizations, may differ, but the objective of all business is the same—customer satisfaction. One's objective may be to deliver quality for preventive inspections, but stringent quality control would serve no purpose in an industry, where, firstly, middlemen rule the roost, and unethical influence mechanisms decide as to whether your product should be pushed. And, secondly, where defective products can be pushed via the same mechanism through quality control officials. But fortunately, this is not always the case. Nevertheless, quality should be tailored to consumer requirements. Quality simply indicates 'conformance to customers' requirements', and not as some RNRIs tend to believe, as conformance to one's own personal standards, or quality in terms of an aesthetic or functional sense, or of the standard abroad. What is the justification for international quality at higher prices, when the market requires lower prices with lower functional efficiency of the product? Quality is dependent on the quality of inputs, in the manner in which inputs are delivered, stocked and converted into a product or service. It depends on the manufacturing or value-added process, on equipment and manpower, and in the way in which the final product or service is delivered to the customer, installed and the after sales services provided. But the latter two quality determinants arise not only from the values of the entrepreneur, but also from the efficacy and ethics of labour, and if this factor of production is not up to the mark, a mere vision of quality means nothing.

Planning, visualizing and allocating time for goal setting is a crucial element in business planning, as is planning for delivering quality. Haren Shah, Dhirubhai Desai and Kapadia, three people in three different circumstances, have emphasized the necessity for vision in business. Haren Shah envisions competition from megaplayers, Dhirubhai Desai sees his company as a Rs 10 billion company by 2000 AD. He has diversified and gone public to mobilize maximum resources to achieve this objective. Thakore envisions the construction industry in Bangalore to reach a stage of slump in a few years' time, as the city is overreaching its capacity, without adequate infrastructure. He is contented. He is a small entrepreneur, and has returned to India to lead a peaceful life, and with his golf and four hours of work, he is confident of maintaining his ROI of 22 per cent, with his quality products and above board dealings.

Intrad Consult Pvt Ltd

Nothing Less Than The Ivy League In Education And Training

A native of Kerala, Krishna Kumar's father retired as Chief Internal Auditor of the Assam Oil Company. Kumar, largely reared in Assam, passed out of the exclusive Rishi Valley Public School, the Indian Institute of Technology and the Indian Institute of Management, and joined a British MNC. The MNC a leading player in the global textile industry, the equivalent of Unilever in terms of market dominance. He was a senior manager, reporting to the company president, when he was selected and sent to Turkey as commercial director of Middle East operations. Later, he moved to Dubai, which was the hub of the Middle East. He set up a profit-centre operation, which he controlled as general manager operations. After 13 years of service with the company, and having spent four and a half years in the Middle East, he resigned and returned to India in mid-1995. Earlier, in March 1995, by virtue of his performance, he was selected to attend an advanced training programme at the prestigious INSEAD (France).

Looking For A Niche Always

Kumar essentially managed areas of general administration and marketing in his 13 years of service. His specialization during his management education was in marketing. 'When you decide on specialization, you should not lock horns with others who are equally competent or trained. An ACA, an ACS or an AICWAI, finance and costing professionals, could perhaps beat an MBA who has specialized in finance, hands down, as we are not trained at all levels of finance, right from preparing vouchers up to financial ratio analysis and evaluation. It is marketing and strategic management that should be an MBA's choice and forte' he says. Consistent with this philosophy of identifying niches, on his return to India, Kumar took up a business that would not put him in competition with Indian entrepreneurs, adept in their business, and confident in their environment. Instead, he got into trading, utilizing his contacts abroad.

Trained To Do Business Anywhere In The World!

'When an NRI comes back to India,' explains Kumar, 'after having lived in the midst of trading NRIs, very successful traders, he has learnt a lot. If you can do business or handle business in Dubai, you can do business anywhere in the world,' he states emphatically. 'Indian traders in Dubai operate at very low margins. Their business lifestyle permits it. They are quite happy to work in 'shacks'. No fancy seven-storeyed office complex for them! They bring in employees from India, at a pittance, and they manage to operate with low margins, as they get away with low overheads. Other nationals, not even the Chinese, can compete with them. Thus, they raise entry barriers,' Kumar elaborates. He has learnt a lot from them. He was also an Indian, but working for a multinational, which had higher overheads. And his success abroad developed immense confidence in himself.

The market was large and diverse, covering 13 countries. He had to deal with Europeans, Iranians, Lebanese, Africans, Indians and Arabs, and cover different market segments, varying right from small tailors to large industrial concerns. In some segments, brands did not matter. 'It was something like selling shoe polish. The brand may not matter very much to consumers so long as the shoe shines,' he explains, 'we had to operate in a very trim fashion.' Selling was the crucial function that he mastered.

An 'Itch' For Challenge Without Entrepreneurship In The Blood

In India, Kumar muses, 'You have a dozen people around you at office who will do everything from household to official chores. Working abroad, regardless of designation, you get your rations yourself, you don't develop an ego problem where sending your own faxes is concerned, everybody knows everybody, you deal at the boss to boss level, and you should know the nitty-gritty of every transaction, even while preparing macro-strategic business plans. My job was to develop the market, and I did it!' he declares. When he joined his office abroad, his company's market share was 8 per cent, and when he left, it was something like 23–24 per cent!

Then came the 'itch'. He felt it was time to move on to a new company, or a new product, or maybe do something on his own. He was looking for something challenging. He realized that he could get a comfortable job in India, or abroad, though maybe not exactly the job he wanted, but something that would help him maintain the standard of living that he was used to while working abroad. In fact, the six months prior to his final return to India, he had been chased by 'headhunters'. 'There is a large corporation in Hong Kong, supposed to be amongst the largest headhunters in Asia . . . we chased each other.' Finally, when he met the boss of the set-up in Hong Kong, he was offered a job by the headhunters themselves to set up an office in India. But he was not interested. Leading Indian textile companies, with some of his former associates in top management positions, would have been keen to accept him. But no!

His decision to do business in India also had other rationale. He left a job in which his company was spending about Rs three million a year by way of his salary and perks, including his keep, accommodation and transport. It was by engaging in business that he could generate an income close to this. Kumar was 37 years old and he was ambitious. Then there was the family factor. He could not let them come down from the standard of living they were used to while abroad. Colleagues of his have come to India to handle MNC operations, relatively 'cushy' jobs! This kind of opportunity may help maintain one's lifestyle, but his ambition was to perhaps eventually set up a macro project in manufacturing, worth several billions, in India. However, initially he decided to get into trading in large volumes of textiles, with low overheads, till he was established.

In India, even today, especially for a South Indian, with a background of professional employment, it is a critical decision to get into business. The extended family system in India, which may include a cousin, three times removed, who could say, 'Oh you're getting into business! You couldn't find a job?' Kumar's family was already in business, hence it was easier, he feels. On his return from the Middle East, he observed that anybody returning from abroad, suffers from a standard of living shock, rather than a culture shock, and that encourages the 'doing business in India' decision, to maintain a higher level of disposable income. Krishna Kumar feels he has developed business acumen by his commercial exposure abroad. 'I was a professional and respected for my business acumen.' Once he decided to do business in India, he worked quickly. He gave a package deal to a chartered accountant to complete all the necessary formalities with regard to the bureaucracy. In a few weeks, he had his RBI code, his export–import code all set.

A Low Investment, But High Competence-Based Option

An NRI coming back to operate in the Indian environment faces the tremendous disadvantage of having to compete with other established entrepreneurs in the market. He believes that he could never have competed with them on equal terms. 'There are options. I could do a one billion rupee project, where I would have minimum interaction with the grassroot-level bureaucracy or labour. If I run a C&F agency, I may have to deal with the same corrupt officials of various regulatory agencies,' he elaborates. 'The last few years abroad have taught me a few good things.' He feels that he would now find it difficult to interact in an unprofessional or unethical manner with staff or with officials of support or regulatory institutions. In this project he is not immediately utilizing his engineering or manufacturing skills, but only his commercial exposure.

In the last couple of years of his stay abroad, Kumar established a rapport with several textile units in South India. They produced quality products with the best machinery, but lacked marketing initiative or contacts. They were rather traditional and conservative in style. 'An entrepreneur from a small town in Tamil Nadu cannot be comfortable with a buyer in Hong Kong,' he explains. The tolerance level of his customers and suppliers was much higher with a person like Kumar, whom they had known over a long period of time. If you go to Singapore and talk to a Chinese as an unpolished Indian entrepreneur, without having established a rapport with him earlier, you would find it difficult to clinch a deal. Now that it is only a few months since his return,

Kumar is involved in playing the role of a middleman, fixing buyers and sellers, for a commission. But he can soon start buying from sellers in India and selling on his own. The second option would generate much higher margins.

At this very early stage, Kumar's business and personal expenses are not clearly demarcated. But his projected turnover in 1997 is about Rs 80 million, with a staff of about four people, and a gross profit of about 5 per cent. 'I will be a very unhappy person if I didn't,' he laughs. Overheads are low and his direct export earnings are tax free. Not bad for a start, he feels!

How The Mind Works . . . And Exploits Scope For Arbitrariness

Krishna Kumar was worried about how the mind of a bank official or the Indian market works. What are the factors that influence them? He wondered? He decided to be a middleman, operating with low overheads, before getting into a manufacturing operation targeted at the Indian market, using India as a manufacturing base, or even buying and selling. He says he has learnt a few good things in his four to five years in the Middle East, working for a British company. He perhaps wants to first acclimatize himself to the poor work ethos at the grassroots level of bureaucracy, the labour structure and the support system. As he says, for example, he would not stand a chance against an experienced Indian entrepreneur who has been doing business in India for years. This, coming from an Indian professional, who has worked in India for eight or nine years before going abroad for less than five years, is significant. The fundamental question is: How does the scope for employing influence mechanics arise? Basically, it is the loopholes and lacunae in the system, combined with social values, that serves as the genus. For example, consider the submission of a project report, seeking term loans for a manufacturing enterprise. The approval of a project report lies in the hands of appraisal officers, and there is some scope for arbitrariness in evaluation. Unethical influences are sometimes brought upon the officials by promoters so that they can themselves reap maximum benefits in term's of repayment schedules or debt volumes. Also, preliminary and pre-operative expenses may normally constitute only 5 to 7 per cent of the project cost. But delays in appraisal increase these expenses, and these delays could affect project cost. Hence the appraisal officer is a key figure at the pre-initiation stage.

How exactly does the scope for using unethical influence arise? For example, to ensure regional development, the minimum contribution from promoters is variable, depending on the location of the project. The government offers incentives in the form of a central investment subsidy, up to 25 per cent of fixed assets, subject to upper limits based on the background area classification of a specific location. Indirect tax incentives are also offered. Requests for equity support may also be considered by financial institutions in the form of the equity participation of institutions, seed capital assistance and risk capital. The 'risk perception' of the project determines the extent of facilities offered by funding institutions, so as to minimise the burden on the promoter to the greatest extent possible.

Secondly, state finance corporations (SFCs) who fund small projects, and industrial development corporations (IDCs) who support most medium-scale investments, all consider the security margin in the project. The margin of security is defined as the difference between tangible assets and term loans, as a proportion of tangible assets, and has fixed guidelines laid down by the IDBI, which provides re-finance to SFCs and IDCs.

Also, some projects may not require much finance by way of fixed investments and, hence, term loans. Nevertheless, they may require a high working capital and margin money component. The Debt Service Coverage Ratio (DSCR) is derived from the cost of production and cash-flow statement. These are prepared after 'assuming' a particular repayment schedule of the term loan taken from financial institutions. These statements are also prepared after 'assumptions' regarding project profitability are made. Appraisal officers finalize them after 'consultations' with consultants with experience in this sector. Indicative profitability ratios of specific industries are also considered, modifying, extending and finalizing repayment schedules.

Hence, the debt equity, promoter's contribution, security margin and DSCR are items which are of crucial relevance to the promoter and the project. Assumptions and discretionary decision making, to some extent, lie with appraisal officers and expert consultants in the sector, who advise them. At times, some promoters use unethical influence mechanisms to get the best deal for themselves, while at times, some unethical officials and consultants exploit promoters. Speeding expenses, and corruption, in some cases, is a likely possibility. But while the scope for unethical exploitation may exist in business and the bureaucratic environment, the cases of most of these RNRIs presented in this book indicate an entrepreneurial breed who are aware of these problems, but rather than complain about it, manage the show with their own values, skills, competencies, and a conviction . . . of making it and sustaining it!

PART FOUR

PART FOUR

Monitoring Recession, Proactive Reactions And Self-Check Mechanisms

The Indian industrial economy has witnessed rapid metamorphosis over the last few years. For example, till the early 80s, Indian brokers were engaged in buying and selling government securities and in playing the role of commission agents in mobilizing fixed deposits for companies. By the mid-80s, lead managing issues became a hot subject. New instruments, such as the concept of rights issues of convertible debentures, to meet working capital requirements, developed. The services sector and the financial sector reached even higher levels by the early 90s.

It is perhaps resources, rather than political will, which remains a hurdle to the effective operation of institutions. This is so, regardless of their being legal institutions, the equity market, lending institutions, or industry support institutions. Systems for effective monitoring and surveillance will take time to develop. There is no dearth of Harshad Mehtas (of the infamous stock scam) wannabes exploring means of exploiting the Indian public. Nor is MS shoes the only dud public issue—plantation firms and non-banking financial corporations disappear overnight on maturity of investments mobilized. Domestic credit rating has hardly helped in many cases.

Due to the stringent collateral requirements of institutions, 'black money' finds it difficult to surface and find its way into productive investment, and the cut-back on government spending, giving due significance to IMF specifications, have all contributed to a recessionary trend in the Indian economy. But this does not make the market any more gloomy than the rest of the world, hit by international recession in many product categories. There are as many ways to make a quick buck as there are ways to make a sustained buck!

For the relatively uninitiated businessman, awareness of consumer buying behaviour is as crucial as awareness of business practices. For example, Lupin Pharmaceuticals has it made with its drugs for tuberculosis, though there are 35 other entrepreneurs, including global giants, in the Indian market. Taking into consideration the months of treatment required for the disease, and the strained financial standing of most patients, who hesitate to stock a month's dosage, Lupin packed a day's dosage of the different necessary drugs in one pack. No retail outlet sells one tablet of each type individually to customers and patients. Lupin spun out a winner.

The Indian economy has been experiencing a slowdown, but certain sectors, such as healthcare, the courier business, commodity trade, fast-moving consumer goods and software are doing well. Marketing rules the roost in most industrial sectors. Be it the car giant Maruti Udyog, or the welding and consumables industry operator RNM, the focus is on customer service, excellent distribution and servicing networks. Instalment payment facilitates and plugging in of different price, quality, preference segments for products, is the name of the game. As is well known, unethical business practices are hardly strange in this environment. Unethical marketing of products is quite common. Securing favourable or exaggerated credit ratings, or testing ratings from firms, so as to promote one's own product, is not uncommon phenomenon. But entrepreneurs can often act as 'mutual' monitoring and regulatory bodies. The recent squabble in the dry cell battery market, with an Indian claimant having a suit filed against them before the Monopolies and Restrictive Trade Practices Commission (MRTPC), is widely known. The claims of the Indian operator of having the longest-lasting battery, on the basis of a third party testing report, was challenged by an MNC competitor and everything short of a public detraction was made by the Indian company. However, while some semblance of monitoring and fair-play may be ensured by the entrepreneurs themselves in the larger-scale category, and in the macro perspective, one cannot pin much hope regarding the same in the small-scale category.

Enough Of Games . . .
It Is War Between And
Within Scales

The days of competing on the basis of license procurement influencing Delhi are (nearly) gone. For example, the Fast-Moving Consumer Goods (FMCG) industry has been witnessing convulsions, be they soap, detergent, cola or other product sectors, such as consumer durables, cellphones and cars. In many product sectors and market segments, multinationals easily overcome domestic opposition, and are soon at each others' throats in their quest for global market share leadership. In the cola wars, the battle is waged through imagery, celebrity endorsements, mega-budget media ads, and cornering of bottles and distribution channels. In the toothpaste industry, it is fought on product features and strength of product lines. Detergents compete on the same front and in segmenting the market, pricewise. Competitive moves by large entrepreneurs against each other on the marketing front is but one mode of competitive assault. In their cases, it is the market element that is vital and it may be taken for granted that they have the best possible management team to handle most other aspects of the project and enterprise. But the competitive success of smaller units whether they are run by RNRIs or Indians, may often crucially depend on many project and management-specific features. Mere development of consumer awareness and loyalty for their product can hardly serve as a unique or isolated focus.

Smaller companies are often initiated and run with equity contribution from promoters, loans from banks, and unsecured loans in terms of credit or funds, ploughed in *benami* by promoters themselves or their relatives. Interest has to be paid for the latter, and hence, operational costs are boosted so as to reduce tax liability. Personal loans taken by cash-short promoters are also often ploughed in as equity. As the enterprise grows, the equity base needs to also develop, so that it can be looked upon favourably by bankers for enhanced funding requirements, or by the public, when going in for issues. Hence, systematic reinvestment of operational surplus . . . after securing them de facto and on paper, is vital. Some cash-strapped entrepreneurs also take personal loans for meeting working capital needs. The interest burden of such cash is often rather high, and they can hardly generate surplus profit after interest, regardless of how much some pay or manipulate figures to avoid paying tax. Hence, cash-short entrepreneurs often find the going tough. In fact, sometimes the phenomenon of being short of cash is wanton. Many smaller entrepreneurs, in their desire to grow horizontally, set up several sister concerns or diversify into other activities. Their surplus cash is used up on such diversifications. One wonders if such practices, which are common in the Indian environment, contribute towards the sustainable development of an enterprise in a fiercely competitive environment. Efficient capital structuring is thus vital. Capital structuring determines the viability of a project and also the price and terms of products sold. With scope for tax evasion and avoidance, advantage of financial leveraging, by maximizing debt finance, assuming sufficient market demand and return on investment hardly exists. And, in the present scenario of domestic and global recession, the focus, in the case of several enterprises, should be on minimizing interest burden . . .

and is not. In fact, many entrepreneurs lay emphasis on securing institutional loans from developmental institutions with minimum equity and collateral requirements. Banks are hardly flexible these days. Institutional loans in such terms are easier to procure, particularly since such credit is sometimes secured through unethical means.

Smaller enterprises can best operate within close proximity to raw material sources and the market, the focus being on credit and debtor payment periods. Small units scarcely operate in volumes that would allow the high interest cost of working capital with long operating cycles, taking costs and prices as relatively fixed. It needs to be ensured that the operating cycle is smaller in terms of inventories, finished goods stock and credit period for debtors. So that, even with high levels of working capital turnover volumes, their interest burden will not be high. These are aspects that few businessmen give serious consideration to.

Operating at lowest feasible fixed costs is an option not only to help the enterprise operate at the lowest break-even point at the crucial teething stage of the enterprise (and of the 'would-be entrepreneur'), but to also avoid labour problems. Employing labour on contract, outsourcing work, and start-up with minimal capital investment costs is a crucial option, which has to be considered in some states in India whose political leanings are particularly socialist, with high levels of labour unrest. In fact, in some such states, and in some sectors, the option of not having a large manufacturing facility, but (for example) allowing labour to manufacture products at their residence or on the premises of a charitable organizations (employing their inmates), is often pursued. But such means can hardly be considered for all industrial sectors. Shoe manufacturers and stabilizer manufacturers sometimes pursue this alternative.

Most smaller-scale enterprises are constituted as sole proprietary or partnership firms. Few operate as even limited companies. The issue is one of control. Also the high rates of corporate taxation and the taxation on dividend dissuades many from going public or being deemed as public, as they grow. Financial institutions and the public prefer more professional management and systems in the organization of their clients. This is an element that warrants consideration . . . a trade-off decision.

Hence, smaller entrepreneurs in India need to focus on getting their functional management system right. The employment of hired or leased facilities and equipment, to the greatest extent possible, converting possible fixed to variable costs, and reducing operational risk, should be explored in a competitive environment. Focus on purchase of raw materials and services on credit to the extent possible, offering attractive trade discounts for spot cash payments, avoiding unsecured deposits which seek cash interest in 'black' money, and attempts to attract equity investment by merchant bankers, are vital options that need to be explored.

Just as it is not necessarily very easy to identify an opportunity, conceptualize and implement a project and manage it, the Indian environment also ensures that it is not very easy to exit from a project or stop running a business. Labour laws in particular are rather unfriendly!

With regard to the marketing front, innovative marketing options need to be adopted by smaller units. They can hardly afford the large resources required to market general consumer goods or several specific categories either. A small pharmaceutical company can deviate from conventional promotion methods of giving expensive gifts, sponsorship of trips abroad and giving lavish parties. Developing, printing and donating scientific books to medical colleges, and aiding researchers and students in their work, are alternative options that will generate consumer awareness, goodwill, company image and credibility. Means by which smaller units can successfully compete with other small firms and with larger units remain aplenty.

Those With A Never-Say-Die Attitude

So much for the general impressions presented in the previous two sections. Our voyage, intra-state and inter-state, in the Indian subcontinent for the Returned Non-Resident Indian 'smaller' entrepreneurial breed, that has been playing truant, would be incomplete if we did not cumulatively capture the rich experiences and impressions encapsulated in their case studies. They are the ones who have had the toughest barriers, given their 'smallness', profile and unfamiliarity with the environment. If they could do it, why could not more of their breed also do it? It is about time we had an overview of the who, the how and the why question of RNRI entrepreneurship in the sub-continent—about their mistakes, lessons learnt by them and advice offered, and their cultural compatibility. Do our hypotheses in Part Two of the book, and the indicative analysis and impressions presented towards the end of each section in Part Three of the book, to facilitate ease in comprehension of hold good? Our limitations, of course, rest on the relatively small sample size. Though we were not specifically focussing on a sampling methodology of enumeration, possible intra-and inter-state diversity, with regard to culture, infrastructure, markets and policy have been sought to be controlled in order to facilitate generalization. Pattern matching of experiences and impressions gives us valuable insights into the RNRI entrepreneurship phenomenon . . . and the environment they operate in.

More Of A Phenomenon, Than Faceless Martyrs

The Returned Non-Resident Indian entrepreneur in the Indian SME sector is not a faceless martyr who has run back from abroad, nor is he someone who is struggling to survive in the entrepreneurial battlefield in the 'abysmal' Indian environment. The impression that is given by these RNRIs is one of confidence, with a compelling urge to do better and better, often without compromising on their values. The RNRI in the SME industrial sector is neither an alien nor a strange species, paddling in vain in murky water. He is a phenomenon who can do and has been doing wonders in and to the Indian industrial economy. Other NRIs, if motivated and *informed*, may well do the same!

A Diverse Basket Of Entrepreneurs And Enterprises

The sectors into which these RNRIs have invested cover a wide spectrum—from computer hardware and software, plastics, soft drinks, electronics, engineering activities, and financial services, to drug-pharmaceutical manufacturing operations. Some have taken up a manufacturing area of operations, while others have entered into trading or service industries, such as housing and the Yellow Pages! We have a Krishna Kumar playing the 'middleman' in trading in textiles, and a Narain who had been involved in trading in tea. The diversity of industry sectors and the phenomenal success of some of them is in itself an indication of their contribution to the Indian industrial economy.

Their initial investments vary from a mere Rs 10,000 in the services industry to several millions at the time of their initiation into the manufacturing industry. Several of them have had meteoric rises in a span of a few years. Many have diversified and created a whole group of companies. Increases in turnovers have ranged from a few million rupees to hundreds of billions. The number of empl-oyees varied from as little as four full-time employees in Thakore's case, to more than a 1000 employees in the case of Desai and Kapadia. Krishna Kumar operated as a one-man show almost. Some have stayed for two years abroad, some for two decades, and some for most of their lives, before returning to India. A few had been based at the most developed economies of the world, while some come in from a typical underdeveloped and unstable Third World economy. Most have entered into the Indian business arena in the erstwhile License Raj. While a few like Shama Bhat, Arora, Krishna Kumar and Pujari entered in the post-reform period after 1991, some were in the process of initiating a business, or were just a month or two into it, in 1995–97, when this study was conducted.

Perceptions Controlled For Diversity

The majority perceptions of these RNRIs, their former NRI typology-wise, particularly in terms of their country of stay (developed/under-developed) and nature of occupation abroad (business/professio-nal), as perceived by the authors, are by no means significantly different. There is no significant divergence regarding their impressions about the infrastructure, the potential for policy change, the bureaucracy, labour laws, or concerning business–labour–bureaucracy-related ethics . . . the environment, in general. Most are bullish regarding the positive side of reform, about increasing levels of market demand and access, competition and liberalization, and are geared to take up the challenge. The fundamentals of doing business in India, be they statutory levies, the potential for policy change, the bureaucratic system, or ethos and values, it seems, have not significantly changed as yet. Though, of course, the market is increasingly becoming the master, with increasing competition.

Doing Business In India: A Corollary To The 'Return To India' Decision

The who and why question of RNRI entrepreneurship in the SME sector may be answered by analyzing the necessary and sufficient conditions for their return to India, and their 'doing business in India' rationale. Our study indicates that the latter is invariably a corollary to the former. The historical and psychological pull factor of coming 'home' are invariably a necessary condition, which, if backed by an immediate push from their country of domicile abroad, due to adverse circumstances, growing children, or the absence of other gainful opportunities, and the pull factor of being independent and being one's own boss, together lead them into the 'doing business in India' decision. The crucial pull, an immediate and sufficient condition being that of an opportunity compatible with their savings and investible or mobilizable funds to do business, or support their decisions.

Historical Pushes And Pulls And The RNRI Entrepreneur: Typologywise

The study validates our hypothesis regarding the nostalgic NRI and the 'doing business in India' decision of most RNRIs in the SME sector. The decision of an RNRI to return and turn to an entrepreneurial career in India is a complex one. Though there is an immediate rationale, and both pushes and pulls, their decision flows out of a number of circumstances and factors, having their genus in the background of the individual and his psyche. These serve as historical pull factors.

Most RNRI entrepreneurs, particularly first-generation emigrants, return to India because of the strong sentimental pull factor of returning 'home'. By 'India', they mean their hometown or state, where they have their loved ones, old friends and contacts. But this serves as a historical rationale—a necessary condition. It does not suffice to ensure their entrepreneurship decision in the sub-continent. Their immediate rationale is either a push factor from abroad or a pull factor from India. And, the latter is invariably an opportunity to do business in India. The push factor from abroad, and negative circumstances, may include currency, political or personal risk, job-related dissatisfaction, or persecution being a 'second class' citizen in a foreign economy and society. Their opportunities may arise from a state-level delegation who have gone abroad, from support from an Indian partner, support either in terms of ideas or finance from other NRIs abroad, or from colleagues and relatives in India. The RNRIs decision to do business is invariably linked to their 'return to India' decision. It is often only in business that their level of independence, freedom of action and ability to maintain the standard of earnings and living that they were used to while abroad, psychologically make it worth their while to productively employ themselves in India. It is not necessarily a 'burning desire' to do something on their own, alone, that pushes most RNRIs into entrepreneurship.

RNRI entrepreneurs seem to come largely from the USA, the UK, Africa, South East Asia and the Middle East. Most of them, first-generation immigrants, return in their 30s and 40s, perhaps due to a phase of 'mid-life crisis', if we are to believe our psychologists. This phase coincides with their having attained some stature in professional life and amassed considerable savings while working abroad, a portion of which they can easily invest in small or medium entrepreneurship in India. Their children are coming of age, are in their pre-teens or lower teens mostly, and they would like to bring them up according to Indian culture and social values. Most have suffered from the 'what does one do in India' syndrome, first, and from the 'can I do business in India?' syndrome, next. But conviction and opportunities, or support, bring them back.

Few declare themselves as 'globalized people', like Pujari does. Few have an objective entrepreneurial inclination that the relatively lower levels of initial competition and investment, cheap manufacturing and labour base, contacts or support, incentives, exemptions and subsidies, in a rapidly developing economy like India's, attracts. Attraction is more emotional than objective and businesslike.

A first-generation emigrant and a first-generation entrepreneur, Kiran Shah always intended to return to India. His ageing and physically ailing parents in India also needed him. He was just waiting for the right opportunity. Haren Shah had it all planned, even before he left. A second-generation entrepreneur, but first-generation emigrant, he was training and saving abroad, just to return and do business in India. Kapadia learnt, what he as an enlightened socialist could learn, from socialist France, the birthplace of the word 'entrepreneur', in terms of skills and perceptions, and returned home to India. He worked for a few years, and when he could mobilize a team, set up a software firm.

A first-generation emigrant and a second-generation entrepreneur, Thakore returned home for 'peace and quiet', once he had reached close to the stage of retirement in his dentistry practice in the United States. He got into business to keep himself meaningfully occupied.

Which Typology Prevails With Regard To RNRI Entrepreneurship?

Of these nth-generation emigrant–entrepreneur typologies, it is the first-generation emigrants, the Haren Shah types, who would like to return to India once they have amassed substantial savings abroad, and who are only waiting for a good opportunity; and the Thakore types, who return to India after spending most of their working life abroad, and only after that take the 'return to India' decision. But this latter typology rarely gets into entrepreneurship 'with a vengeance' in the SME category, if at all! It is more a means of keeping oneself occupied.

A few like Mukherjee are second-generation emigrants from abroad. Having been born, having worked and done business in Africa and the United Kingdom, and having had only one opportunity to visit India for a holiday, and for a 'wider' family reunion, there really was not 'much' emotional affinity to India. Neither did Narain, whose circumstances were similar, have any particular emotional attachment to India. The fact that both of them chose places like Pune and Bangalore, advantageous both from the perspective of economies of location, or perhaps a socio-climatical backdrop to live and do business, provides evidence of this fact. Most second-generation emigrants have an objective outlook regarding their location of operations and settling down, rather than a subjective bias towards locating themselves and their enterprise close to their kith and kin, language and sub-culture in the country. However, some second-generation businessmen, like Haren Shah, prefer a location in their own state. But generally, the second-generation emigrant is more objective. This merely indicates that the 'pull' factor of home need not always be taken as an indisputable attraction for second-generation 'emigrants' like Mukherjee or Narain, or even to some first-generation emigrants like Pujari. An individual's psychology and circumstances play a big role in their decisions.

Immediate Pushes And Pulls: A Sufficient Condition . . . Elaborated

As indicated above, the historical, necessary pull factor of India may be reinforced by a number of immediate factors. Hemrajani's decision was influenced by possible burglary attacks on 'outsiders,' and the risk of currency fluctuations in an economically not very sound African economy. He was not earning in 'good old dollars,' nor did he feel the psychological pressure, worth a trade-off, with a relatively high paying job abroad. Chandresh Parikh was on the verge of acquiring an English or American nationality for himself and his immediate family when his wife but endorsed his opinion, 'Why live like a second class citizen in the West when you can live comfortably in India?' Prabhakar returned with job-related dissatisfaction, and Arora returned due to the war in Kuwait. Neither had thought of finally settling down anywhere but India!

But there were other immediate rationale regarding opportunities ensuring their permanent resettlement and their doing business in India. Prabhakar took over his family business at the insistence of his father, Arora had two partners, old friends, who were willing to risk time and money on the project.

Immediate opportunities for doing business in India may be several. Haren Shah had a promised market, Desai followed the Gujarat entourage on its return from a promotional tour to the United States, Chandresh Parikh had the seed of an idea implanted by colleagues in the paints industry in the sub-continent and the support of three committed partners.

The largest attraction is the presence of a reliable partner in the sub-continent to handle what an NRI has heard of as the 'harrowing' phase of pre-initiation of a project—often the offer of partnership, or informal support to follow-up on the time-consuming pre-initiation phase, especially in manufacturing projects. In the absence of such an immediate option, the NRI may never seriously try to take up the option of doing business in India, and only return to India after retirement. In their 50s, they return for 'peace and quiet', and not necessarily to set up a business where they may have to work '18 hours a day'—the Returned Non-Resident Indian Association in Bangalore has several 100s on their list. Many of them are doctors from abroad. Most seem to be close to retirement and some have retired from active work, few are looking for a really serious business option, a make or break decision. One may, at most, look at their business decision as a post-retirement means of keeping themselves occupied. Thakore works four hours a day, and perhaps plays golf on the rest of the days. It is his background, skill and competence, and not mere sweat and strain that have brought him success in business. Not many RNRIs can be as competent or lucky.

Now that we have validated our hypothesis and fundamental propositions with regard to NRI typologies and syndromes, specified in Part One of this book, let us consider how an NRI or RNRI latches onto an idea.

The 'How' Question Of Opportunity Identification

Once the decision to do business in India is made, the NRI, during visits, makes personal enquiries, establishes contact with industry and bureaucracy, and focusses on a business idea, often linked to one's work experience, background, skills and contacts. The specific idea sometimes comes from the entrepreneur himself, who strives to link it to his skill, training aptitude and resources. Business identification is sometimes facilitated by personal perception of market demand, consultants, colleagues in India, the promise of a foreign market by NRIs abroad, or from one's background. Prabhakar took over his family business and consultants gave an idea to Arora and Pujari. Kiran Shah was promised a market by a colleague in India, Lalwani by one abroad. Chandresh Parikh had the broad problem and idea conceptualized by suggestions from colleagues and future partners in India. Dr Shama Bhat and Dr G.R. Patel had worked on the product abroad. Patel had developed processes and catalysts, and Bhat had worked in the area of AIDS research for years in his University in USA. Dhirubhai Desai had assistance in idea generation from the promotional delegation from Gujarat. Bhaskar worked together with other NRI partners abroad, established buying arrangements with contacts abroad and established his business in India.

Krishna Kumar had contacts abroad. He had work experience in the marketing and administrative functions of a textile company, a world-class organization. He established contacts with sellers in South India, and decided to be a middleman on a private basis. Thakore's family background was in real estate development. He had experience in the same business in the US, even while practising dentistry alongside. He decided to do the same in India. His investment in a hospital project was something he got into because of his area of specialization. But when it was not picking up, he picked up the 'ready' alternative of property development. Kapadia had worked in software development in India and abroad. As an employee, he understood the business, established contacts and went into it on his own, supported by reliable and committed professionals like himself from his place of work in India.

Narain was a businessman. His family background was business and he had been always looking for new opportunities. From trading in tea to operating cinema houses in India, his operations were diverse. A casual suggestion from an acquaintance started him bottling a cola drink in Maharashtra. Hemrajani, in Nigeria, while scanning newsletters and magazines related to the chemical industry, came across something interesting. The per capita consumption of plastics was observed to be low in India—his decision was made.

Hence, once the decision to do business in India is made, opportunity identification is only a matter of time . . . or chance. If the idea is not given to them, by consultants and potential partners in India or abroad, the RNRI often narrows down on one himself.

The 'How' Question Of Market Entry

Formal partnerships and informal support seem to be backed by frequent visits to India in the period before final re-settlement and commencement of operations. The time lag in opportunity identification, procuring statutory clearances and institutional incentives before enterprise initiation seems to be utilized in this fashion. This is particularly true in the case of manufacturing entrepreneurs seeking term loans, and not entrepreneurs considering the services sector. This seems to be the most favoured methodology.

Kiran Shah had the financial partnership and the moral support of three partners, family friends who had their own businesses to look after, but who helped him and bolstered his confidence. He was worried about the business idea and about the marketability of his modems. Hemrajani had the support of his brothers in India, who though not businessmen themselves, helped him during the pre-initiation running around period. Being a finance professional himself, it was not really difficult for him to prepare and submit a project report. Chandresh Parikh had Indian partners, who had experience in the broad industry related to his idea. They also did the necessary spade work, even though he did not himself visit India several times a year in the couple of years before project initiation, to personally follow up developments.

Dr G.R. Patel returned to India and initiated the business with 'no contacts'. But he had gone through a lot of literature and done his homework. Those like Pujari, Shama Bhat and Dhirubhai Desai, who invested in the medium-scale industry category, faced few hurdles in the pre-initiation phase. Maybe it is the perception of support institutions of SSI, maybe it is the project viability potential of a medium-scale unit, regardless, they found the pre-initiation stage relatively smooth. In fact, though the others employed reputed consultants to prepare and submit project reports, Desai did it himself and initiated his project in a record time of three months. Of course, he had come to India at the 'special invitation' of a state-level promotional delegation to the USA.

Basant had his elder brother to handle the initiation and management of the enterprise for over a decade, while he ploughed in funds. Bhaskar, Krishna Kumar, Arora, all had the pre-initiation formalities assigned to a consultant as a sort of a package deal. Those who had it relatively easy were Prabhakar, who returned and took over the business from his father, and Bijalalli and Krishna Kumar who entered the services sector, seeking no funds from financial institutions. Their projects were on in no time.

The ideal strategy for initiating a manufacturing enterprise, it seems, is to employ a well-referred and competent local consultant to smoothen the process of initiation. He need not serve only as a mere liaison agent to route 'speed' money. His years of expertise in this job, in the particular environment, is in itself worth the investment. The presence of reliable partners, perhaps a relative, if not a formal association with a colleague or partner, who will do the running around until project initiation, is of great help. The RNRI could just come and take over the business. He would not have to spend his time waiting. But this is with regard to manufacturing options. Krishna Kumar, who played the role of middleman on a commission basis through his export firm, gave a 'package' deal to a chartered accountant. The statutory requirements and licenses were all completed in about a couple of months.

The lucky ones get their manufacturing concern-related proposal through in three months, the not so lucky ones may have to wait for a year or two. The unfortunates, like Mukherjee, may have to struggle for several years.

The Environment Is Different To That In The Developed West(?)

On entering the Indian environment, it may be easier to consider it with an open mind. The rather stringent ethics of a first-generation RNRI returning after a decade or more of staying in a developed country, may at times have to compromise with itself. The social environment is perceived to be extremely different for the unacquainted RNRI. Informal speed money is routinely employed from jumping a queue in buying a transport ticket, to buying property. Cognizable offences are sometimes dropped by payment of hush money. To those uninitiated to business speed money, all this may seem shocking. But for RNRIs who have done business abroad, particularly in other developing countries, 'business is business'. Given the plethora of subsidies, term loans, and exemptions offered to a new unit, evidence of corruption or unwarranted delays may be perceived even at the business pre-initiation stage. But 'where in the West do you get these benefits?' Often it is due to defective project report preparation and information that delays occur. And if you have to pay for it, it is only what you deserve, say some.

But the fact remains that though studies on a 10 point scale have ranked corruption in India as twice as much of that in the US, it is not necessarily the norm. RNRIs from African and other developing economies may find the incidence of corruption by no means alarming. Though the 'how to go about doing it' and 'through whom', in particular cases, is a query that several new RNRIs could have asked to gain additional or speedy benefits for their enterprise, few have! Some RNRI entrepreneurs with exposure to doing business abroad, feel that unaccountable speed money often goes down the drain. This is the difference, they claim, between corruption in India and some other developing countries. 'In India the job is often not done, and if it is, it is done improperly or inadequately,' declare many, who for obvious reasons would not like to elaborate or be quoted. Many of the successful entrepreneurs, however, claim that these are versions blown up beyond proportion.

Credibility And The 'True' Entrepreneur

Many first-generation entrepreneurs often face criticism from well-wishers in India when they declare their intention to do business in India. It is the RNRIs' own competence that is usually questioned. Independence, education or success while working abroad does not ensure that necessary business acumen has been gained. Most firms that are not doing very well are manned by first-generation RNRIs with mere expertise in some specific functional area of management, perhaps technical, personnel or financial. They have not had the opportunity to gain the overall rounded managerial expertise that is required by an SME owner-manager. Mere possession of certain entrepreneurial competencies does not guarantee success in business, if there is a dearth in relevant hard skills. Some are not doing very well due to exogenous policy change, or due to the adverse fallouts of the erstwhile License Raj. Many who continue confidently, despite enormous exogenous adversity, have learned the tricks of survival on the job, and backed with strong entrepreneurial competencies, remain bullish about their entrepreneurial future. Such people, though reeling under or recovering from adversity, do not try to shift the blame of their own misplanning at the stage of project identification and market entry, to the environment or the institutional framework. They speak of a confident future—and do not try to blame past adversities on anyone and everything but themselves!

Problems In The Identification And Entry Stage

The existing sources of information are perceived to be sadly lacking in specific product-market-locational-project details. Ideas, concepts and innovations, new to the Indian economy have better potential to succeed in the SME sector. However, demand characteristics and forecasting in specific market segments are difficult to estimate, and are hence often ignored. Consultants are criticised as often being nothing more than liaison agents, who ensure or speed up the registration and project initiation process and the release of subsidy or term loans from financial institutions. Most of them are incapable of even this! Market reports, either readily available or from 'affordable' market research consultants within the SME RNRI budget, may not only be misleading, but even dangerous. Promotional programmes conducted abroad, seeking to attract NRIs, are largely perceived to give an overly rosy picture of the idea of doing business in India. For example, the single window clearance system does not seem to have made most of their lives any easier.

Role Model Entry

Other than Mukherjee, who had to wrestle with the License Raj, most non first-generation entrepreneurs considered seem to be doing well. Among the first-generation emigrants, the 'nostalgic' ones are most likely to return to India, ones who have amply displayed entrepreneurial talents, done business abroad or in India, seem to glide into doing business here with aplomb.

Atul Sood's case serves as an ideal example, reiterating the broad similarities that cut across the cases in Part Three with regard to the historical background and immediate factors facilitating the 'return to India' and 'business in India' decision, and the process of opportunity identification and market entry.

A Role Model And His Entry

Atul Sood hailed from a family that ran a flourishing ice-slab production and distribution business in Mumbai. After schooling in India, Sood went abroad to the USA on holiday. His uncle, who was playing host, suggested that he take a snap entrance test. He took it and was admitted to the MBA programme at Michigan. He displayed entrepreneurial tendencies at a very tender age. At Michigan, he was a member of the entrepreneur's club. He observed that the alumni, particularly the South East Asians, were willing to pay a good price for memorablia, particularly T-shirts, ties and such other items carrying the university logo. An idea was formed. Sood invested $500 in this business and set up a store. It did very well. When college authorities objected to the use of the university logo, he met and convinced them that it was a temporary venture and that it was doing the college good. He promised to hand it over to another student on his passing out. He kept his promise and sold it to the highest bidder for $10,000. Sood then worked for an automobile company. He became its youngest vice-president. He was well and truly settled in the USA. But given his family background, the urge to do business was always there, lying dormant. He believed that the ideal time to switch from employment to entrepreneurship was when he was comfortably placed in his career and not after retirement. The itch became stronger as he neared his 30s. His familiarity with the Indian environment and his family business background pointed to India as the best place to do business. Competition, and his having no particular competitive advantage over the American entrepreneur, helped him make up his mind. India it would be! An immediate opportunity arose when his boss in the USA, who was of Indian origin, became interested in doing business in India. He, unlike Sood, was a US citizen, and personal circumstances would not permit him to return to India for good, at least in the short run. He put in money and 'Artig' was formed.

Identifying the opportunity was not easy. Sood had considered a variety of options, including apple juice concentrates and aqua culture. Ultimately, he decided on the manufacture of ice cubes. His family owned several ice factories in Mumbai. He was familiar with the technical and managerial aspects of the business. He had observed the rapidly growing popularity, over the years, for ready crystal-clear ice cubes in the USA. He believed that similarities in lifestyle and consumption patterns existed between the US market and customer segments in major Indian cities. Maybe it would do well in India? He investigated the market, viz., Mumbai, during his periodic visits to the city. His family contacts in potential customer industries helped him. The study boosted his confidence. His family also possessed storage facilities. It was all perfectly set. He returned in 1995, and set up a 60-tonne capacity plant at a project cost of Rs 40 million. Everything was smooth. He intended to tap the household consumer market through middlemen who could undertake direct deliveries. He would himself directly focus on the institutional market of restaurants, bars and parlours. His product and concept of crystal-clear ice, which had a small pore in it through which impurities drained themselves away, was new to the business environment. He was confident.

While planning his entry, Sood had also planned for his personal and family needs, housing, education for the children and his social life. He avoided getting into the mental frame of blaming the system for anything and everything. He knew that project information was available in a decentralized fashion in India. He was also aware that the Indian economy was plagued by technology, market, statutory levy and professionalism-related problems. Reliable and accurate informational databases were not available with a mere telephonic 'tinkle'. But he also realized the advantage of relatively low competition. And, the fact that it is only setting up a business in India that seems a lot more tougher, managing it would not be all that difficult. It is just the initial impetus, the starting phase, that largely makes or breaks an entrepreneurial adventure!

Not all cases could serve as role models, but most of the cases in Part Two contain some similarity with Sood's case.

A Comedy Of Errors And The Tragedy Of The Environment!

Many RNRIs have suffered at the hands of the support system, the bureaucracy, policy change, and from the relatively dismal bureaucratic, business and labour ethos in the Indian environment.

Problems seem to have arisen with regard to *opportunity identification*. This is particularly true regarding data from official information sources being available in a decentralized manner, and is grossly inadequate. The onus of project identification and indicative viability, hence, invariably lies with the entrepreneur. In the case of some inexperienced RNRIs, the project once initiated, soon goes haywire—at least initially. Market projections, business practices and technical line balancing may go out of hand. But most are of the committed kind, who have got into business with a vengeance, and, hence, wriggle out of trouble. Most major hurdles arise at the pre-initiation and teething stage of an enterprise. Perhaps the entrepreneur was acclimatizing himself to the environment or trying out his skills in entrepreneurship! This confirms the belief that it is the launching of the business that is the most difficult part of the 'doing business in India' option.

Bureaucracy and red-tapism have taken its toll. Time lags in procuring statutory clearances, government provision or infrastructure or utilities in time, or of the quantum required, delayed dispersal, if at all (!), of subsidy, and some levels of corruption, particularly at the grassroots, have enhanced lags in project initiation and aggravated teething problems.

Some had been cajoled to pay 'speed' money, for example, by underlings of the utilities department. Most first-generation entrepreneurs worry that for years they have not done anything like this. How can they now? Negative impressions flow abroad, and the relatively cool attitude of support institutions in some cases, particularly towards those who enter the SSI category at lower investment levels, seem to lend credence to these warnings.

Some entrepreneurs urge a flexible approach towards the authorities. A closed mind and one's own ingrained impressions about delays and institutional problems, including the widely perceived problems of corruption and delays, serve no purpose. Authorities are hard-pressed themselves, and the lower rungs of the industry support system have little incentive to undertake extraordinary efforts to speed up their work or promote industry.

Propelling One's Way Into Business . . . Over The Table

Some RNRIs, finance professionals themselves, concede that rather than prepare and submit the project report themselves, the employment of a local consultant with contacts in the bureaucracy, could have perhaps helped speed up the process of disbursement of term loans and initiation of the project. But the possibility of the existence of such avenues does not imply that one has to do it. It may have taken time, but they did it with absolutely no speed money involved. A local accredited consultant, being a person who prepares project reports as a professional, would know exactly how to tailor the project to the requirements of regulatory and support authorities. It need not necessarily imply that illegal payments are being made. Those RNRIs using unethical means may often get away with defective projects at the initiation stage, but only till the market gets them.

Second-generation entrepreneurs laugh away corruption. They believe that developing countries may perhaps have a 'bit more corruption than the developed ones'. India may perhaps have a bit more than some other developing economies. This may sound shocking for first-generation entrepreneurs, particularly those who have not done business in, say, Africa, and in some sectors in the West. But 'business is business,' the second generationers declare. The problem, it seems, is regarding corruption at the grassroots level, which is not that evident in developed economies. Second-generation entrepreneurs also 'pooh-pooh' the excuse of corruption as one that dissuades the 'business in India' option. Some have seen nothing of it! The most important point is the NRIs image and presentation of himself. Once his credibility is established with appraising officers and others in the support system, there is not much likelihood of delay in approvals or sanction. It is often questionable projects and questionable promoters who are either exploited by corrupt officials, or by those who make use of the 'speed' money option themselves, as a means of correcting defects attributable to themselves or their projects. In fact, some believe complaints from NRIs and RNRIs may be attributed to the overly rosy picture painted for the NRI when they initially explored the 'business in India' option. NRI firms get a few priorities here and there, say with regard to land allotment. Nothing more! In some cases, the support officials may not seem very enthusiastic when the entrepreneur actually gets into the business of initiating the venture. The fact remains that returning from abroad with reasonable funds, and setting up a competitive project, perhaps a medium-scale one, is one matter, and coming in with a few hundred thousand rupees, and trying to get into some field, where even local entrepreneurs are finding it difficult to survive, is another issue altogether. It is all a question of credibility, which is shown in terms of the amount one is willing to risk, the homework one has done, and the display of commitment one shows to see the project through.

The study indicates that there are widely prevalent negative impressions abroad, often exaggerated. In fact, corruption, or what there is of it, is 'often' at the grassroots, and at the lower levels of the bureaucratic hierarchy, and smaller firms face the brunt of it at the pre-initiation stage. Their projects are often not very viable on the face of it. Their bargaining power is low, and they find it difficult to directly deal with senior officials. With a larger project, things can be smoother. The bureaucracy is the master often till the initiation stage of an enterprise. Beyond this phase, an SME may not have much to do with the support system, as long as the 24 different types of returns are submitted and loans due are repaid on time!

The Environment, Business Systems And Practices Encapsulated

The *potential for policy change* has been omnipresent, and hence, while long-term vision is something that most RNRIs possessed, strategy and planning was mostly short term. A project that cannot withstand policy change is hardly sustainable. But then, changes in policy may be predicted to some extent by vision and careful environment scan. Interest rates, import duties, exchange rates and demand may all vary with policy change, and reduction in tariff barriers and increased competition from abroad need to be anticipated and hedged against.

Labour, particularly the less skilled and uneducated staff and the blue-collar types, may have to be handled with some strictness. Constant monitoring and accountability need be maintained and ensured. The level of professionalism amongst white-collar employees and their work ethos is relatively a lot more superior.

The *business environment* in most sectors of the Indian economy has hardly been kind to the RNRIs. Delayed payments have to be taken in the 'right spirit' and ignored, so as to avoid scaring away other potential buyers: A sort of distorted public relations imperative! Personnel in distribution outlets and large buyer segments have to be encouraged by 'special incentives'—money under the table basically! All have faced problems of bad debts and irrecoverable dues. Not surprising, as often even court summons are avoided, by exploiting loopholes in the system and by payoffs. The system is hardly in a position to monitor or implement rules of a free and fair competitive market environment. Enforcing contractual obligations is a time-consuming and costly affair. Narain has had competitors buying up his bottles before peak seasons, so as to hurt his sales. Adulterated and fake cola drinks have been put into his cola bottles. Chandresh Parikh believes that some traders, middlemen in his business, adulterate products and sell them to customers, so as to gain higher margins. Quality control officials can invariably be bought!

Further, most entrepreneurs confide, one has to compete with Indian businessmen who follow the practice of double-book bookkeeping, and not mere double-entry bookkeeping. Indian competitors may pay lower taxes and lower levies, and can afford lower margins—the 'grey' market, where evading and avoiding various levies is often the norm in many sectors, rather than the exception. Competitors may reduce the burden of the incidence of regulatory norms and overheads by various measures, sometimes by means of unaccounted cash transactions and by signing up labour for higher wages on paper. The labourers are happy to get a job and entrepreneurs are happy to pay lower amounts of wages and lower amounts of tax by diverting profits into overheads on paper. Beyond statutory limits, labour are largely hired on a part-time or contract basis, so as to avoid the incidence of labour legislations, which are unnecessarily cumbersome and expensive and give labour more bargaining power.

The environment, it seems, is about the same in India and in a relatively unstable developing economy. There are social and economic upheavals every few years, and the state of the infrastructure and ethos, for example, is not very dissimilar. From their observation of businessmen in India and administrative provisions in the small-scale category, some RNRIs are not surprised with the high incidence of evasion and avoidance of tax. The 'black' economy is significantly developed by the business class, and one cannot condemn it absolutely, as most businessmen realize that several expenses in business cannot be shown on the records, and the incentives to show book profits are not attractive.

Now, the *environment may have its limitations*, but then, several of the 'not-doing so well' projects suffered from defective market and environment analysis, and to some extent, sustainable ideas. In some cases, the entrepreneur, unfortunately, does not seem to have possessed well-rounded managerial exposure, or entrepreneurial competencies, at least at the project initiation or teething stage. Hence, it is a mix of defects in the environment and with the project, due to which problems in the pre-initiation, initiation or teething stage arises. Beyond this stage, persevering qualities and gains from 'learning by doing', turn RNRI entrepreneurs into successful businessmen in the Indian environment.

A project with high asset specificity, low value-added production process, low margins, one supplying uncompetitive import substitutes, or one oriented towards seeking incentives, neglecting the market and technical conditions, can hardly do very well. Kiran Shah returned, to manufacture computers, banking on the word of mouth promise of a colleague for a large order, in a country where even contracts on paper are not easy to enforce! He set up a firm with high asset specificity, producing a relatively low value-added component to imported inputs. Haren Shah too made the latter error. Either of the two errors could have killed Kiran Shah's venture. Both the Shahs suffered with the onset of reduced import tariff barriers since 1991. Of course, the quality of the products could be ensured only through their high import content. Given their small scale of operations, neither could afford to integrate backwards. Hemrajani got into plastics, sometimes seen as the 'easiest' of all sectors, with potential for the non-technically qualified person. But the industry was one that operated on low margins, and where networks and connections played a critical role. Business practices and contacts were crucial elements in the industry. One can blame dismal ethics and policy changes for that. But the fact remains that Hemrajani had not counted on the fierce competition and high bargaining power of distributors in his industry, which he should have. Dr G.R. Patel returned 10 years late, as he himself confesses, his process technologies and catalysts for chemical processes faced excessive domestic competition and could not stand up to it.

Infrastructural and utility-related problems in his firm only added fuel to the fire and put the firm in trouble. Several entrepreneurs, who have gone through problems at the teething stage of their enterprise, had fundamental problems with their project—the non-provision of promised incentives, such as capital subsidy and infrastructure, for instance.

RNRI Entrepreneurship In A Nutshell: Hard Ones Crack . . . Business!

You have met the RNRI entrepreneurs. You have followed their adventures to independent enterprise, sharing their successes and failures, witnessing their triumphs, and learning how they overcame adversity. The main objective of this pioneering research effort was to understand certain elements in the RNRI entrepreneurship phenomenon, in order to give a correct idea of the business environment to the nostalgic NRI, the first-generation emigrant, entrepreneur or businessman, so that he can take a calculated decision whether to do business in India or not.

In the good old License Raj of yesteryears, lags in procuring statutory clearances and paperwork took its toll, so as also did policy change and dismal business and labour ethos, which have not been easy to anticipate and hedge against. But often, it is not the environment alone which is to blame regarding the dismal performance of a unit. The entrepreneur, perhaps due to his unfamiliarity with the business and bureaucratic environment, his inadequate exposure to business, dearth of entrepreneurial competencies, or managerial skills in all the functional aspects of management, may not be blameless. While there have been poor performers, there have also been the 'tremendous' achievers!

In spite of economic reform in 1991, the vestiges of a controlled economy remain, while competition from larger entrepreneurs, especially those from abroad, has been increasing. Quality and commitment-conscious entrepreneurs use their own values as a source of competitive advantage, while remaining wary of relatively dismal business and bureaucratic ethics and institutional limitations regarding market rules.

Due to the poor record of the institutional environment, particularly with regard to implementing the promised offers and incentives of support institutions, projects should be formulated on business sense, rather than on 'promised' institutional support. Often, even if the latter materializes, the project could suffer from other business-related diseconomies.

Integrating Jacks Into Strategy

The strategies adopted by RNRIs are varied. Some may go in for an expansionist strategy, seeking incentives and new opportunities to maintain a diversified portfolio, as a precaution against market risk. Those with a definite competitive advantage and proprietary knowledge, follow a stabilization strategy. In the small-scale sector, going in for a retrenchment strategy may require an entrepreneur to forget his entrepreneurial adventure in India. Unique means have therefore been adopted by some persevering entrepreneurs, to avoid writing off their business—and very successfully too. Being something of a 'jack' of most trades seems to have facilitated an expansionist strategy, while having a 'jack' for each trade in the management team seems to have led to a stability strategy. Forward integration in terms of marketing products, and outsourcing inputs, have helped ensure low fixed overheads and a lower break-even point, lowering project cost and enabling the firm to remain price competitive; a myopic approach of fostering too many small firms has been avoided, with a flagship company with a respectable statement of accounts and performance, to mobilize external finance to fuel growth.

Panacea To A Dismal Bureaucracy

The bureaucratic and business environment may be dismal in terms of ethos in some cases. But one need by no means adapt to and exploit the environment. By merely being aware and cautious, one can do well. Credibility, entrepreneurial and managerial skills, serious planning at the initiation, teething and growth stage of an enterprise, would ensure a sustained, if not a tremendous performance. Conservatively financing a project in terms of its capital structure, and employing the services of experienced and competent consultants could help one understand business practices in specific sectors, and investing in a good professional market researcher is one that may be well worth the money spent.

Confident Of The SSI Option?

Several of the cases presented in this book are about second-generation entrepreneurship, which is almost an automatic decision once the NRI decides to return to India. But the rationale of the first-generation entrepreneur to take up business arises from several pull and push factors. A crucial, implicit element seems to be the confidence of a self-made individual, who has learnt to survive and thrive in an alien environment, and is used to some levels of independence. If he could make it on his own in an alien environment, he can do it in India too. It is the confidence, will and potential for sincere hard work of the NRI that makes the decision easier. But getting into the small-scale sector is by no means necessarily an intelligent decision. Incentives and exemptions from the extortionate tax regime and other policies cannot make up for the implicit disadvantages of an SSI in the Indian environment. Of course, the investment decision is industry and manufacturing or service sector specific, and standard guidelines on viability can by no means be prescribed.

Entry Is A Necessary Precursor To Start-Up!

There is a safe entry stratagem by which an entrepreneur would not have to give up his standard of living abroad, while simultaneously keeping the option of returning and doing business in India alive. One could serve as a financial partner to a firm in India and return at the stage, perhaps years later, when the firm is well on its way to growth. The motive for doing business in India may arise due to one's own characteristics, background, or partnership support in India or abroad. It is not merely a means of maintaining one's standard of living, but also a need for achievement. If money is assumed as the major rationale, so be it. Regardless, a systematic methodology of entry and business planning must be followed.

The starting crises, the greatest killer of enterprise, may arise from a cash crisis, but the genus may be often traced to problems in the marketing function. The market is increasingly the master. The best option may be to take over one's own family business. But how many have the fortune of one awaiting them!

It is perseverance that has taken most of the successful entrepreneurs presented in this book to new and greater heights. An innovative idea, perhaps one adapted from the West, regardless of it being linked to one's training or background, can, if pushed by sheer hard work, in itself lead to success.

Within The Environment And Without

Business in India could well be a 'piece of cake' for non first-generation entrepreneurs, especially if they have done business in India or abroad earlier. One may just retire into business. But, one's business family background and previous experience in the field could easily lead to success. In fact, those who have been doing business all their lives look down upon new first-generation entrepreneurs and ridicule their foibles and lack of commitment. The former have the experience and the financial muscle, and invariably do well.

But financial clout is by no means an imperative for successful entrepreneurship. A professional, by virtue of his highly developed skills and contacts abroad, can bank on them and start and run a globally competitive enterprise, employing India as a cheap manufacturing-service base. Without doubt, one unfamiliar with the environment, especially if he has not done business before in India, or in a developing economy, and does not possess a family background in business, may be handicapped. He may take some time to learn how the minds of people in the bureaucratic and business environment work. The system is such that there remains scope for exploiting it and being exploited by it. One could try an opportunity where interaction with the system and environment is the least. One could perhaps focus on the export market, be aware and careful while doing business with one's own strong ethical values, or adapt and change with the environment. The 'black' economy could be as high as 50 per cent of the total economy!

30

The 'How' Question Of Doing Business In India

Some RNRIs have been following a policy of flexible manufacturing and a high value-added composition of imported and domestic inputs, to face progressive competition. They focus on service, maintaining goodwill and a good image with regard to all players in the market, so as to create a niche and entrench themselves. They have learnt the importance of familiarizing themselves with a 'specific' business environment. The environment is such that managerial excellence and a wealth of resources, without familiarity with the latter, would yield naught. The environment, ethos and values are different from those of a developed economy of the West, and, some RNRIs may not be culturally fit to adapt to the environment. However, it is by no means necessary to *change*. Environmental awareness is as essential as it is to be wary, but it is not essential to change one's orientation. One's values, commitment to obligations and emphasis on quality could ensure a sustained competitive advantage.

The problem of delayed payments and bad debts in the business environment, that effects cash flow and working capital management, can be tackled, but not by taking recourse to legal remedy, which should be a last resort, and is a time- and resource-consuming option. One should instead identify and deal with reliable parties with care. Competitors may evade and avoid taxes and labour legislations, and employ unethical, even illegal means for improving their own returns above or below board, or for destroying your initiative. The 'black economy' is estimated to be at least about $ 30 billion a year. This is the environment one has to compete in. However, entrepreneurial competencies and sound managerial strategies can ensure growth and success. Maintaining a sound, credible image is crucial at all stages of growth. But knowing the mind of the market is also crucial. In some sectors in the North the demand and competition is price based, in the South, it is quality based, and in the West it is a mixture of both. Budget-to-budget planning, rather than long-term planning prevails in India. Labour ethos, particularly among the less skilled and almost illiterate people, is lacking, and labour laws are biased towards labour—a deadly combination. Motivation and employing a 'carrot-and-stick' approach may be the answer.

From all the cases, there evolves a sort of ideal methodology that applies to the entire process of doing business in India.

The Ideal Methodology

During visits, potential RNRIs could make personal enquiries, establish contacts and focus on a business idea. Business identification may come from colleagues in India offering an idea and a market to an NRI abroad, or NRIs from abroad offering the same to an RNRI or Indian, the second may also involve funding support. The specific idea should preferably come from the entrepreneur himself, and he could strive to link it to his skills, training and resources. Unless a financially qualified professional, he could give the duty of preparing a project report to a consultant, preferably one with 'contacts' with support institutions. Identification of the right person for the job may be facilitated by the suggestions of experienced colleagues, entrepreneurs or officials in the region. Family, friends or potential partners can follow up on the formalities of initiation, ensuring that papers keep moving to the final project appraisal and approval, registration and sanctioning of term loan. At this stage, the RNRI could return home and take over the mantle. A time span of a year or two may be normal for the whole process to reach finality.

The would-be entrepreneur can increase the frequency of his visits to the sub-continent over this period and maintain a constant flow of correspondence with relevant institutions. Indian partners, if nothing else, help maintain morale and provide moral boosts during the sometimes harrowing pre-initiation stage.

If one has the opportunity to return along with a promotional delegation at the state level, incorporating ideas linked to their broad suggestions, it may be easier to initiate the manufacturing process in a matter of a few months. While one's broad locational decision is invariably pre-decided, to be one's hometown or state, the specific location must be decided after considering institutional assistance and subsidies, but not at the cost of the market and other project logistics-related rationale.

The utility of an established consultant with contacts in hastening the pre initiation formalities should not be underestimated. The procedures and guidelines in Indian industry are at times stringent and problem-ridden. For example, if one is not too careful about one's project report, it may spell doom—an organization manufacturing diagnostic kits is not a drug company, but an equipment-manufacturing unit. The time taken for formalities to be cleared for a drug company may kill the unit even at the teething stage.

A smaller medium-scale investment focussing on a new product with scale economies is more likely to succeed. Smaller and smaller medium-sized firms often succeed by a focus or niche strategy, the faster growing one's focus on diversification, depending on the stage of the product's lifecycle. Success is ensured by presentation skills, building a solid image, and recognising marketing as the key functional area—all need to be supplemented by hard work and positive thinking. Success would also be ensured by constant innovation or by maintaining one's competitive advantage with a focus on service and value offered to customers. New ideas, new concepts, focussing on quality, and a righteous approach to the business environment may also meet with success.

A variety of influence strategies, name dropping or interacting with the top echelons of support institutions directly, threatening adverse media publicity, or formal complaints to superiors, could all serve to ward off the possible influence of corruption. Those who have returned immediately, following investment promotional teams from India, constantly taking officials into confidence, while preparing error-free and thorough project reports for appraisal, and going in for at least a lower medium-scale investment project, invariably gain extra co-operation from support institutions. This is especially so if officials are convinced of the sincerity, 'credibility', and potential of the RNRI, his project, and his contribution to Indian industry. He is not just another SSI entrepreneur seeking incentives and benefits from resource-scarce institutions, and who is more likely to fail, with low commitment or competence, and is mentally positioned with one foot abroad—one who may well leave without a trace. Economic reform and liberalization, while easing investment formalities, may imply enhanced competition and danger for those not adequately prepared or overconfident. Reforms do not mean that institutional systems, in terms of value systems, change overnight. It is, in fact, the widely accepted dismal value systems at the grassroots level in terms of corruption, its eager acceptance by its beneficiaries, and the absence of common civic sense that shocks those who are easily shocked. However, while one may perceive oneself as unfit in this socioeconomic culture, many learn to change, to their own benefit. As an alternative, by persistence and righteousness, one can successfully fight against the disease in the system. Part Two of the book gives instances of many entrepreneurs who have done the latter and succeeded.

Constant innovation, with a focus on service, trying to be one up on policy change and its implications to one's project, can help. One must realize that marketing is a crucial functional component of any project. It is better to firm up a short- or medium-term marketing tie-up, even if relatively unfortunate, if one is not too sure or confident of demand. Similarly, excessive reliance on one buyer or specialized machinery, which cannot adapt to market and demand variation, is dangerous. One needs to guard against project cost/cash outflow-increases over the preliminary project pre-initiation stage, due to delays in registration, license formalities and bureaucratic lags, or lags in the availability of infrastructure or utilities.

'Verbal' contracts are a joke and dangerous in a country where sometimes even agreements on paper are difficult, time-consuming or costly to enforce. Labour management, with a 'carrot and stick' approach is essential. The scores of agencies that a businessman has to deal with while doing business in India are timekillers and the mental strain, especially if the officials are callous, is great. Failure or lackluster performance in business is quite possible because of various exogenous factors, in spite of entrepreneurial skill, competence and resources. RNRIs approaching the environment with a closed mind, particularly with regard to social, business and institutional norms and ground practices, will find it difficult to adapt to the environment.

Planning in the SME sector, while being largely budget to budget earlier, needs to shift towards anticipating progressive reforms, its pace and sequencing. The latter may significantly affect planning initiatives. Vision and a focus on quality is a sustainable approach. But it is necessary to be careful while defining quality. It is useless to focus on high quality, perhaps with imported components and low value addition, when your customer is cost conscious and not quality conscious, or when the country is opening up to outside competition.

Most vociferous critics of the Indian environment are relatively unsuccessful entrepreneurs. The big success stories included in Part Two of this book are extremely bullish about the business scenario and the economy, and pooh-pooh criticisms from dissenters, attributing the latter's impressions to their incompetence. In business in India, it is also prudent to have a suspicious mind and wait for people, support institutions and fellow businessmen or employees to prove themselves before trusting them. Given the relative dearth in labour ethos, a 'carrot and stick' approach needs to be employed. Empowerment has worked in some cases, but is not necessarily the ideal personnel stratagem. Employees from the South of the country are in general perceived to be more sincere, efficient and less 'troublesome' than those from the North. Out-of-state labour seems more committed and sincere.

Given India's social system, personal relations and business should be kept as far away from each other as possible. This is true specially in the case of partnerships. Ego conflicts, misunderstandings, unprofessionalism and subdued drive may arise at the strike of a match.

The skills required to do business in India include marketing and creative ability. This is not merely with regard to the product, but for creating goodwill, liaising, networking, presentation and public relations in general. The success stories understand the need for presentation and maintenance of an image, even a flashy one, at times, though they display conventional Indian conservativeness with regard to market competition, handling labour with strictness and meeting obligations when it comes to the management of their enterprise. The business style in India, while ideally being professional in outlook, is different from that of developed economies, as it also warrants a considerable focus on efficiently dealing with the external environment, including the state bureaucracy and in anticipating policy change.

Being registered as an NRI project with the authorities does not serve as an underwritten guarantee for a successful business project. Some priority in infrastructure, provision of utilities and in social resettlement is offered. Regardless, invariably it is the project, the market and their competence that determines success. One must not expect things on a platter. A single-window clearance system does not imply that institutions do your homework. While several RNRI firms lose out at the pre-initiation stage, they also do so due to various starting crises. Those RNRIs who have a well-rounded managerial experience, have independently handled projects, worked in global environments, as businessmen or employees, are worldly wise, broad or open-minded, and possess sound business sense, can perform miracles doing business in India.

It seems to be due to a lack of serious motivational drive, with one foot abroad, and one in India, and expecting support and success on a platter, that many RNRI business ventures fail at the pre-initiation stage, or succumb to sickness. Those who do not do their homework pay for it. Of course, if one has the indomitable will of most of the entrepreneurs presented in this book, extraneous factors do not really matter much!

31

Policy And RNRI Entrepreneurship

Policy, unfortunately, is today progressively looking for the NRIs investible funds, and not necessarily for an RNRI SME entrepreneur, who may not have the right kind of well-rounded experience to set up or manage an enterprise on his own. Let them get into business as sleeping partners with somebody who is able and willing, seems to be the logical underlying policy. But if this is the policy, it is rather myopic, and if it had been strictly implemented, we would have gone without the brains and contributions of people like Bijahalli, Dhirubhai Desai, Kapadia, Dr Patel or Dr Bhat. The fact is, India needs both the NRI and his dollars. Some people may argue that the initial time lag in project initiation can be used to check on their commitment and entrepreneurial competence. RNRIs operate on the same plane as Indian entrepreneurs do, so why give them any special advantages is a relevant question. This is a matter of debate. The question is how desperately do we want them!

Though a large business house has the political and business clout to perhaps overcome adversities and limitations in the environment, they also have other countries as investment options. The policy maker should try to make the environment more favourable. But it is bound to take time, even with the best will in the world. Therefore, the requirements of the NRI investor or big-time entrepreneurs should not be ignored. It is just that it is not going to be very easy to attract entrepreneurs with global options in the short term, and perhaps even in the medium term. The environment cannot be made globally attractive in a day!

The fact remains that few RNRIs in the SME sector have come back only for policy incentives. But this does not mean that we should just let sleeping dogs lie. Those who have it in them to return, survive and thrive in an environment where competition is opening up by the day, will do it, preferential policy or not. Maybe we do not need the others. All these are debatable issues. It is, in fact, the institutional structure, the bureaucracy, archaic laws, and business and bureaucratic ethics that have to change. Policy initiatives encouraging better monitoring, disclosure rules, or greater accountability, cannot change a bureaucratic or business culture overnight. So, should we let the system sort out the diehard RNRI entrepreneurs, the boys from the men? Or should we develop a system so that RNRIs are equipped with potential to develop into strong and productive entrepreneurs? In turn, encouraging more to return.

National resource centres, such as the EDI, which have strived to pioneer Entrepreneurship Development (ED) programmes throughout the developing world, have institutionalized a three-month ED programme. Competence verification, idea generation and project preparation, all pre-initiation activities, the major hurdles in the 'doing business in India' option can be comprehended, and often completed, by attending these programmes. But awareness on this option is marginal. Presenting the environment as it is to NRIs abroad, disseminating awareness regarding training require-ments, particularly for first-generation would-be RNRI entrepreneurs, are all imperatives. This book may also be viewed as one seeking to provide a preliminary introduction to doing business in India to the discerning NRI.

References

1. *A Handbook for NRIs*, Nabhi Publications, New Delhi, 16th Rev., 1997.
2. *Asian Development Outlook*, 1996 and 1997, Oxford University Press Ltd., New York, 1996.
3. Tranitkar, Ajit and Mallika Conductor, *In Search of Identity—The Women Entrepreneurs of India*, EDI, Ahmedabad, 1992.
4. Barrow, Colin, Robert Brown, Liz Clarke, *The Business Growth Handbook*, Kogan Page Ltd., London, 1995.
5. Batra, G.S. and Narinder Kaur, Ed. *New Economic Policies in Developing Countries*, Vol. 5, Management of Economic Crises, Anmol Pub. Pvt. Ltd., New Delhi, 1996.
6. Bhattacharya, B., Satindev Palaha, *Policy Impediments to Trade and FDI in India*, Wheeler & Co. Ltd., New Delhi, 1996.
7. Awasthi, D.N. and Sebastian Jose, *Evaluation of Entrepreneurship Development Programmes*, EDI, Ahmedabad, 1996.
8. Gupta, Uttam, 'Patriotism alone cannot lure the NRI', *The Indian Express*, Ahmedabad, 2 December, 1997.
9. Hajela, Kuldeep K., *A Complete Guide for Non-Resident Indians*, Jaico Pub., Mumbai, 1995–96.
10. Monthly Newsletter, *Indian Investment Centre*, Various Volumes, 1994–96.
11. Colliers, Jardine and David G. Jackson, *Asia Pacific Business Guide*, McGraw-Hill Book Co., Sydney, 1996.
12. Jose, Sebastian and Sanjay Thakur, *Not Born—The Created Entrepreneurs*, EDI, Ahmedabad, 1994.

13. Kaur, Narinder, *New Economic Policies in Developing Countries,* Vol. 6, Indian Economic Policy: Structural Adjustments, Anmol Publications Pvt. Ltd., New Delhi, 1994.

14. Kanji, Gopal K. and Mike Asher, *100 Methods for Total Quality Management,* Response Books, New Delhi, 1996.

15. Malik, O.P., India Abroad News Service, 'India's credit rating still BA-2; Moody's no to review', *The Economic Times,* 1 June, 1994.

16. Malik, O.P., India Abroad News Service, 'No review of ratings: Moody's', *Business Standard,* 31 May, 1994.

17. Murty, Krishna M., 'NRI Investments: Impediments galore', *The Observer,* Mumbai, 17 February, 1997.

18. Murty, Krishna M., 'Policies that can influence NRIs', *The Observer,* Mumbai, 24 February, 1997.

19. *Open Learning Programme in Entrepreneurship,* Entrepreneurship Development Institute of India, Ahmedabad, 1995.

20. Patel, V.G., *The Seven Business Crises: How to Beat Them,* Tata McGraw-Hill, New Delhi, 1995.

21. *Performance Improvement Programme,* Entrepreneurship Development Institute of India, Ahmedabad, 1991–92.

22. Phansalkar, S.J., *How Not To Ruin Your Small Industry,* Response Books, New Delhi, 1996.

23. Press Trust of India, 'Indian not alluring enough for NRIs', *The Observer,* 1 October, 1996.

24. Press Trust of India, 'NRIs can mobilise up to $ 50 billion', *The Indian Express,* 12 July, 1996.

25. Senger Harro Von, *The Book of Stratagems, Tactics for Triumphs & Survival,* Penguin Books, New York, 1993.

26. United News of India, 'NRI meet on investments today', *Business Standard,* 23 December, 1996.

27. Van Horne, James C. Wactiowicz and M. John, *Fundamentals of Financial Management,* Prentice-Hall of India Pvt. Ltd., New Delhi, 1996.

28. Patel, V.G., *Entrepreneurship Development Programme in India and its Relevance to Developing Countries,* EDI, Ahmedabad, 1970.

Index

About The Authors

V. Padmanand, an economist and management professional, is currently on the Faculty of the Entrepreneurship Development Institute of India, Ahmedabad, He holds M. Phil. degrees in economics from the University of Cambridge and the Centre for Research in New International Economic Order (CReNIO). He has many research publications to his credit besides considerable experience of industrial consultancy work. He currently heads the Thrust Area, 'Performance and Growth of Existing Entrepreneurs' at EDI, Ahmedabad, and overseas business growth related national projects under the auspices of development banks and international projects under the United Nations Industrial Development Organization (UNIDO, Vienna).

P.C. Jain has been senior faculty at the Entrepreneurship Development Institute of India, Ahmedabad, and specialises in business policy and strategic management. A Ph.D. from the University of Delhi, he has published a number of research papers and was also the editor of *Handbook for New Entrepreneurs*, which secured the DMA-Escorts best book award for 1998. He is presently associated with the Sri Ram College of Commerce, University of Delhi.